Startling Strangeness

Startling Strangeness

Reading Lonergan's Insight

Richard M. Liddy

UNIVERSITY PRESS OF AMERICA,® INC.
Lanham • Boulder • New York • Toronto • Plymouth

Copyright © 2007 by
University Press of America,® Inc.
4501 Forbes Boulevard
Suite 200
Lanham, Maryland 20706
UPA Acquisitions Department (301) 459-3366

Estover Road
Plymouth PL6 7PY
United Kingdom

Library of Congress Control Number: 2006931314
ISBN-13 978-0-7618-3604-9 (cloth : alk. ppr.)
ISBN-10 0-7618-3604-7 (cloth : alk. ppr.)
ISBN-13 978-0-7618-3605-6 (paperback : alk. ppr.)
ISBN-10 0-7618-3605-5 (paperback : alk. ppr.)

∞™ The paper used in this publication meets the minimum requirements of American National Standard for Information Sciences—Permanence of Paper for Printed Library Materials, ANSI/NISO Z39.48-1992.

"Remember who your teachers were."

(I Timothy 3, 14)

Contents

Preface

Each of us speaks and acts out of an horizon. One person speaks and acts out of an horizon that is narrow and un-nuanced. Another speaks and acts out of a broader and deeper horizon: she brings to her speaking and acting historical nuance and an openness that goes far beyond prejudice. Such a person has an operative philosophy that is open to greater expanses of reality and she can field questions and challenges in many areas.

This is what it meant by a "philosophy": that is, a framework for thinking about life and the universe. And all of us, whether we know it or not, have some philosophy—whether it be narrow and superficial or broad and deep. This book will reflect on such implicit philosophy in the light of Bernard Lonergan's *Insight: A Study of Human Understanding* as well as in the light of my own wrestling with that book and the change that happened in me as a result of that effort.

The book, especially in its central section, will involve a significant amount of "theory," that is, long chains of reasoning that reflect the long chains of reasoning in *Insight*. But all such chains of reasoning, if they are to have any credibility at all, must flow from human experience, specifically the experience of human understanding. And this is why I have written this book in a narrative form. It involves my own upbringing, my encounter with Lonergan as my teacher in Rome, and most of all, my experience of at first not understanding and then coming to understand what *Insight* is all about.

Because it is a narrative, this book involves what some might call "luck" and others "divine providence" or "grace." St. Thomas Aquinas held that understanding involved a passive element, a receiving of intelligibility into the mind. Besides the wrestling with a text and the human effort to know, there are also moments of "reception," of "getting it," of "catching on." This book is essentially the story of my "getting it," of coming to understand what Lonergan's *Insight* was all about—and what I am about.

The inspiration for this book came during the mid-1990s when I was a Senior Fellow of the Woodstock Theological Center at Georgetown University. Woodstock's mission is to reflect theologically on contemporary problems: economic, social and political. In order to do that, however, the Jesuits and their collaborators at the center realized that they needed an over-arching philosophical-theological framework within which to think about such complex contemporary issues. Bernard Lonergan's philosophy and methodology provided just such a framework. And since I had studied Lonergan's thought since my student days in Rome in the 1960s, I was invited to join the center. It has been for me a wonderful experience of collaborating with men and women of expertise in various fields in the light of the Christian Gospel.

Such stimulating reflection sent me back to my own roots, to my first encounters with Lonergan as his student in the 1960s, and especially to my intense study of *Insight* in the mid-1960s. So powerful was that experience that it has remained as an undercurrent to my life to this day. With the reading of that book some intellectual center of gravity shifted within me. My intention in writing this present book is to share that experience with others and in that to invite them to think about their own implicit philosophy, their own operative notion of themselves. The use an autobiographical approach is a way of helping others to enter into my own thought, Lonergan's thought—and their own. The title of the book comes from Lonergan's line in *Insight* where he notes that anyone who comes to understand what he is writing about will have an experience of "startling strangeness."

As I finish writing this book I want to thank various persons who have been especially helpful in encouraging me to stick to the task at hand, a task that at times seemed quite daunting indeed. I am grateful to His Eminence, Theodore Cardinal McCarrick, former Archbishop of Newark, who gave me a leave-of-absence to work at the Woodstock Theological Center, as well as to the present Archbishop of Newark, John J. Myers, for continuing my assignment at Seton Hall University. I am also grateful for the friendship and support of the Archbishop of Newark Emeritus, Peter Leo Gerety. I am very grateful to Msgr. Robert Sheeran, President of Seton Hall University, for his friendship through the years and his support of the Center for Catholic Studies. The launching of the Lonergan Institute at Seton Hall as part of that center is just one step in the Gospel's entry into contemporary culture and the Lord's desire to have a say in all the areas of human life. I am grateful to the priests community of Seton Hall University and to my brother priests for their support. I am grateful to all the faculty I have worked with at Seton Hall in departments and committees, etc., who have been so open to depth-reflections on human life; and to the students at Seton Hall, whose desire for wholeness so inspires my journey. I am grateful to Russell and Marge Francisco for their computer help; and to Professor William Toth and all the staff of the Center for Catholic Studies who have put up with me while I wrote this book.

I am especially grateful to James O'Connor, S.J., the director of the Woodstock Theological Center, who invited me to join the center, as well as to Gasper LoBiondo, S.J., the present director, and all the fellows and staff of the center through the years. In particular, I want to thank William Walsh, S.J., and John Haughey, S.J.—good friends who, by their taking Lonergan seriously, reinforced my conviction that I was on the right track. I also want to thank my family, especially my sister, Marie Therese Liddy, who has proofread and edited this book and made a number of helpful suggestions; also, my sister-in-law, Colette, and my nieces and nephews who help me remember my roots. I also want to thank my friends. I have been thinking of Jesus' words in St. John's Gospel: "I have called you friends because I have made known to you what I heard from my Father." We tell our friends what we hear in our hearts. Perhaps this book is one step in that sharing; but it is not the only one. Many other steps have come before and, hopefully, many more will come in the future.

Finally, I want to thank the University of Toronto Press. Robert Doran, S.J., and the Estate of Bernard Lonergan for permission to quote from the works of Bernard Lonergan.

Introduction

In July of 1964, after having studied in Rome for four years, I returned, a young Catholic priest, to my home in New Jersey. I was twenty-six years old. Soon afterwards my bishop, Archbishop Thomas A. Boland, called me in to talk about my future. He was a kind elderly man and he told me that the authorities wanted me to teach at "Darlington," the local Catholic seminary, and consequently I would be returning to Rome at the end of the summer to work on my doctorate. "What would you like to teach," he said, "philosophy or theology?"

"Theology," I responded immediately.

"Well, we don't need anyone in theology," he said. "We'd like you to study philosophy."

Well, at least he asked!

And I was distressed by the assignment. For one thing, I had been away from home for four years and my trunks carrying all my belongings—mostly books—were on the high seas coming towards America. Now here I was being sent right back to Rome for three more years of study. I could hear the pain in my father's voice when I told him the news on the phone.

But there was another reason I was distressed at the prospect of studying philosophy. I wasn't sure I believed in it.

I had studied scholastic philosophy in my early seminary training and that was chiefly "metaphysics"—the study of the structure of the universe according to Aristotle, Saint Thomas Aquinas and the ensuing scholastic tradition. But during my years in Rome the Second Vatican Council had begun and during that time scholastic philosophy had become, in the minds of many, quite discredited. Where previously official documents of the Catholic Church were couched in scholastic terminology—"matter" and "form," "substance" and "accident"—the Council preferred a whole new way of talking. Pope John XXIII's intention in calling the Council was to make a leap forward—"*un balzo innanzi*"—from ancient ways of thinking and speaking to new and contemporary ways of communicating to the people of our own day.[1] The manner was to be more personal, more "existential," more pastoral. Consequently, aside from an occasional reverential nod toward scholastic philosophy, the Council barely paid attention to it. A whole new way of looking at things had entered into the minds of many and the ground had shifted from under the scholastic philosophy I had learned when I first entered the seminary.

And so I remember lying on my bed in my family's home that summer of 1964 and wondering if there was anything to philosophy at all. Priest friends of mine were already involved in interesting pastoral work in the inner cities of America, and that's where I really wanted to be—not relegated to some back room in a library in Rome.

But that's in fact where I ended up. I said "Yes" to my superiors and took the *USS Constitution* back to Rome in September of '64. It was a wonderful trip as the boat was filled with American college students singing 1960s "hootenanny" songs of freedom and love. Sister Mary Luke Tobin of the Sisters of Loretto was on the ship on her way to the Council as an "auditor" and she led a number of stimulating discussions on all the innovations the Council was undertaking. On the way, the ship stopped in Madera in the Azores, Gibraltar and Casablanca, finally arriving at Naples.

But when I finally arrived in Rome and began studying philosophy, my distress continued. That fall I took a number of courses needed for the "Licentiate" in philosophy—roughly equivalent to a Masters. I learned a lot more scholastic philosophy as well as being exposed to other philosophies, such as existentialism, phenomenology, Anglo-American philosophy, etc. But none of this really touched me and I continued to wonder about the whole viability of anything called "philosophy."

Those courses required a lot of intense study. The previous summer I had taken comprehensive exams in theology covering the four years of study and now, within a year, I was responsible for a second set of comprehensive exams. I feared a breakdown and one sunny but chilly January day as I walked by the Trevi Fountain, I remember saying to myself,

> After I get through these courses, I am never going to sit in on a course I don't want to take again. I am only going to take courses I want to take—courses where I believe I can learn something genuinely new. I am going to seek out the best stuff I can find.

And the best "stuff" I could find was the work of Fr. Bernard Lonergan, S.J. I had had Father Lonergan for theology two years previously and much of what he had taught went right over my head. He was highly esteemed by many of the students, but difficult to understand. I remember a classmate, David Tracy, saying to me, "If you're going to study any philosophy, study Lonergan—he's the best."

And that's what I did. For several years, while my friends and classmates worked in the streets of Jersey City and Newark, in a dimly lit room at the back of the library of the Casa Santa Maria in Rome, I read Lonergan's *Insight: A Study of Human Understanding*. It was a 785-page book and sometimes while I studied it in the late afternoon Rome's electric supply would experience a "brown-out," a dimming of the lights—a fitting symbol I felt for the enlightenment I was seeking.

And enlightenment did come. Not in the sense that I arrived at all the answers, but in the sense that I happened upon a few personally appropriated answers that through the years have proved central to my life. In this book I would like to describe that process of enlightenment, occasioned by Lonergan's *Insight*. Even now, almost forty years later, I can remember where I was and what I was doing on that late afternoon in Rome as a long study of *Insight* came to a head.

But how can I describe that experience? Later in this book I will describe it very specifically, but let me initially characterize it as "strange." In his introduction to the Western canon Harold Bloom singles out "strangeness" as the characteristic of the truly "great books."

> With most of these twenty-six writers, I have tried to confront greatness directly: to ask what makes the author and the works canonical. The answer, more often than not, has turned out to be strangeness . . . Walter Pater defined Romanticism as adding strangeness to beauty. . . . The cycle of achievement goes from *The Divine Comedy* to *Endgame*, from strangeness to strangeness. When you read a canonical work for the first time you encounter a stranger, an uncanny startlement rather than a fulfillment of expectations. Read freshly, all that the *Divine Comedy, Paradise Lost, Faust Part Two, Hadji Murad, Peer Gynt, Ulysses,* and *Canto general* have in common is their uncanniness, their ability to make you feel strange at home.[2]

In the introduction to *Insight*, Lonergan also characterized as "strange" the experience of those who understood what his book was all about. The book is about fostering an "insight into insight," that is, an insight into one's own ability to have insights or acts of understanding. Of that breakthrough he writes: "one has not made it yet if one has no clear memory of its startling strangeness."[3]

Still, though strange—so much so that it has marked me to this day—it was also an experience of "coming home." As Bloom put it, a great work makes you feel "strange at home." And that was Lonergan's intent.

> The present work is not to be read as though it described some distant region of
> the globe which the reader never visited, or some strange and mystical experi-
> ence which the reader never shared. It is an account of knowledge. Though I
> cannot recall to each reader his personal experiences, he can do so for himself
> and thereby pluck my general phrases from the dim world of thought to set them
> in the pulsing flow of life.[4]

Especially in his later writings Lonergan refers to the intellectual breakthrough his book seeks to foster as an "intellectual conversion." He does not
use this term in *Insight,* perhaps because of its religious overtones and his
audience is "anyone of a sufficiently cultured consciousness." Nevertheless,
elsewhere he will speak of this moment of startling strangeness as a conversion.

> Intellectual conversion is a radical clarification and, consequently, the elimina-
> tion of an exceedingly stubborn and misleading myth concerning reality, objec-
> tivity, and knowledge. The myth is that knowing is like looking, that objectivity
> is seeing what is there to be seen and not seeing what is not there, and that the
> real is out there now to be looked at.[5]

That is the negative side. That is what intellectual conversion is *from.* The
positive side is that it opens one up to a whole new notion of reality. Whereas
the cognitional myth tends to conceive reality in terms of "the world of immediacy" that can be seen, heard, touched, tasted, smelt and felt, intellectual
conversion introduces one to "the world mediated by meaning" that is known
only by accurate understanding and true judgment. An appreciation for such
a world of meaning includes an appreciation for the "long chains of reasoning" that lead us beyond what is merely apparent to what is so: to what the
scientist discovers and the philosopher meditates on. But all such chains of
reasoning can only make full sense if they are rooted in a breakthrough to
reason itself.

Lonergan once wrote of "the neglected subject" that is so fascinated by the
transcendence of truth as to forget that truth exists in minds. Or "the truncated
subject," for whom the reality of one's self can be beyond the horizon of
one's self. There can be a major disconnect between what one thinks one is
and what one truly is. But the elimination of such inadequate positions is not
easy. It involves an experience of startling strangeness.

> The transition from the neglected and truncated subject to self-appropriation
> is not a simple matter. It is not just a matter of finding out and assenting to a
> number of true propositions. More basically, it is a matter of conversion, of a

personal philosophic experience, of moving out of a world of sense and of arriving, dazed and disoriented for a while, into a universe of being.[6]

Such was Augustine's experience as he journeyed through his young adult years until at the age of thirty-one in the spring of 386 someone gave him "some books of the Platonists" that gave him the key to himself. As Peter Brown spoke of the contribution of these philosophers:

For the Neo-Platonists provided him with the one, essential tool for any serious autobiography: they had given him a theory of the dynamics of the soul that made sense of his experiences.[7]

So there is a significant amount of history in this book, as my life from the 1940s through the 1960s intersected with that of Bernard Lonergan and with the history of the times. So also there are "long chains of reasoning"—for the world *is* mediated by meaning: insights, judgments, beliefs. But all such writing of history and all such philosophizing are rooted in the experience of the self-appropriation of the knower. And of such this book desires to be an example.

And so, sometime around the spring of 1967, after wrestling with *Insight* for over a year, I had such a startling and strange experience as Lonergan speaks about. It is the clear memory of that experience some forty years later that has given rise to this book. For that moment opened up innumerable other moments in my life and thinking. It was a turning point that precipitated a whole series of turning points. I will describe that experience in chapter thirteen. The chapters leading up to that will describe the context for my reading of *Insight* in the mid-1960s and some of the "long chains of reasoning" that I found in that book.

OBJECTION

But let me immediately speak to an objection: that it seems like the height of arrogance for a relatively unknown person to write autobiographically. What possible value could such an autobiographical essay have? "After all, you are certainly not on the level of your mentors and teachers: Lonergan, Newman, Augustine, Plato, etc." Yet my response can only be that at the present stage of human development, philosophical and human questions cannot but involve an element of autobiography. As Newman put it, towards the end of the 19th century, "in these provinces of inquiry egotism is true modesty."[8]

I am what I am or I am nothing. I cannot think, reflect, or judge about my being, without starting from the very point which I aim at concluding . . . I cannot avoid being sufficient for myself, for I cannot make myself anything else,
and to change me is to destroy me. If I do not use myself I have no other self
to use . . . What I have to ascertain are the laws under which I live. My first
elementary lesson of duty is that of resignation to the laws of nature, whatever
they are; my first disobedience is to be impatient at what I am, and to indulge
an ambitious aspiration after what I cannot be, to cherish a distrust of my pow-
ers, and to desire to change laws which are identical with myself.[9]

At this point someone might rightly ask, "So what? What's the point? What
good does it do to have had such an experience?" And no better response can
be given than Lonergan's own "mantra" in the introduction to *Insight*:

Thoroughly understand what it is to understand, and not only will you understand the broad lines of all there is to be understood but also you will possess
a fixed base, an invariant pattern, opening upon all further developments of
understanding.[10]

In other words, if you understand yourself correctly, you will understand
the structure of the universe correctly. You will not be a materialist. You will
not reduce the universe to electro-chemical events understood materialisti-
cally, as do many scientists and neuro-biologists. You will not reduce the
universe to what can be known by physics, biology, psychology, sociology or
any of the other empirical sciences.

Nor, on the other hand, will you be caught in a pseudo-spiritualism that
reduces spiritual realities to imaginary ones. You will not be caught in any
fundamentalism that reduces the complexities of life to a conservative or
liberal mantra. Not seduced by talk-radio, you will instead be committed to
a nuanced and differentiated vision revealed by developing understanding,
correct judgment and grounded belief.

This is no little thing—to have an angle on "all there is to be understood" as
well as "a fixed base, an invariant pattern, opening upon all further developments of understanding." One will not be easily fooled by slogans. One will
not be misled by "pie in the sky" political promises. On the other hand, one
will be passionately committed to truth and to the reality revealed by truth.

And for one who has glimpsed the infinite act of understanding behind
every act of human understanding, the whole enterprise is bathed in and motivated by a transcendent dimension.

Our subject has been the act of insight or understanding, and God is the unrestricted act of understanding, the eternal rapture glimpsed in every Archimedean
cry of "Eureka."[11]

THE PLAN OF THE BOOK

The plan of this book, then, is to set out my encounter with Lonergan as a student in Rome in the 1960s and, within that context, to describe my reading of *Insight* and my breakthrough to understanding his thought—and my own. *Part I: The Way to Insight* describes the context I was coming from: pre-Vatican II Catholicism in mid-twentieth century America and the neo-scholastic philosophy that I experienced in the seminary as well as my studies in Rome during the Second Vatican Council and my early encounters with Lonergan as my theology professor. It also describes my graduate studies in philosophy and my doctoral dissertation on Susanne K. Langer, the immediate context within which I picked up *Insight* and began to read it seriously.

Part II describes my reading of *Insight*. It involves the intricate analyses of mathematical and scientific understanding as well as common sense and reflective understanding. It leads up to what Lonergan calls "the self-affirmation of the knower," the invitation for the reader to verify in herself the analyses of understanding he has outlined. It also includes all that flows from that self-affirmation: the notion of "being," objectivity and an outline of metaphysics. Finally, it outlines the ethical and theological implications of the self-affirmation of the knower.

At the time I read *Insight*, I vaguely saw these implications as flowing from "an insight into insight." But having it all come together was a very personal itinerary—which I describe in *Part III: Insight into Insight* This part highlights the "labyrinthine ways" my mind traveled as I wrestled with *Insight* and the "startling strangeness" that came over me that afternoon in Rome as I realized what *Insight* was all about—and what I was about. In the final chapter I recount some of my encounters in later years with Lonergan, not only as a teacher but also as a friend. I also draw out some—only some—of the cultural implications of "an insight into insight."

A suggestion. One might read *Part I* and *Part III*, the more narrative parts, rather quickly. But *Part II* is a description of my reading of Insight, a process that took a good part of a year. One might take one's time in reading this part and, as Lonergan pointed out, the process of growing self-understanding outlined there is a slow process best accomplished in a group setting where we can help one another in our growing understanding.

NOTES

1. Bernard Lonergan, "Pope John's Intention," *A Third Collection* (Mahwah, NJ: Paulist Press, 1985), 226.

2. Harold Bloom, *The Western Canon: The Books and Schools of the Ages* (New York: Harcourt Brace and Co., 1994), 3.

3. *Collected Works of Bernard Lonergan* (hereafter *CWL*) Vol.3, *Insight,* ed. Frederick Crowe and Robert Doran (Toronto: University of Toronto Press, 1992), 22.

4. *CWL 3 Insight*, 13 (xix).

5. Bernard Lonergan, *Method in Theology* (London: Darton, Longman and Todd, 1972; reprinted by University of Toronto Press, 1990), 238.

6. Bernard Lonergan, *A Second Collection* (London: Darton, Longman & Todd, 1974; reprinted by University of Toronto Press, 1996), 79.

7. Peter Brown, *Augustine of Hippo* (Berkeley and Los Angeles: University of California Press, 1969), 168.

8. John Henry Newman, *A Grammar of Assent* (London: Longmans, Green, & Co., uniform edition, 1913), 384.

9. Newman, *A Grammar of Assent,* 347. See also 385-386: "In spite of oppositions and conflicts among people on matters philosophical, ethical and religious, still a serious inquirer: . . . brings together his reasons and relies on them, because they are his own, and this is his primary evidence; and he has a second ground of evidence, in the testimony of those who agree with him. But his best evidence is the former, which is derived from his own thoughts; and it is that which the world has a right to demand of him; and therefore his true sobriety and modesty consists, not in claiming for his conclusions an acceptance or scientific approval which is not to be found anywhere, but in stating what are personally his grounds."

10. *CWL 3 Insight*, 22 (xxviii).

11. *CWL 3 Insight*, 706 (684).

Part I

THE WAY TO *INSIGHT*

Chapter One

Amateur Philosophizing

1. AN AMERICAN CATHOLIC FAMILY

I always wanted to be a priest—at least as long as I can remember. Obviously many "scripts" influenced this desire—for we are products of our family and our times. My mother, for example, though never overtly or in a heavy-handed way, certainly longed for me to be a priest. At the same time I was attracted to the life. I hold within me an early image of Father Thomas Gillick, one of our parish priests, intently serving Holy Communion to parishioners kneeling at the altar rail of our parish church of Our Lady of the Valley in Orange, New Jersey.

I was born in that town in 1938, and grew up in West Orange, the son of Irish American parents. With the exception of my mother's mother, who emigrated from Ireland in the 1880s, my other grandparents had all been born in America. Both my parents were from large families; and both were very devout Catholics.

I once visited the little village in County Clare from which my great grandfather on my father's side had emigrated in the late 1840s at around the age of fourteen. There I read in the church record of the times when Catholics were not allowed to have their own church, and so they attended Mass in each other's homes. Many times the houses were so crowded that they had to stand outside in the rain. For me, that is an image of how the spark of Catholic faith passed on to me. It was a vibrant faith, certainly not unconnected to social struggle, that leapt the ocean and passed on to my parents, my sister, Terry, my brother, Joe, and myself.

This "being Catholic" was not just a cultural thing. There was something more. Very early in my life my mother would bring me to our parish church and explain to me the meaning of the stories depicted in the stained glass

3

windows. And it was not at all unusual to see my father, a teacher, football coach and public school administrator, sitting quietly, with beads in hand, reciting the Rosary.

My father once told my mother that he was disappointed that Our Lady did not seem to be answering his prayers. That night, at a raffle in the parish hall, he won a beautiful statue of the Virgin Mary, a statue that remains in our family to this day.

The depth of our family's faith was reflected in the *Memorare*, the ancient prayer recited at every family Rosary:

> Remember, O most gracious Virgin Mary,
> That never was it known,
> That anyone who fled to thy protection,
> Implored thy help or sought thy intercession,
> Was left unaided.
> Inspired by this confidence,
> I fly unto thee, O Virgin of virgins, my Mother.
> To thee I come, before thee I stand,
> Sinful and sorrowful.
> O Mother of the Word Incarnate
> despise not my petition,
> but in thy mercy hear and answer me. Amen.

And we had much to pray for. My parents had experienced the great Depression and now in my early years the nation was engaged in the Second World War. My earliest memories involve a dark feeling overshadowing a bright sunny day as an older boy told me the frightening news of the war—I think it was around the time of the attack on Pearl Harbor. And perhaps because of the emotions involved, I have a vivid memory of standing with my family on the platform of Pennsylvania Station in Newark as a band played and my uncle Jim, my father's brother, headed off to war and to the invasion of France.

Typical of our family prayers was the following prayer from Saint Ignatius which we would recite together as we drove home from early morning Mass.

> Soul of Christ, sanctify me,
> Body of Christ, save me,
> Blood of Christ, inebriate me,
> Water from the side of Christ, wash me,
> Passion of Christ, strengthen me,
> O good Jesus, listen to me,
> In thy wounds, hide me,
> At the hour of my death, call me . . .

I had little clear idea of what prayers like this really meant, but I felt that they had a very deep meaning. At least they meant that God the Father, Jesus, his Mother, and the saints were very present to me. According to Catholic belief, such faith was a gift, a grace. Basically, it is "caught, not taught." Such faith is a way of looking at life with "the eyes of the heart." I "caught" such a faith from my mother and father.

Certainly the stories I heard from the religious Sisters of Saint Joseph at Our Lady of the Valley School just extended and deepened the larger narrative within which I was coming to understand my life. So also the friendliness and yet "mystical" authority of the local parish priests deepened in me the awe and admiration my whole family felt for the Catholic priesthood.

At the same time there was a reverence for intellect. My father's family in particular, inspired by "Grandma Liddy," had all graduated from college and was committed to education. Born Margaret Mary O'Brien in Morristown, New Jersey, in 1885, Grandma Liddy recalled her step-mother, Bridget Anglin, who had run a girls' finishing school in Ireland, talking about the renowned "Doctor Newman." When almost a century later I heard this from my aunt Mary, it struck me as strange how the great English writer, John Henry Newman, had through his books eventually become a great friend of my own mind and heart.

My mother also, a high school graduate, was an avid reader. A friend from college recently told me how amazed he was at the number of books my mother had around our house. And at an early age I remember rummaging through encyclopedias in our house and reading there articles about the structure of the atom. "Wow!" And also "chemistry experiments" with a friend, Hughie Devore, whose father at the time was the football coach at Notre Dame. It was obvious to me that the world was far larger than the immediate world around me. It seemed full of endless possibilities.

Such innate trust in reality found expression in play and sports, in hikes and friendships and, as I grew, in music. The music of my teenage years, which I often listened to on the "record player" as I lay on our living room floor, was romantic—the ballads of the forties and fifties. But it was also classical. I remember making the conscious decision to "stay with" a piece of classical music: to "let the music lead me" as I followed the long, intricate patterns of Beethoven or Tchaikovsky. To truly listen, to allow one's hearing to be "caught" in the rhythms, tensions and resolutions of "Swan Lake," seemed to be a freedom, a liberation, "a moment in and out of time." Years later I would write a doctoral dissertation on the American philosopher, Susanne K. Langer, and her philosophy of art.

Obviously, as I look back on it now, I was of a decidedly introspective temperament. Though I loved sports, especially playing them with my older brother, Joe—I still remember the thrill of catching my first fly ball!—I particularly loved "the inner world," the world of books and thoughts and music and art. I got involved in the external world of the people around me and I would do my best at it; but I was most comfortable in the unseen world.

Bernard Lonergan writes of "the world mediated by meaning," that is, "the far larger world" than the world of immediacy, that we get to know by questioning, understanding, judging and believing. It was this world I came to be truly interested in. And as I grew up and moved from elementary school to Seton Hall Prep, the local Catholic boys high school, and thought about my future, I "tried on" other callings besides the priesthood—the law, for example. But nothing ever "fit" like the priesthood. And so, even as a freshman in high school, I joined the seminary program for those who were thinking of taking this direction in life.

Among other things, we were very specifically encouraged to spend time in prayer; and, while sitting before the large crucifix in Our Lady of the Valley Church or kneeling before the Blessed Sacrament during "Forty Hours Devotions," the feeling I had for so long would return. I definitely felt a sense of "vocation," of "God calling me" to head in the direction of the priesthood.

Of course, during my high school and college years I wrestled a great deal with this decision. The idea of not pursuing one of the beautiful Catholic girls whom I knew involved, even then, an immense sacrifice. For, like other young men, I fell in love. I was knocked off my pins by a young lady a year behind me in school, someone I nervously took to high school dances. She was very quiet too and we did not talk too much!

And besides, I still felt this mysterious "call" to continue on toward the priesthood. As Dag Hammerskojld once wrote of his own "vocation":

> I don't know Who—or what—put the question, I don't know when it was put. I don't even remember answering. But at some moment I did answer "Yes" to Someone—or Something—and from that hour I was certain that existence is meaningful and that, therefore, my life, in self-surrender, had a goal.[1]

That "Yes!" had to be repeated again and again in my life through the years. For even at the time there were intimations of future sufferings and loneliness. The decision to continue on to for the priesthood, to move from high school to the college seminary program, emerged from a process of personal wrestling that involved my whole being. Francis Thompson's poem, *The Hound of Heaven*, whose 180 lines I memorized completely at one time during those high school years, spoke to my heart:

> I fled him, down the nights and down the days;
> I fled him, down the arches of the years;
> I fled him, down the labyrinthine ways

Of my own mind; and in the mist of tears
I hid from him, and under running laughter.
Up vistaed hopes I sped;
And shot, precipitated,
Adown Titanic glooms of chasmèd fears,
From those strong Feet that followed, followed after.
But with unhurrying chase,
And unperturbèd pace,
Deliberate speed, majestic instancy,
They beat—and a Voice beat
More instant than the Feet—
"All things betray thee, who betrayest me."

Though filled with foreboding, the poem's ending represented a great promise:

"All which I took from thee I did but take,
Not for thy harms,
But just that thou might'st seek it in My arms."

This image of running from, but being pursued by the living God, only deepened as around 1954 I read a novel by Ethel Mannion entitled *Late Have I Loved Thee*. In this novel the conversion of Saint Augustine forms the background for the narrative of a modern young man who leaves a reckless life to becomes a Catholic priest. At the same time, in the university we were also reading Augustine's *Confessions* and memorizing some of his Latin words:

Sero te amavi, pulchritudo, tam antiqua et tam nova, sero te amavi.
    Late have I loved thee, O Beauty ever ancient, ever new, late have I loved thee!

And I was absolutely thrilled, as many still are, by Augustine's words,

Fecisti nos ad te, Domine, et inquietum est cor nostrum donec requiescat in te.
    Thou hast made us for thyself, O Lord, and our hearts are restless until they rest in thee.

Though my own life's journey was not at all as dramatic as was Augustine's, still his "story" spoke to my heart. I still have the well-worn copy of Frank Sheed's translation of the *Confessions* which my mother had bought and which I picked up around our house. It is marked and underlined and there are notes in the margins. My own journey to appropriate my Christian faith was certainly intensified by that early encounter with Augustine's deep desire.

2. "A REASON FOR THE FAITH THAT IS IN YOU"

As the years passed, my "wrestling with God" became more and more intellectual. It was the 1950s and I was in my teens, and such a subtle affair as
the decision to become a priest had to—in some real way—make sense. Even
then, so rarified a decision, a decision so seemingly contrary to the outside
culture, needed to be backed up with an intellectual framework. For there
were obviously those outside the tight confines of my Catholic world who
believed different things than Catholics believed. I had Protestant and Jewish
friends from families in our neighborhood. I even read about those for whom
religious belief made no sense at all. It was obvious to me that the Catholic
way to live life was not the only option.

Furthermore, Catholics in general were slowly being assimilated into the
great movements of the American nation. Not only did members of my family
fight in both World Wars, engendering in us a deep sense of patriotism, but
the great movements rooted in the Enlightenment were having an effect not
only in the public schools where my father taught, but also in the Catholic
schools that I attended. If Catholics were to survive in this country, they had
to partake in the increasing specialization of knowledge that gradually was
breaking down the classical European educational system.[2]

Still, because I wanted to become a priest, I took the "classical track"
in Seton Hall Prep, an education consisting largely of the Greek and Latin
works with a smattering of mathematics and science. Similarly, at Seton
Hall University all those preparing for the priesthood majored in classical
languages. Our Greek teacher was Father William Halliwell, a relative of the
famous—for some, infamous—Will Durant, the popular historian who had
also attended Seton Hall. Father Halliwell was a tall thin gray-haired man
with a very eccentric wit, who in the midst of teaching would suddenly yell
out a question, such as "Old or young?" It took a while to catch on that someone had just spoken of "senators," the cognate of the Latin "senex," an older
person. This was not only a very effective method for keeping people on their
toes; it was also a great encouragement to study Skeets *Etymological Diction-
ary of the English Language*, an essential companion to Halliwell's classes.
In addition, Halliwell actually expected us to read Euripides' tragedies and
Plato's *Apologia* in Greek! Flunking my first exam in his course was a great
incentive to learning Greek.

Also, major political and cultural issues were in the air, and occasionally
those issues surfaced in my university classes. In a history course with Father
John E. O'Brien, for example, we read Crane Brinton's *The Makers of the
Modern Mind*, which catalogued the philosophies and cultural movements
that prepared the soil for "modernity."

In the widest terms the change in the attitude of Western men toward the universe and everything in it was the change from the Christian supernatural heaven after death to the rationalist natural heaven on this earth now—or at least very shortly. But the clearest way of realizing the greatness of that change is to start off with a very basic modern doctrine that is unquestionably new—the doctrine of progress. Belief in progress, in spite of the two world wars of our generation and the grave economic crisis of the thirties, is still so much a part of the way young Americans are brought up that very few Americans realize how unprecedented that belief is.[3]

It was during those years that I began to search out books that centered on "the reasons" for my Catholic faith." I remember questioning:

Why would a person who was not a Catholic, perhaps not even religious at all, change and want to become a Catholic? Why take on all this "baggage:" the specter of hell, meatless Fridays, Sunday obligation, Mass in Latin, a strict moral life, confession? Even celibacy? What really made "converts" tick? What went on in them? Were they for real?

This interest in religious converts—their journeys and their reasons for becoming Catholics—their stories—certainly reflected the questions I was asking myself. Was not their wrestling with faith amidst a secular world only a mirror of what I myself was wrestling with? that is, a secular world that seemed at times to get along quite well without all this Catholic folderol?

And so among my reading at the time were numerous "conversion stories," narratives of persons who had not been religious at all, or "not even Catholics," who eventually had undergone such a radical change in their lives as to become Catholics.[4] Such were the stories of Dorothy Day, Avery Dulles, Raissa Maritain, A. J. Cronin, Alexis Carel, Anne Freemantle, Clare Booth Luce.[5] All, in one way or another had tried to put into words the grounds for their decisions. And in the background of all of these stories loomed the secular world whose focus was decidedly "this worldly," with at least an indifference to, if not a denial of, "the Beyond."

That great secular world involved elements that were decidedly anti-religious, perhaps especially, anti-Catholic. At the time, Paul Blanshard's books attacking the Catholic Church as il-liberal and at root un-American were receiving a lot of attention. I remember my father talking about "that Paul Blanshard!" And my sister remembers my father coming home shaken one night from a Board of Education meeting in the city of Newark where he felt his Catholic faith had been attacked.

In short, we as Catholics were coming of age in America. Our families had fought in its wars and were participating in its public and civil institutions. And yet, to some degree, we kept a distance. We continued to preserve our own Catholic schools where the Catholic religion was freely taught and where all other things were seen in relation to Catholic faith. And beyond our own community there was "the modern world" often characterized by an anti-religious and indeed, anti-Catholic "animus."

In the face of these great cultural movements, the Catholic stance tended to be defensive. And I was defensive. I remember defending Senator Joseph McCarthy's anti-communist campaigns largely because he was a Catholic. And the image of Cardinal Mindszenty's harrowed face condemned to prison by the Hungarian Communists seared the Catholic soul. Perhaps the age of the martyrs was not over.

And so it is no wonder that my decision to become a priest would be filled with much questioning. Such questioning was both soul-searching and "world-searching." A friend from college recently recalled the many nights we stayed up in the Seton Hall dormitories arguing about these issues:

- Is there a God?
- How do you prove it?
- Who's to say?
- What does science have to say on the issue?

For many today these questions are no longer in fashion. Much of the "postmodern" world considers them to be questions arising within a particular Western context. Outside of this context the questions are meaningless. But for me these were real questions; in fact, they were "life and death" questions. If there is no God—really—why be a priest? In fact, if there is no God, why be good? Moral? Ethical? Was Dostoyevsky correct, "If there is no God, everything is allowed?"

It would be some years before I would feel adequate to handling these questions. But they were my real questions. They rolled around in my feelings and sometimes I articulated them to myself and to others. Karl Jaspers once described this "amateur philosophizing" in the following way.

Philosophizing is the activity of thought itself, by which the essence of the person, in its entirety, is realized in the individual. This activity originates from life in the depths where it touches Eternity inside Time, not at the surface where it moves in finite purposes, even though the depths appear to us only at the surface. It is for this reason that philosophical activity is fully real only at the summits of personal philosophizing, while objectified philosophical thought is a preparation for, and a recollection of, it. At the summits the activity is the inner action by which I become myself; it is the revelation of Being; it is the activity of being oneself which yet simultaneously experiences itself as the passivity of being-given-oneself.[6]

Something in those words would have rung true in me as I struggled as a young man with my self and my "vocation." They expressed the deep struggle—in part, a philosophical struggle—that was mine. Within what Lonergan calls "the dialectic" of opposing viewpoints, one is thrown back on oneself and the question of one's own existence. This is the question of one's own "self"—who one thinks one is and who one really is—the implicit self-knowledge at the core of our knowing and deciding. It is the implicit philosophy that only later finds expression in explicitly philosophical positions.

For the most part, all I had were questions. But the questions led to reading—and significant books began to come across my path. "When the pupil is ready, the teacher appears." As I mentioned, in our house there were always books lying around by folks who had also wrestled in one way or another with these deep questions of the human heart. One book that exercised a powerful influence on me was Thomas Merton's *Seven Storey Mountain*. Published in 1949, I read it in the early 1950s. It was the story of a young man's conversion to Catholicism and eventually to becoming a Trappist monk. The power of that bestseller in the early 1950's lay not only in its literary character, but also in Merton's presentation of the "reasonable" nature of his decisions. He had thought these things through and he had followed out the direction of his thought. In the mid-1930s his study of medieval history coincided with his own inner search. One day he picked up Etienne Gilson's *The Spirit of Medieval Philosophy* and read there:

> Beyond all sensible images, and all conceptual determinations, God affirms Himself as the absolute act of being in its pure actuality. Our concept of God, a mere feeble analogue of a reality which overflows it in every direction, can be made explicit only in the judgment: Being is Being, an absolute positing of that which, lying beyond every object, contains in itself the sufficient reason of objects. And that is why we can rightly say that the very excess of positivity which hides the divine being from our eyes is nevertheless the light which lights up all the rest: *ipsa caligo summa est mentis illuminatio* [that very exceeding darkness is itself the enlightenment of the mind].

Merton comments on this quote from Gilson:

> I think the reason why these statements, and others like them, made such a profound impression on me, lay deep in my own soul. And it was this: I had never had an adequate notion of what Christians meant by God.[7]

What was Gilson's language about? "The absolute act of Being in its pure actuality?" What was this? Was this language run amuck, the "be-witching" power of words? Or was there some deep meaning in this way of speaking? I did not know, but I certainly wanted to know. What was this that I was trying to get at? Who was this "God" who, especially in prayer, I felt was "calling" me?

Such were the topics of my questioning, my reading and my late night discussions in the college dorms with my friends. I was looking for words to explain "God" and the world to myself—and myself to myself. Though on occasion, especially in moments of crisis, I was tempted to unbelief, mine was a believing *praxis*. I was from a deeply believing Catholic family and I had already made commitments in line with that belief. In some sense perhaps I had already "fallen in love with God," the object of all I yearned for.

But I wanted to know who it was that I was in love with. I wanted to know who this being was and what "he" was doing—in me and in the world. My intellectual questioning did not interfere with my basic faith; in fact, it gave it a vibrancy.

A saying my father would sometimes repeat to my brother, Joe, my sister, Terry, and myself captured this combination of faith and questioning that would play such a large part of my life. It was a saying he had heard from his parish priest as a young man in Bernardsville, New Jersey. "Monsignor McKeon always used to say to us: 'Have a reason for the faith that is in you.'"[8]

That is what I was seeking: the "reason" for the faith that an invisible and incomprehensible God was calling me on a journey into the future beyond any horizons I could envision. It was certainly a journey beyond the pale of ordinary life.

3. SCHOLASTIC PHILOSOPHY

The desire to have "a reason for the faith that was in me" thrilled at the prospect of the formal study of philosophy when I entered the major seminary at the age of twenty in 1958. Immaculate Conception Seminary was located in an idyllic country area of northeast New Jersey, called "Darlington." It was an ideal location for prayer, reflection and study.[9] It included some 1600 acres of woods and lakes for hiking, swimming, ice-skating, etc. And within this beautiful setting there was the common life. There was the daily schedule with its rising at 5:30 am, meditation and Mass, and then off to a regulated day of class, meals, sports, study and prayer until you sank exhausted into bed at "lights out" at 10 pm. All was regulated by the seminary rule: "Keep the rule and the rule will keep you."

Common liturgical prayer was a major part of this regimen. In addition, during a rare free moment, one would steal into the beautiful dimly lit chapel for "a visit" and perhaps taste for a moment some consolation. All was in function of that future desired yet fearful day when one would lay prostrate on the floor of the cathedral before the bishop and commit oneself to the infinite God and to his people forever. Gradually you watched as the men in the classes in front of you began to be ordained.

Characteristic of the time and the place was the uniform, the black cassock, filled with symbolic meaning. The military discipline and regimen, the emphasis on authority guided by the universal law of the Church, the continuing prominence of Latin in our prayers and even in our textbooks—all conspired together to make you feel you were part of a universal church that was the repository of an unchanging tradition come down from the past. We had little awareness that many of the things that we attributed to "immemorial tradition" were in fact products of the Church's own more recent battle with the Enlightenment. We had little historical sense.[10]

Of course, there were some aspects of "the system" that even at the time we felt were just "too much." We were so cut off from the culture around us that I remember feeling quite specifically that I did not know if I could make it. Some of it was just "not me."

And, of course, the world of psychology was looked upon with great suspicion. "Freud?" And we were not encouraged to put into words what we were feeling. We survived by prayer, sports and friendships. And also by a great deal of humor—often at the expense of the faculty and administration! And yet, at the same time, many of us did as much reading as the schedule allowed. Though we were cut off from "the world," still, in a sense, that world was present to us.

Classicist Culture

The meanings that informed our lives at the time could be captured by the phrase, "a *classicist culture.*" Such a culture was characterized by the assumption that there was just "one real culture."

> It was the fruit of being brought up in a good home, of studying Latin and Greek in school, of admiring the immortal works of literature and art of the classical period, of adhering to the perennial philosophy, and of finding in one's laws and institutions the deposit of the prudence and the wisdom of mankind.[11]

This was how my superiors and teachers in the seminary tended to see things. It was a way of thinking rooted in classical culture and persisting into the twentieth century.

> It was named simply culture. It was conceived absolutely, as the opposite of barbarism. It was a matter of acquiring and assimilating the tastes and skills,

the ideals, virtues, and ideas, that were pressed upon one in a good home and through a curriculum in the liberal arts. This notion, of course, had a very ancient lineage. It stemmed out of Greek *paideia* and Roman *doctrinae studium atque humanitatis*, out of the exuberance of the Renaissance and its pruning in the Counter-reformation schools of the Jesuits. Essentially it was a normative rather than an empirical notion of culture, a matter of models to be imitated, or ideal characters to be emulated, of eternal verities and universally valid laws.[12]

Even though there were some cracks in the wall—and I could begin to "feel" them at the time—nevertheless what my teachers and I considered "culture" were the meanings and values set out once and for all in the classical past and handed on to us in the present. On this view, the unity of the Catholic faith tended to be seen as "everyone doing the same thing as it has always been done": for example, the Mass in Latin everywhere throughout the world. Its motto was that of the Vatican Cardinal Ottaviani: "*Semper idem*": "always the same." It also consisted in everyone subscribing to the correct formulae that had come down unchanged from the past: not only a common Creed, but even the memorized answers in the catechism. Connected to this view were the locked bars of "The Cage" in the seminary library, the repository of the books on the Index of Forbidden Books. We were not to be contaminated by exposure to heterodox views.

All of this was connected to what has been called the "banking" theory of learning in which the teacher "deposits" a carefully circumscribed amount of learning into the minds of passive students.[13] No effort was made to find out what we as students saw in the teaching that might influence a change in a teacher's methods. There was little to no mutuality.

Within the Church the Catholic clergy were the special carriers of this classicist culture. And it easily gave rise to a "clericalism." Since there is but one normative culture,

> . . . that one culture is not attained by the simple faithful, the people, the natives, the barbarians. None the less, career is always open to talent. One enters upon such a career by diligent study of the ancient Latin and Greek authors. One pursues such a career by learning Scholastic philosophy and theology. One aims at high office by becoming proficient in canon law. One succeeds by winning the approbation and favor of the right personages. Within this set-up the unity of faith is a matter of everyone subscribing to the correct formulae.[14]

But was this really what Catholicism was about? Often during those two years at Darlington I sensed that "something was missing." At the same time, it was true that, beneath the externals, I sensed a life.

Such classicism . . . was never more than the shabby shell of Catholicism. The real root and ground of unity is being in love with God—the fact that God's love has flooded our inmost hearts through the Holy Spirit he has given us (Rom. 5, 5).

Classical Philosophy

> But besides the meaning and value immediately intuited, felt, spoken, acted out, there is to any advanced culture a superstructure. . . . Besides the meanings and values immanent in everyday living there is an enormous process in which meanings are elaborated and values are discerned in a far more reflective, deliberative, critical fashion.[15]

The theory that articulated and defended this Catholic classicism consisted in Neo-scholastic philosophy. That philosophy formed the scaffolding, not only for Catholic theology, but also for all of Catholic education.[16] Obvious examples were the categories of "substance" and "accidents" used to explain Christ's presence in the Eucharist, and also the distinctions of "nature" and "person" used to explain the two natures and one person in Christ. The language of Scholastic philosophy constituted the whole superstructure of Catholic theology. All Catholic seminarians were required to study at least two years of such philosophy before beginning the study of theology.[17]

Looking back on it, it was an amazing requirement. No other professional, except university professors of philosophy, are required to study philosophy prior to their specifically professional studies. Why us? Why were we expected to study it? Why this emphasis on philosophy for future priests?

It seems that this required study of philosophy flowed from the conviction that the Christian vision of things could fit into a rational account of the universe. The study of philosophy implied the possibility of human reason analyzing human life in such a way as to grasp the "reasonableness" of the Christian vision. This insistence on the importance of philosophy implied that "the meaning of life" could be reasonably and rationally articulated in such a way as to in some sense "make sense" of the Christian mystery as the ultimate answer to life's questions.[18] There was at least some coherence between the Christian "answer" and human questions. This in fact had been a characteristic of Christianity from its earliest days when Christian apologists sought to articulate the meaning of the faith in terms of current philosophies.

Of course, it was a particular type of philosophy that we were asked to study—generally called "scholastic," or "neo-scholastic." Its basic tenet, at least in its major thrust, was an adherence to the teachings of St. Thomas Aquinas. Although Thomas' philosophy had gone in and out of favor since the thirteenth century, modern scholasticism owed a great deal to the influence to Pope Leo XIII's 1879 encyclical, *Aeterni Patris*. Leo's letter was a response

to the conflicting philosophical currents of the nineteenth century. As movements rooted in the Enlightenment seriously undermined the influence of the
Church in many areas, the Church fought back by a "return to Aquinas." Neo-
scholasticism was the Church's philosophical response to the great skeptical,
atheistic and agnostic philosophies of the eighteenth and nineteenth centuries,
the philosophies that accompanied and in large measure invoked the authority
of the scientific revolution.[19] Leo XIII's aim had been to strengthen contemporary Catholic thought by the influence and example of Aquinas. Just as
Thomas and his followers represented a principle for the transformation of
medieval culture, so it was hoped, the re-discovery of Thomas would provide
the principles for the transformation of the modern world.

And so, besides continuing to learn Latin and Greek, we were directed
toward the classical philosophers, Plato and Aristotle, and to their Christian
transformations in Augustine and Aquinas. We were encouraged "to hear the
accents of the Eternal in the temporal."[20] The reading of Plato and Aristotle,
of Augustine and Aquinas, was an effort "not to forget": to allow the rebirth
in us of what had happened in the minds of the classic writers. Our own efforts at authenticity were the condition for understanding the tradition and
that tradition itself could contribute to our own authenticity.

> Hence all appropriation of tradition proceeds from the intentness of our own
> life. The more determinedly I exist, as myself, within the conditions of the time,
> the more clearly I shall hear the language of the past, the nearer I shall feel the
> glow of its life . . . the new sound it makes in old thoughts.[21]

At least I got a "glimmer" of that call to authenticity found in the ancient
texts.

What was a much more difficult task—more difficult than we imagined
at the time—was understanding what this tradition really meant in its own
historical context. For example, how can we understand Aquinas in the context of his own times rather than as prismed through the eyeglasses of later
centuries? Classicist practice too easily gave way to facile interpretations of
Thomas, interpretations that historical scholarship, even among Catholics,
was beginning to challenge.

> When the study of Aquinas was enjoined on all students of philosophy and the-
> ology, what was envisaged was the assimilation of the basic tenets of Thomistic
> thought. But the first concern of historical scholarship is not to set forth and con-
> vince readers or hearers of the profundity of an author's thought, the breadth of
> his vision, the universal relevance of his conclusions. That sort of thing may be
> allowed to pad a preface or to fill out a conclusion. But the heart of the matter is
> elsewhere. It is a long journey through variant readings, shifts in vocabulary, en-
> riching perspectives—all duly documented—that establish as definitively as can

be expected what the great man thought on some minor topic within the horizon of his time and place and with no great relevance to other times and places. Only from a long series of such dissertations can the full picture be constructed—a picture as accurate as it is intricate, broad indeed but with endless detail, rich in implications for other times if only one has the time to sort them out, discern the precise import of each, and infer exactly what does and does not follow."[22]

In other words, the real point of historical scholarship was not primarily to vanquish opponents, but to come to understand historical figures in the context of their own times. But such a process can, in the long run, heighten oppositions in the present. Leo XIII's insistence on "returning to Thomas" eventually highlighted the fact that different "Thomas's" emerged as different interpreters brought different personal horizons to the interpretation of Thomas' texts.[23]

A Classicist View of Knowing

While undervaluing the historicity of the ancient texts, neo-scholasticism at the same time emphasized "logic." This emphasis on logic resulted in a pronounced tendency to "verbalism" or "conceptualism," that is, the use of words without any effective control on their meanings. A purely logical presentation did not necessarily convince. One could be very logical in all one's deductions, but at the same time, one's "principles," one's starting points, one's assumptions, might be confused.

And so there was this decidedly negative side to the philosophy we were presented. Some of our professors found it enough to give us "the party line"—sometimes called "non-historical orthodoxy." Some professors had no special training in philosophy and their courses followed the approved textbooks, thus passing on to us the concepts that had been passed on to them—without the meaning.[24]

This lifelessness was especially characteristic of what we were taught about what it means "to know." The terms of our "rational psychology" were taken largely out of Aristotelian metaphysics. It was a "faculty psychology," speaking mostly of "intellect" and "will" as "potencies of the soul." While paying little or no attention to consciousness or self-awareness, the "acts" of these potencies were related to their objects merely through the metaphysical categories of efficient and final causality.

Thus we were told that the process of knowing consists of acts of sensation followed by the two activities of "simple apprehension" and judgment. The first of these takes place through the activity of the "active intellect" grasping the forms of things—the "dog-ness" of a dog, for example—and impressing this concept or "expressed species" on the "possible intellect." This first act of the intellect was followed by a second act which is judgment. For the most part, neo-scholastic philosophers considered this second act to be a "composition or division," that is, the connection of a predicate to a subject or the negation of a predicate to a subject. Somehow all of this added up to a "realist" philosophy that maintained the ability of the human mind to know reality. As Ross Perot spoke of the NAFTA treaty as "that sucking sound from the south," so our rational psychology tended to picture the human mind as "sucking" concepts out of things and comparing them with each other to see if they resembled reality "out there."

This was an intuitionist view of knowing in which we somehow intuited the correspondence or our minds with reality. But somehow we were never led us to ask why we would not need another intuition to see if our previous intuition objectively corresponded to reality. It was a theory that implied infinite regress—the need for ever higher "looks" to check out the objectivity of previous "looks."

Indeed, although I could memorize this system for exams, I had no clear idea of what the scholastic terms—"potency and act," "essence and existence"—really meant. Years later a friend recalled to me his great surprise when, after much studying, he realized that what Thomas Aquinas really meant by "the active intellect" was our human capacity to wonder and to ask questions!

4. ETIENNE GILSON AND THE PROBLEM OF THE BRIDGE

Nevertheless, there was one very positive influence on my two years of studying philosophy. One of our teachers, Msgr. Joseph Przezdziecki—affectionately known as "Joey Prez" or "Prezzy"—had studied at the Pontifical Medieval Institute in Toronto. From Prezzy we got a sense of reading the actual texts of the great philosophers. In a pronounced Polish-American accent Prezzy would read a text from Aristotle or Aquinas, and then proceed to march back and forth in front of the classroom reflecting on or wrestling with the position enunciated in the text. He himself had studied under the renowned historian of philosophy, Etienne Gilson, and it was Gilson who had impressed upon him the importance of studying the primary texts themselves.

Gilson (1884-1978) was a Catholic layman whose writings and teachings, especially on medieval philosophy, found an audience far beyond the confines of the Catholic community. In many ways Gilson's commitment to the historical method, a detailed study of historical sources in their original languages, symbolized the new historically conscious culture that was challenging the classicist model in the Church.

Gilson's reputation during his lifetime was *non-pareil*: unsurpassed respect for and trust in advanced scholarly research and commitment to the primacy of the oldest materials, read always in the language in which they were written down, in view of what the original author intended to say, and with critical distrust of intervening interpretations. He wanted medieval studies to make a fresh start, functioning primarily at the post-graduate level, rediscovering the riches of a neglected and only too often despised Christian civilization between late classical times and the early Renaissance.[25]

Son of Catholic parents, Gilson studied philosophy at the Sorbonne in Paris under Henri Bergson. His doctoral thesis was on Rene Descartes, the pivotal figure in the move from medieval to modern philosophy. In 1913 he received a university appointment at Lille where he taught his first course on "The System of St. Thomas Aquinas." Later he would abandon the notion that philosophy could be systematized at all. "He accepted the Thomism of Thomas the philosophizing theologian. He did not admit even the possibility of a systematic Thomism, especially a Thomism reached largely through commentators and interpreters."[26]

Gilson achieved an international reputation and in 1936 he delivered the William James Lectures at Harvard, later published as *The Unity of Philosophical Experience*, a book Przezdziecki required us to read. It was this work which helped convince the great historian of culture, Eric Voegelin, of the epochal role of the thought of Thomas Aquinas.[27]

For Gilson the first and most fundamental of all notions is the notion of Being. Metaphysicians fail when they invest a particular determination of being with the universality of being itself; and the most tempting of all the false first principles is: that *thought*, not *being*, is involved in all my representations. Here lies the initial option between idealism and realism, which will settle once and for all the future course of our philosophy, and make it a failure or a success. Are we to encompass being with thought, or thought with being?

This was heady stuff. It was confronting modern philosophy head on and taking a stand. During the course of his career Gilson's emphasis shifted from the history of thought to metaphysics. This shift was caused less by his disagreement with modern idealists than by his rejection of the "critical realism" of certain neo-scholastics who were using Immanuel Kant's "critique of knowledge" to explain the realism of Aristotle and St. Thomas. He wrote a number of articles hostile to this Catholic "critical realism," culminating in his 1939 work, *Réalisme thomiste et critique de la connaissance.* [28]

So it was no surprise that our major adversary during those two years of philosophy was Immanuel Kant, the eighteenth century German philosopher who raised the question of the very possibility of knowing anything at all. Kant's project was in a real way an outcome of Descartes' efforts to specify "the foundations of knowledge" after those foundations had been shaken by the nominalism and skepticism of the later Middle Ages and by the successes of the new sciences

In addition to the thinking subject, the *res cogitans*, Descartes also posited a *res extensa*, material substance extended in space. Subsequent modern philosophy tended to emphasize either one or the other of these two foundations of knowledge. One stream, epitomized by the Scotsman, David Hume (1711-1776), emphasized *res extensa,* the sensitive foundations of knowledge and issued in modern empiricist philosophy. For Hume sensitive experience is the only genuine source of human knowledge. As a consequence, there really is no material or immaterial "substance"; all we really have access to are bundles of sense data. In addition to sense data, there are just our natural habits of mind by which we attribute "substance" to a certain set of experiences, or "causality" to a certain conjunction of events. A "cause" is merely our expectation that things will be conjoined in a certain way in the future. There is no permanent structure to things; there are only transitory experiences: the "blooming buzzing confusion" of primitive sensitive experiences linked together by mental habits.

Immanuel Kant (1724-1804)

The second stream flowing from Descartes and emphasizing the *res cogitans*, the thinking subject, is epitomized by Immanuel Kant. This stream issued in modern idealism and phenomenology. It was Hume's remarks on causality that roused Kant from his "dogmatic slumber," that is, "the realist assumption" that the mind could know things in themselves. If the causal relation cannot be experienced *a posteriori*, that is, after the fact, as Hume maintained, then the notion of causality must be contributed by the mind itself. It must be *a priori*. Kant extended this notion of the *a priori* to all necessary connections between concepts. His concern became "the conditions of the possibility" for knowing anything at all.

To explain these conditions Kant held that all our knowing takes place through "the forms of space and time" and the "*a priori* categories of understanding"—for example, unity, reality, causality, substance, etc. These are the intellectual "eye-glasses" through which we view the world. Consequently, since we have no intellectual "intuitions"—the only intuitions we have are sensitive—we cannot really know whether our knowledge arrives at "things in themselves." All we can really know are things prismed through the forms of our own understanding.

Where Descartes' dualism of *res cogitans* and *res extensa* led Hume to the empiricism of emphasizing *res extensa*, it led Kant to the idealism of emphasizing *res cogitans*, the central importance of the knowing subject. Since modern science has taken over the explanation of the empirical world of sense, philosophy's new role would be "the critique of knowledge," that is, the exploration of those aspects of human interiority that give rise to the world of science on the one hand and the everyday world of common sense on the other. Since there is no way of knowing what is "beyond" the objects of our sense experience, any metaphysical view of "the whole" is a chimera. The existence of God and the demands of morality are merely "postulates of our practical living."

The Problem of the Bridge

Przezdziecki adopted Gilson's refutation of Kant, that is, a direct counter-avowal. Gilson fiercely maintained that Kant's philosophy goes contrary to the common-sense convictions of the human person, especially the conviction that we do indeed know things in themselves. Our knowledge is evidently objective and Kant's ending point, the destruction of metaphysics, proves the error of his starting point, the idea that we can critique knowledge. We cannot start with the subject and end up in the real world.

As Gilson and Przezdziecki saw it, the basic issue was "the problem of the bridge," how to get from "in here" to "out there"; that is, how to get from our subjective activity to reality. Gilson and Przezdziecki solved this "problem of the bridge" by dogmatically asserting an "intuition of being," that is, an immediate spiritual perception of existing reality. Thus, Gilson asserted that over and above sensitive perceptions and intellectual abstractions there exists an intellectual vision of the concept of being in any sensible datum. It is this concept of being that is predicated in perceptual judgments of existence. It follows that realism is possible if and only if we perceive reality. In other words,

. . . if Prof. Gilson agrees with Kant in holding that objectivity is a matter of perception, if he differs from Kant in holding that de facto we have perceptions of reality, one must not think that he attempts to refute Kant by appealing to a fact that Kant overlooked. Prof. Gilson's realism is dogmatic; the course he advocates is ". . . the blunt reaffirmation of the dogmatic realism whose vitality was denied by Kant's critique."[29]

Gilson's dogmatic realism made sense to me. I can remember very vividly walking home one day from "the Mansion," the seminary classroom building, and reflecting with a friend on this idea of intellect as a "bridge" to reality:

You're over there; I'm here. How could I not validate human knowledge by asserting this? How could Kant maintain what he does? His critique just doesn't make sense! You're there; I'm here; I know you're over there. How could anyone not be a realist?

What I did not realize at the time was that both Kantianism and Gilsonian Thomism rested on the same assumption: namely, that the mind can only reach reality by taking a look at it. Kant denied we have such a mental faculty; Gilson countered that we did.

> Jack or Jill is invited to raise a hand and to look at it. The hand is really out there; it is the object. The eye, strangely, is not in the hand; it is some distance away in the head; it is the subject. The eye really sees the hand; it sees what is there to be seen; it does not see what is not there to be seen. That is objectivity.

Such is what Bernard Lonergan called the "naive realist" position on knowing; it has its strong points, but it also has a weakness.

> The strength of the naive-realist position is its confidence in the validity of human knowing; its weakness is its inability to learn.[30]

This emphasis on being certain, on refuting any skeptical attacks on the possibility of knowing, interfered with really figuring out what knowing in fact is. In our two years of philosophy we never spent any time examining how people who are successful in knowing things in fact know. Never were we directed to analyzing the operations of mathematicians and scientists who during the last several centuries have so greatly extended our knowledge of the natural world.

Years later I discovered that at the same time as I was studying classicist philosophy in the seminary, Bernard Lonergan was describing the roots of the system I was learning. In a lecture from 1961 he described a philosophical emphasis on the certainty of knowledge without a corresponding emphasis on understanding what in fact knowledge is.

> In the nineteenth century there began to appear, and there may still exist, books on epistemology that took their starting point in the existence of knowledge. Universal skepticism is self-contradictory; because it is contradictory, knowledge exists. But just knowing that knowledge exists is knowing something very abstract.

A philosophy, built upon such an abstract view of human knowing will give rise to "the Catholic ghetto."

> What kind of knowledge exists? What is the knowledge that exists? If you express the knowledge that exists abstractly, what will follow? You will have a mere abstraction, and it will give rise to alienation. It will give rise, for example,

to what has been called the Catholic ghetto. Catholics have held on to this idea of knowledge, while the rest of the world pays little attention to it. Merely to assert the existence of knowledge without saying as fully as you can what knowledge is, is to utter an abstraction, which gives rise to alienation.[31]

In other words, the alienation that Catholics began to articulate in the 1960's had some of its roots in a view of knowing that kept them from linking their faith with all the complex dimensions of human knowing and human living. A false or inadequate knowledge of human knowing kept Catholics from knowing themselves and from knowing others. Such could be alienating.

Since the rise of the modern sciences, however, there had emerged new concrete ways of understanding the world and new ways of understanding human history that were obviously very successful. If Catholics did not take these new ways of knowing very seriously, their accounts of what it meant "to know" would be "out of it" and they would contribute to the alienation of the Catholic community from the rest of the modern world.

In general, then, the traditional neo-scholastic philosophy courses did not encourage thought. Philosophy of its nature was supposed to be an appeal to human reason, certainly one's own reason. But the very idea of a "party line" eviscerated this idea of thinking for oneself. As Karl Jaspers said of the early philosophy courses he took in the university:

> The lectures offered nothing of what I sought in philosophy: neither the fundamental experiences of Being, nor guidance for inner action or self-improvement, but rather, questionable opinions making claim to scientific validity.[32]

5. INTIMATIONS OF CHANGE

Nevertheless, even in Darlington, even as I studied neo-scholastic philosophy, I was becoming aware of changes in the Church around me. Someone spoke to me about a French Jesuit paleontologist by the name of Teilhard de Chardin who was bravely trying to bridge the gap between Catholicism and the modern sciences. I became vaguely aware that Catholic writers, especially in Europe, were seeking to enter into dialogue with modern philosophy. Thus, lingering in the library one Sunday afternoon in 1959, I came across the work of Joseph Donceel, a Belgian Jesuit who had been greatly influenced by the school of Scholastic philosophy at Louvain, Belgium. That school's chief luminary, Joseph Maréchal, S.J. (1878–1944), had sought to initiate a dialogue between the philosophy of Thomas Aquinas and Kantian philosophy. I remember wondering why we were not being exposed to these writers.

Other currents were in the air. In a summer course Father Prezdzcki intro-

duced us to the Dane, Soren Kierkegaard, the inspiration for modern existentialism, and his appeal to personal authenticity in the face of any alienating intellectual system. I was attracted by and mystified by his mysterious words on
the break-up of his engagement to Regina Olsen, "If I had faith, I would have
married Regina." Kierkegaard himself was a person of deep religious faith,
but I gradually became aware that the twentieth century's major responses to
his call for authenticity were the agnostic and atheistic philosophies of Martin
Heidegger and Jean Paul Sartre.

Newman in *The Idea of the University* claimed that it was better to have too
few classes than too many, for students can often learn more from each other
than they can from the classroom. That was my experience at Darlington.
Among us there were a number bright young men who were widely read and
they directed me to very interesting writers, many of them French Catholics.
The novels of Leon Bloy, Francois Mauriac and Georges Bernanos gave me
a sense of the challenges of living the Catholic faith in the modern world. For
them faith was as much concerned with what went on outside the church as
it was with what went on within.

I began to read biographies of Catholic intellectuals and "how others had
done it." One that made a tremendous impression was Louis Bouyer's *The
Spirituality of John Henry Newman*. Newman was a very religious man, but
he was also very much of an "amateur philosopher." I read Bouyer's book
during a retreat, and from that time on, Newman became a companion of my
intellectual life.

I also read a biography of Charles De Foucauld, the Frenchman who at the
end of the nineteenth and early twentieth century dedicated himself to living
the contemplative life in the midst of the poor Islamic people of northern
Africa. He was killed by a band of marauders, but his life inspired the birth
of many communities, among them the Little Sisters of Jesus whom I was
to soon meet in Rome. De Foucauld's spirituality touched me deeply and his
inspiration has remained with me through the years. His life proclaimed the
need to live the Gospel in the midst of the world.

I also read at the time a biography of Edith Stein, the young Jewish intellectual and disciple of Edmund Husserl, who in 1922 became a Catholic
and eventually a Carmelite sister. Eventually martyred by the Nazis at Aus-
chwitz, Stein's life and writings became for me a great inspiration for a life
of faith—and intellect.

And so I left the two years of philosophy introduced to some of the basic
names and themes in the history of philosophy. I had been introduced to the
classical philosophers. In its fundamental positions the neo-scholastic philosophy I studied was fiercely anti-materialist, anti-Kantian and anti-atheist. But
it did not stick. It did not succeed in doing what it is the aim of philosophy

to do: to provide a personally appropriated language for understanding the world and ourselves. And the reason it did not stick was that its presuppositions were classicist.

> Fourthly, there is the collapse of Thomism. In the thirties it seemed still in the ascendant. After the war it seemed for a while to be holding its ground. Since Vatican II it seems to have vanished. Aquinas is still a great and venerated figure in the history of Catholic thought. But Aquinas no longer is thought of or appealed to as an arbiter in contemporary Catholic thought. Nor is the sudden change really surprising. For the assumption on which Thomism rested was typically classicist. It supposed the existence of a single perennial philosophy that might need to be adapted in this or that accidental detail but in substance remained the repository of human wisdom, a permanent oracle, and, like Thucydidides' history, a possession for all time.[33]

Not that there was no need for philosophy in the new age that was being born. But there was now a new context. The perennial philosophical issues had been transformed into a new key.

> In fact, there are a perennial materialism and a perennial idealism as well as a perennial realism. They all shift and change from one age to the next, for the questions they once treated become obsolete and the methods they employed are superseded.

NOTES

1. Dag Hammarskjold, *Markings* (New York: Knopf, 1966), 205.
2. For an excellent analysis of "the new learning" as distinct from the classicist education, see Bernard Lonergan, *CWL 10, Topics in Education*, ed. Frederick Crowe and Robert Doran (Toronto: University of Toronto Press, 1993), 15 ff.
3. Crane Brinton, *The Shaping of the Modern Mind* (New York: New American Library, 1953), 118. See Bernard Lonergan, "Theology in Its New Context," *A Second Collection*, 56-57: "Coinicident with the origins of modern science was the beginning of the Enlightenment, of the movement Peter Gay recently named the rise of modern paganism. Moreover, while this movement is commonly located in the eighteenth century, the French academician Paul Hazard has exhibited already in full swing between the years 1680 and 1715 a far-flung attack on Christianity from almost every quarter and in almost every style. It was a movement revolted by the spectacle of religious persecution and religious war. It was to replace the God of Christians by the God of the *philosophes* and, eventually, the god of the *philosophes* by agnosticism and atheism. It gloried in the achievements of Newton, criticized social structures, promoted political change, and moved towards a materialist, mechanist, determinist interpretation no less of man than of nature."

4. There were, for example, a series of books edited by John A. O'Brien from Notre Dame in which various converts to Catholicism recounted their particular stories. See *The Road to Damascus* (1949) and *Where I Found Christ* (1950).

5. Many of these converts to Catholicism reflected a Catholic literary revival that took place between the 1930's and the Second Vatican Council. On this "Catholic Revival," see Philip Gleason, *Contending With Modernity* (New York: Oxford University Press, 1995), 146 ff. For another view of the "Americanization" of Catholics, see Charles R. Morris, *American Catholic* (New York: Random House, 1997). More recently, on the tremendous influence of converts to the Catholic faith in England and the United States, see Patrick Allitt, *Catholic Converts: British and American Intellectuals Turn to Rome*, (Ithaca, NY: Cornell University Press, 1997).

6. Karl Jaspers, "On My Philosophy," *Existentialism from Dostoyevsky to Sartre*, ed. Walter Kaufmann (New York: World Publishing Co., 1972), 139.

7. Thomas Merton, *The Seven Storey Mountain* (New York: New American Library, 1952), 171-172.

8. See *1 Peter* 3, 15-16: "Always be ready to make your defense to anyone who demands from you an account of the hope that is in you."

9. Anthony Kenny, noted philosopher and master of Balliol College, Oxford, writes of his time in the Catholic seminary in England as the best educational experience he ever had: "I have never since been as well read, in the sense of retaining so much literature in my head at the same time." *A Path From Rome* (Oxford: Oxford University Press, 1986), 41.

10. Raymond Hedin in his book on seminary training and priesthood highlights this fact that we had no sense of history, of the fact that the seminary was historically created and conditioned and that it could *change*: ". . . We were told nothing of this history while we were students, lest it become 'mere' history to us, one actual course of events among other possibilities, and thus be reduced from absolute to relative status; for us, the contingencies of history were buried under the claims of timelessness." Raymond Hedin, *Married to the Church* (Indiana University Press, 1995), 26.

11. "Revolution in Catholic Theology," *A Second Collection*, 232.

12. "The Absence of God in Modern Culture," *A Second Collection*, 101. See also 92: "Culture was conceived normatively. It was a matter of good manners and good taste, of grace and style, of virtue and character, of models and ideals, of eternal verities and inviolable laws." The whole ethos was summed up by the title of a book by a Jesuit, James J. Walsh, *The Thirteenth: Greatest of Centuries* (1952).

13. See Sara Castro-Klarén, "The Paradox of the Self in *The Idea of the University*," *The Idea of the University*, ed. Frank Turner (New Haven: Yale University Press, 1996), 323 ff.

14. *Method in Theology*, 326-327.

15. "Belief: Today's Issue," *A Second Collection*, 91.

16. See Philip Gleason, *Contending With Modernity*, *passim*.

17. That requirement lasted up until the Second Vatican Council, after which for some years the demand for prior philosophy was significantly attenuated. Recently there has been an effort to reassert the importance of philosophy in the training for the priesthood. See Bernard Lonergan, "Questionnaire on Philosophy: Response,"

CWL, Vol. 17, *Philosophical and Theological Papers 1965-1980,* ed. Robert Doran and Robert Croken (Toronto: University of Toronto Press, 2004), 352-383.

18. See David Tracy, *America,* October 14, 1995, 18: "People in this country too easily forget simple things, for example that it was the philosophy departments of Catholic universities that kept philosophy pluralistic in this country. They weren't taken over, as so many secular departments in this country were until recently, by ana-lytical philosophy. It's been the philosophy departments of the great church-related, chiefly Catholic, institutions that kept alive philosophical forms that can help one think about religion and give one ways to approach theology. This is an intellectual benefit for the culture as a whole, as well as for the Catholic Church."

19. That indeed something was needed in the nineteenth century is evident from Bernard Lonergan's blunt lines in the early 1960's: "Thus I should maintain that the crop of philosophies produced sine the Enlightenment are not open to revealed truths because they possess no adequate account of truth." *CWL 4 Collection,* ed. Frederick Crowe and Robert Doran (Toronto: University of Toronto Press: 1988), 186. See also *Method in Theology,* 317: After outlining the cultural changes brought about during the last four centuries by science, scholarship and philosophy, Lonergan states: "These changes have, in general, been resisted by churchmen for two reasons. The first reason commonly has been that churchmen had no real apprehension of the nature of these changes. The second reason has been that these changes commonly have been accompanied by a lack of intellectual conversion and so were hostile to Christianity." On the failure of churchmen to recognize the end of the classicist world, see B. Lonergan, *A Second Collection,* 94.

20. See Karl Jaspers, "On My Philosophy," 138: "We can ask primal questions, but we can never stand near the beginning. Our questions and answers are in part determined by the historical tradition in which we find ourselves. We apprehend truth from our own source within the historical tradition. The content of our truth depends upon our appropriating the historical foundation. Our own power of generation lies in the rebirth of what has been handed down to us. If we do not wish to slip back, nothing must be forgotten; but if philosophizing is to be genuine our thoughts must rise from our own source."

21. Jaspers, "On My Philosophy," 133-134.

22. "The Scope of Renewal," *CWL 17 Philosophical and Theological Papers 1965-1980,* 283.

23. Gerald McCool describes the various schools of modern Thomism. See *Catholic Theology in the Nineteenth Century: The Quest for a Unitary Method* (New York: Seabury, 1977); and *From Unity to Pluralism: The Internal Evolution of Thomism* (New York: Fordham University Press, 1989).

24. Karl Jaspers, "On My Philosophy," 134: "Concepts which were originally reality pass through history as pieces of learning or information. What was once life becomes a pile of dead husks of concepts . . . "

25 L. K. Shook, "Gilson, Etienne Henry," *New Catholic Encyclopedia, Second Edition,* Vol. (Washington, D.C.: 2003) 227. A recruit in the first World War, Gilson was taken prisoner in Germany where he continued his early study of "Christian phi-losophy" and also learned Russian from other Russian prisoners. After the war he was

named full professor at the Faculty of Letters at the University of Strasbourg. There he published several works on medieval philosophy. In 1926 a chair in medieval philosophy was created for him at the Sorbonne in Paris where he taught courses on Thomas and Thomism, on St. Bonaventure and on the origins of modern philosophy.

26. Shook, 228.

27. See Eric Voegelin, *Autobiographical Reflections*. Ed. Ellis Sandoz (Baton Rouge, LA: Louisiana State University Press, 1989) 25; 95.

28. English translation, *Thomist Realism and the Critique of Knowledge*, tr. M.A. Wauck (San Francisco, 1986.) After the outbreak of World War II, Gilson's interests became increasingly theological and ecclesiastical. He was disturbed that Père Chenu's brochure on theological method had been placed on the Roman Index; and was soon equally disturbed at attempts to condemn Henri De Lubac's *Le Surnaturel*. In 1948 he published what some consider his masterpiece, *L'être et l'essence* (English: *Being and Some Philosophers*, Toronto, 1949).

29. "Metaphysics as Horizon," *CWL 4 Collection*, 196.

30. "Cognitional Structure," *CWL 4 Collection*, 214.

31. *CWL*, Vol. 5, *Understanding and Being,* ed. Elizabeth Morelli and Mark Morelli, revised and augmented by Frederick Crowe (Toronto: University of Toronto Press, 1990), 12-13.

32. Jaspers, "On My Philosophy," 132.

33. "The Absence of God in Modern Culture," *A Second Collection*, 110.

Chapter Two

Rome 1960–1964

1. ROME AND VATICAN II

Misgivings about some dimensions of seminary life—and about myself—took a back seat when in 1960 the seminary faculty recommended to my Archbishop that I continue my preparation for the priesthood at the North American College in Rome. It was an exciting prospect: travel, exposure to other cultures, especially to Italy, and of course, proximity to the successor of Peter, at that time the charismatic Pope John XXIII. Pius XII had died in 1959 and the Church had taken a most unexpected turn with the election of this short ample man from Bergamo who proceeded to call the twenty-first Ecumenical Council of the Church. Something was afoot; something was in the air; something was happening. It was exciting, but I did not know exactly what "it" was.

And so in September of 1960 I traveled to Italy on the ocean liner, "*Cristoforo Columbo*." It was a joyful and fun trip—meeting seminarians from throughout the United States also headed to Rome. A week later we arrived in Naples where we were met by older students from the North American College and given a two-day tour of the Naples-Sorrento-Amalfi area. Finally, we arrived in Rome and the North American College.

The college was a large post-World War II marble building on the Janiculum Hill with an imposing view of Rome and Saint Peter's. It was a monument to the triumph of the United States and the connection of American Catholics to the See of Peter. At the time it was presided over by its rector, Archbishop Martin J. O'Connor, a large man who carried himself with great ecclesiastical dignity. He incarnated the classicist worldview if ever there was one.

I was to stay in Rome for seven years, including the whole period of the

Second Vatican Council, returning home only during two summers. During my seminary years there I was to deepen the habits of discipline and piety I had adopted at Darlington, but at the same time we enjoyed more freedom to explore Rome and Italy, its historic monuments—and its restaurants! We explored Europe for a month each summer.

It was a heady time to be in the Eternal City. Things were in motion both within the Catholic Church and beyond. Not only had Pope John called the Council but America had a dynamic Catholic President with a flair for oratory who had initiated such things as the Peace Corps. On a European tour in early 1963 President Kennedy visited the College and shook hands with everyone. He asked me where I was from and I almost forgot!

Everywhere one looked, it seemed that change and hope abounded. Although my archbishop, Archbishop Thomas Aloysius Boland, returned from the first session of the Second Vatican Council with the reassurance, "Don't worry, nothing will change," still many things were changing. It was wonderful to be a young seminarian in Rome during those days. Frequently bishops and leading theologians from around the world would come to the North American College to give lectures on what was at stake in the Council. And a few blocks away, over at Saint Peter's, armed with a press card from my local newspaper, I was occasionally able to work my way in to the Council sessions. And virtually every day after those sessions I would attend the English-speaking press briefings in the USO Center not far from St. Peter's. Staffed by Council participants and expert "*periti*," those briefings were mini-courses on the Church's developing theology.

I remember one day reporters asking about discussions going on in the Council on the role of Mary in the Church. One theologian responded: "It's simply a case of the 'minimalists' versus the 'maximalists.' The maximalists want to attribute to Mary every conceivable dignity and the minimalists want to attribute to her as little as possible." Immediately the Redemptorist priest, Bernard Haring, one of the great moral theologians of the century, responded: "I think it would be a great disservice to the Church to look at this issue as one between the minimalists and the maximalists. The issue is one of truth: the truth of Mary's role in the mystery of salvation—and that is what the Council Fathers are trying to clarify." The next day the headline in the *International Herald Tribune* read "Council Fathers Split on the Role of Mary" and the first lines explained: "Yesterday the Council split between the minimalists and the maximalists." So much for "spin!"

Still, it was an exciting time. The discussions and conflicts going on the aula of St. Peter's were mirrored in our studies at the Jesuit Gregorian University. "The Greg" was a forbidding looking stone building in the center of Rome to which the various Jesuit provinces in the world contributed some of their brightest professors. When I began my classes there in October of 1960, I was immediately overwhelmed as I listened to the professors lecturing in Latin! I had known that the classes were supposed to be in Latin—but here they really were! And as we listened that first day to the Canadian Jesuit, Fr. Rene Latourelle, a fellow student from New Jersey, Jim Herbert, leaned over and traced the design for a tick-tack-toe game on my notepad! Eventually, however, after a couple of months of some intense study, we began to realize that we were even chuckling at the professor's jokes in Latin!

The framework for our studies was, obviously, classicist. The major emphasis was on "dogmatic theology," that is, the articulation and defense of the dogmas of the Church against all adversaries. The focus was on the clear articulation of the certitudes proclaimed by the Church, certitudes to be memorized and proclaimed by future priests. For clarity, all of theology was divided into various treatises. Each treatise normally was the work of one semester: "The One God," "The Triune God," "God Creating and Elevating," "The Word Incarnate," "The Blessed Virgin," etc. Again, for clarity, the substance of each treatise was divided up into a limited number of short, one-sentence "theses." Twenty to thirty theses commonly constituted a single course and the daily lectures in Latin progressed through the theses one at a time and in sequence.[1] Each thesis was followed by the definition of its terms. A typical thesis, for example, read:

> *Ex doctrina Novi Testamenti constat unum eumdemque Jesum Nazarenum et (1) verum hominem esse, et (2) multipliciter divina participare, et (3) verum esse Deum.*
>
> "From the teaching of the New Testament it is evident that the one and the same Jesus of Nazareth (1) truly is a man; (2) in a variety of ways participates in divine things; and (3) truly is God."

The thesis and the definition of its terms were followed by the "theological note." For example, was this thesis infallibly held? defined by an ecumenical council or a Pope? the clear teaching of the Scriptures and tradition? Or was it rather the "opinion of theologians?" the "better theologians?" or only a probable opinion?

There followed the list of adversaries: everyone from "the Saduccees" of Jesus' time to contemporary writers. These adversaries were often just listed without any serious attempt to understand their teachings in their own historical context. Next, there was the "argument" in defense of the thesis and the argument was taken from the three sources: 1) Scripture; 2) Tradition and 3) Reason. The arguments from Scripture were regularly taken from "proof-texts," that is, individual Scriptural texts taken out of their original historical context. Similarly, the arguments from tradition were taken from "Denziger," a collection of conciliar and papal teachings, again set out without much notice of the historical contexts in which those texts originated. Finally, there was the argument from "reason," usually set out in the form of an Aristotelian syllogism. Sometimes it was noted that the proof from reason was only *de convenientia*, that is, concerned only with the "fittingness" of a particular revealed doctrine. Finally, there were responses to objections, again set out in syllogistic fashion.

The student was expected to memorize this structure and all the bits and pieces that fit into it. The exams in the major courses usually took place in June, at the end of the entire scholastic year, and these were oral exams administered by our Jesuit professors in Latin. For some months before the exams we would wander in pairs around the grounds of the North American College practicing our Latin responses. It was clearly a classicist structure. To quote Quentin Quesnell:

> Clearly this Scholastic thought world was one that put an extraordinary premium on logic, clarity, the mechanics of exposition, on precise divisions and subdivisions of material. It presupposed the possibility of perfect and exact definitions of everything . . . [2]

We had little awareness that this set-up originated in the seventeenth century in reaction to the Enlightenment. "When modern science began, when the Enlightenment began, then the theologians began to reassure one another about their certainties."[3] As Bernard Lonergan would describe this set-up some years later:

> It would be unfair to expect the theologians of the end of the seventeenth century to have discerned the good and evil in the great movements of their time. But at last we may record what in fact they did do. They introduced "dogmatic" theology. It is true that the word "dogmatic" had previously applied to theology. But then it was used to denote a distinction from moral, or ethical, or historical theology. Now it was employed in a new sense, in opposition to scholastic theology. It replaced the inquiry of the *quaestio* by the pedagogy of the thesis. It demoted the quest of faith for understanding to a desirable, but secondary, and indeed, optional goal. It gave basic and central significance to the certitudes of faith, their presuppositions, and their consequences. It owed its mode of proof to Melchior Cano and, as that theologian was also a bishop and inquisitor, so the new dogmatic theology not only proved its theses, but also was supported by the teaching authority and the sanctions of the Church. Such a conception of theology survived right into the twentieth century, and even today in some circles it is the only conception that is understood.[4]

2. HISTORICAL CONSCIOUSNESS

Nevertheless, in spite of the demands of "the system," the times themselves led us to read voraciously outside of the official textbooks. The bookstore at the North American College did a booming business importing books from all over the world, especially from England. Key books marked my early time in Rome. One was Francis X. Durwell's *The Resurrection*, a work that used the latest biblical scholarship to focus on the central role of the resurrection of Jesus in the early Christian message. Another work that touched me was *Liberty and Law in Saint Paul* by Stanislaus Lyonnet, S.J., a popular professor at the Pontifical Biblical Institute in Rome. Lyonnet explained St. Paul's teaching on the liberty of the Christian by invoking the teachings of Thomas Aquinas on the Holy Spirit as liberating the Christian from the bonds of legalism. It was a delight to read Thomas' words: "Wherefore the letter, even of the Gospel would kill, unless there were the inward presence of the healing grace of faith."[5]

For these and similar teachings Lyonnet got into trouble with conservative circles in Rome, especially located at the Lateran University, and for a period was even removed from teaching. I remember vividly one of our professors, Fr. Maurizio Flick, S.J., coming into class one day and vigorously defending him against "the cowardly attacks of those at another university in this city"—to the cheers of the students!

Then, on the verge of the Council, there was the young Hans Kung's *Reform and Reunion*, a visionary view of the ecumenical possibilities of a renewed Catholic Church. I read that book at the villa of the North American College at Castel Gondolfo, the Pope's summer residence, where all of us went for summer vacation. There, living in a room with three other class-mates—David Tracy from Connecticut, Ray Wicklander from Chicago and Dennis Sheehan from Boston—we discussed late into the night what was happening in the church—and in us.

There was also Bernard Haring's seminal work in moral theology, *The Law of Christ*, which aimed at moving Christian preachers and teachers away from a legalistic ethics. Teilhard de Chardin's name was also very much in the air in those days and I was moved by his *The Divine Milieu*, a dynamic vision of Christ from an evolutionary perspective.

Nor was our reading limited to religious writers. I began to read more and more of the existentialist philosophers and works of contemporary psychology. Among the latter was Carl Roger's *On Becoming a Person* with its—for me—refreshing emphasis on "being in touch with one's feelings." Now that was something new!

Finally, we all kept in touch with the underlying "political" conflicts within the walls of St. Peter's by gobbling up the various "Reports from Vatican City" in *The New Yorker* magazine by the pseudonymous "Xavier Rynne"—who turned out to be an American Redemptorist priest.[6]

Even at the Gregorian, in spite of the classicist framework, new historically conscious perspectives were emerging. In fact, the emphasis that really intrigued me was historical: the actual historical formation of the Scriptures, the rooting of the liturgy in early history, etc. The history of a subject brought it alive, put flesh on it, situated it in the context of real people and their real lives. In my first year I was particularly intrigued by Fr. Rene Latourelle's course on the distinctiveness of each Gospel writer's account of the story of Jesus. Later I was enthralled by a course on the infancy narratives in the Gospels of Luke and Matthew. Subsequently, I did my licentiate thesis, the equivalent of an M.A., on the use of the psalms in the discourses of the *Acts of the Apostles*.

These courses and studies seemed to bring the Scriptures alive. There were meanings here that I had never imagined before, meanings woven together by persons rooted in the Hebrew Scriptures and in particular historical faith communities. Whether it all "really happened" as I had previously "imagined" it to happen—that question took second place in comparison to the meanings being revealed.

Such studies brought history alive in ways I had never before experienced. I remember being enchanted when a work of immense historical erudition, *Augustine the Bishop*, by F. Van der Meer, was read to us in the seminary dining room during retreat. Among other things, that book vividly recreated the excitement of the Easter vigil as experienced in Augustine's church in northern Africa in the early part of the fifth century.

I hardly realized it at the time but my historical studies—whether of the Hebrew Scriptures, the New Testament or later church history—were connected to a massive cultural shift in the Catholic Church that was at the same time, about a mile away, being solemnly recognized by the majority of the bishops in the aula of Saint Peter's. I hardly realized that both what I was studying and what was taking place in Saint Peter's were moments in a great cultural shift that was taking place in the Western world—away from "classicism" to "historical consciousness."

This movement to historical consciousness was closely linked to modern science's emphasis on understanding the empirical data, only now the data were not the data of sense, but rather the human meanings originating in particular human persons and communities. Especially from the eighteenth century onward, scholars of history had aimed at meticulously assembling and interpreting these past creations of the human family. First applied to the classics of Greece and Rome, and then to the study of early Christianity, historical scholarship finally in the twentieth century came to be applied—even among Catholics—to the study of the Sacred Scriptures.

Such a way of looking at things was a far cry from the classicism that only focused on "human nature" and missed the myriad ways human nature is lived out. Without denying human nature, it added the quite distinctive categories of the human person as an historical being, "an incarnate subject."

> Such terms refer to a dimension of human reality that has always existed, that has always been lived and experienced, that classicist thought standardized yet tended to overlook, that modern studies have brought to light, thematized, elaborated, illustrated, documented. That dimension is the constitutive role of meaning in human living. It is the fact that acts of meaning inform human living, that such acts proceed from a free and responsible subject incarnate, that meanings differ from nation to nation, from culture to culture, and that, over time, they develop and go astray. Besides the meanings by which man apprehends nature and the meanings by which he transforms it, there are the meanings by which man thinks about the possibilities of his own living and makes his choice among them. In this realm of freedom and creativity, of solidarity and responsibility, of dazzling achievement and pitiable madness, there ever occurs man's making of man.[7]

Such historical consciousness was a far cry from the classicist culture which had influenced my early studies. For far from emphasizing the one Latin culture that was the norm for all others, historical consciousness emphasized the diversity and distinctiveness of cultures. Far from looking down on this diversity, historical consciousness reveled in such differences and invited scholars to truly try to understand and even respect others "in their otherness." "Pluralism" was being born within the Catholic community.

This explosion of historical consciousness gave rise to many movements. Ironically enough, Leo XIII's call to "Return to Thomas!" encouraged the historical study of Thomas in his "other-ness" from modern culture. I have mentioned Etienne Gilson's scholarly historical studies of medieval culture, philosophy and Aquinas. In addition, the burgeoning studies of the Fathers of the Church and of early Christianity revealed to scholars the vibrancy of the liturgy in early Christianity, thus giving rise to the liturgical movement. Concomitantly, people came to a greater awareness of the importance of the diverse local churches and local communities within the universal Church.

All of these movements had been germinating within the Church since the nineteenth century, but not without a great deal of resistance. Fear of "subjectivism" and relativism gave rise to the condemnation of the heresy of "Modernism" by Pope Pius X in the early years of the twentieth century.

At the time, precisely for these emphases, all professors of Catholic theology were required to take the "Oath Against Modernism" as a pre-requisite to their teaching. Even the great nineteenth century figure of John Henry Newman, who emphasized the study of history and the development of Christian doctrine, was treated with reserve.

Nevertheless, the study of Church history, the study of the Scriptures, the "reaching out" to diverse cultures, the rediscovery of themes such as "the Church of the poor," the dignity of the laity, etc. — all these themes had been germinating here and there within the Church for over a century. But all these movements only found "official" expression in the great Council that took place in the Vatican from 1962 to 1965. John XXIII was the Pope and, for some reason, this humble man felt that this was the time for a great "aggiornamento," a great "updating," to take place.

All of this gave us as students the profound feeling that an old world was breaking up and a new one was being born—and we could be part of that new world. In the classicist culture which in many ways we were all still experiencing, stability was the central emphasis: the unchanging essences of things.[8] But we were also experiencing something new and something new within the Church. As Newman put it: "In a higher world it is otherwise, but here below to live is to change and to be perfect is to have changed often."[9]

3. FOUNDATIONS?

> Classical culture cannot be jettisoned without being replaced; and what replaces it cannot but run counter to classical expectations.[10]

In many ways the Council represented a revolt against the type of scholastic philosophy I had studied at Darlington. Again and again during the Council, when the bishops wanted to characterize an approach that they would not take, they would characterize it as "scholastic," and by that they meant an approach couched in the terms and methods of Aristotelian philosophy and syllogistic reasoning.

And when they were asked what positive approach they would take, they invariably spoke of it as "pastoral," that is, an approach that cared about "communicating" with people: not only those within the church, but also the great mass of humanity beyond the confines of the Catholic Church. Thus, the opening message of the Council was a *"Message to Humanity."*

> We take great pleasure in sending to all people and nations a message concerning that well-being, love and peace which were brought into the world by Christ Jesus, the Son of the living God, and entrusted to the Church.

Thus, one of the central words for understanding the Council was "dialogue": dialogue with other Christians, dialogue with non-Christians, dialogue with "the modern world," and even with atheists. Even the church's dialogue with herself in the Council was seen to be in function of her dialogue with others. To entrust the Word of God to others she had to use a language that was understandable to them. Scholastic language was not even used by other Christians. The scholastic mode of thinking and speaking was inappropriate in this dialogue because it was not a language in which most contemporary people, Christian or non-Christian, thought about themselves and their world.

In order to be pastoral, then, and dialogical, the Council fathers and theologians would often use terms such as "personal," "existential," "experiential." In this, particular modern ways of philosophizing were influencing the Council. We already mentioned existentialism with its emphasis on human interiority and human decision-making. The French Catholic writer, Gabriel Marcel, in his book, *Homo Viator*, which emphasized the distinction between looking at life as either "a problem to be solved" or, "a mystery to be lived," illustrated the compatibility of such emphases with religious living. "Phenomenology," a philosophical method associated with the writings of Edmund Husserl, focused on various dimensions of human interiority while "bracketing" questions of existence. Edith Stein, whom we mentioned previously, found her way into Catholicism through her phenomenological studies under Husserl. Pope John Paul II was later to be greatly influenced by this phenomenological method, in particular by the writings of Max Scheler (1874-1928), who emphasized the levels of human feelings and human community.

Perhaps the word most often used to describe these new ways of philosophizing was "personalism." For these various influential ways of thinking took as their starting point, not a theory or a system, but the concrete acting, feeling, responsible person. They were based on the conviction that any valid thought about the human person must begin from the human person's own inner experience. This approach had been prefigured in Catholic thought in the nineteenth century by John Henry Newman in England and in France by the layman, Maurice Blondel (1861-1949). Followers of Etienne Gilson might feel that beginning with the human person's own inner experience was a dead end, but other Catholic thinkers disagreed. They felt that to create a valid philosophy in the context of our own times, you must begin with the human person's own appropriation of his or her own inner life.

This was a cultural situation which neither Aristotle nor St. Thomas Aquinas had anticipated. It was the situation of modern science and modern historical scholarship. It was the situation of modern philosophy from Descartes on with its emphasis on introspective questions: What is the human person? What is human thought? What is human consciousness? Human interiority? It was a situation that thinkers in the tradition of Aristotle and St. Thomas had to take into account if they were to link their philosophical understandings with "the joy and hope, the grief and anxiety of the people of this age, especially those who are poor or in any way afflicted."[11]

How to do that was the trick. Without the accomplishment of that trick, intellectual schizophrenia was the order of the day. On the one hand, there was a scholastic theory or system employed to talk *ad intra* within the Catholic walls; on the other hand, one spoke a totally different language when one went to the office, the business, the physics laboratory, the school, the theatre. How was the Church to speak with all these worlds?

And so it was no wonder that questions began to arise. They began to rise in me.

> Is there any integrating language here? What's the "correct" philosophy? Is it "personalism?" "phenomenology?" "existentialism?" Is there not a danger here of "throwing the baby out with the bath water?" Is there not a danger of becoming lost in an endless relativism? an "incommensurable pluralism" in which it is impossible to communicate from one culture to another? "You do your thing in your culture and I'll do mine in mine—but never the twain shall meet?"

And, as the Second Vatican Council went on, it seemed evident that two contradictory tendencies were emerging, two tendencies that were almost inevitable.

> There is bound to be formed a solid right that is determined to live in a world that no longer exists. There is bound to be formed a scattered left, captivated by now this, now that new development, exploring now this and now that new possibility.

At the time I certainly would have belonged to "the scattered left." And yet, it seemed, a third alternative was needed.

> But what will count is a perhaps not numerous center, big enough to be at home in both the old and the new, painstaking enough to work out one by one the transitions to be made, strong enough to refuse half measures and insist on complete solutions even though it has to wait.[12]

We didn't know it at the time but we sensed it—we sensed we were in the midst of massive changes. Just the depth of emotion generated in people: that "those conservatives" were the embodiment of all that was evil and "progress" and "being up to date" and being "progressive" were the embodiment of all that was good.

But we didn't know the nature of what was happening: that it was primarily a question, not of faith but of culture. For a new kind of culture was being born and that new kind of culture was being accepted by the Church as a carrier of faith today.

NOTES

1. Quentin Quesnell, "A Note on Scholasticism," *Desires of the Human Heart: An Introduction to the Theology of Bernard Lonergan*, (NY: Paulist Press, 1988), 145.

2. Quesnell, 147.

3. "Theology In Its New Context," *A Second Collection*, 55.

4. *A Second Collection*, 57.

5. Thomas Aquinas, *Summa Theologiae*. I-II, q. 106, a. 2, c. Quoted in Stanislaus Lyonnet, *St. Paul: Liberty and Law* (Rome: Pontificio Istituto Biblico, 1962) 244.

6. Xavier Rynne's narratives in the *New Yorker*, still interesting reading, can be found in his Vatican Council II (New York: Farrar, Straus and Giroux, 1968). For the confession of the "real" Xavier Rynne, see Francis X. Murphy, "Out of the Catacombs," *America*, September 11, 1999, 15-17.

7. *A Second Collection*, 60-61.

8. "So its philosophy was perennial philosophy, its classics were immortal works of art, its religion and ethics enshrined the wisdom of the ages, its laws and its tribunals the prudence of mankind. Classicist culture, by conceiving itself normatively and universally, also had to think of itself as the one and only culture for all time." *A Second Collection*, 93.

9. John Henry Newman, *An Essay on the Development of Christian Doctrine* (London: Longmans, 1894), 40.

10. *CWL 4 Collection*, 245.

11. *Pastoral Constitution on the Church in the Modern World*, 1.

12. *CWL 4 Collection*, 245.

Chapter Three

Lonergan the Teacher

Encounter is . . . meeting persons, appreciating the values they represent, criticizing their defects, and allowing one's living to be challenged at its very roots by their words and by their deeds.[1]

When I first met Bernard Lonergan, soon after I arrived in Rome in 1960, he was a fifty-six year old Jesuit from Canada teaching theology at the Gregorian University. Among the older students, he enjoyed the reputation of being the most brilliant of our professors, though he was considered very difficult to understand. I first laid eyes on him in a Roman restaurant, *Il Buco*, where he was having dinner one "free day," that is, Thursday, with some of the older American students. He struck me at the time as a very unassuming man, somewhat corpulent, with a grandfatherly mien. William Shea once described him in this way:

> Bernard Lonergan looked like a man who knew what he was doing and enjoyed it. In the score of times I saw him I could not take my eyes off him. That is understandable, perhaps, because he was the big man in my small world. But he was not what one would expect a great teacher to be. He had none of the sense of theatrical drama, no flash, no bamboozle, none of the Great Man aura. He had a monotonous voice; his hands shook distractingly; he looked overweight, not at all prepossessing in his physical appearance, and he had little physical grace. Oddly, then, it was a pleasure listening to him and watching him. I think it was because he was very smart and clear about what he was doing, and he did it with pleasure. In the academic world one does not often run into really smart people, though one regularly does run into intelligent and capable people. I had the conviction, both from the time I read *Insight* and from the first time I listened to him lecture and answer questions, that he was the smartest person I had run into.[2]

But where had Lonergan come from? What was the history of this brilliant teacher with a pronounced Canadian accent? For at the time none of us knew much of his background. We did not know of his early "nominalism" and iconoclastic attitude towards much scholastic philosophy. Nor were we aware of the influence of Cardinal Newman on his thought, nor that of Plato and Augustine. We were much more aware of the fact that he was steeped in the writings of Thomas Aquinas, having written his doctoral dissertation on the notion of "grace" in Aquinas and later his first book, *Verbum: Word and Idea in Aquinas* on Thomas' cognitional theory. Certainly none of us were aware of his early "intellectual conversion" experienced while studying theology. We knew little of the details of his intellectual journey.

Nor did we know that during his student days in Rome in the 1930s Lonergan had been slated to teach philosophy, but in 1938 the Rector of the Gregorian University had written to his Provincial in Canada asking that he do his further studies in theology.

> Fr. Lonergan has left a splendid record behind him here; and we shall be happy to see him back for further studies. I would suggest—supposing his own preferences are not too strong for one field rather than the other—that he devote himself to Theology. In that Faculty there are hundreds of English-speaking students, who will be needing his help in the future.[3]

As it turned out, my classmates and I were among those English-speaking students, many sent by American bishops, whom Lonergan would teach in the 1950s and 1960s. But during the 1940s, after his return from his studies in Rome, Lonergan had returned to an earlier interest in modern science and mathematics. In this he had the help of his friend, Fr. Eric O'Connor, who had just returned from Harvard with his Ph.D. in mathematics.

> When I began teaching at L'Immaculee Conception [in 1940], Fr. Eric O'Connor returned from Harvard with his Ph.D. in mathematics and began teaching at Loyola College in Montreal. Later in a conversation it transpired that he was having difficulty in his efforts to teach; I asked him whether he was using the highly formalized methods then in vogue. He said that he was and I suggested that he concentrate on communicating to his students the relevant insights and that on this basis the students would be able to figure out the formalizations for themselves. My suggestion worked. The result was that I had an expert mathematician who also knew his physics (during the Second World War he helped out at McGill University and taught quantum theory there) whom I could consult when writing the earlier chapters of *Insight*.[4]

Another factor from the 1940s that presaged his writing of *Insight* was an adult education course that he taught at the Thomas More Institute in Montreal after the end of the war in the fall of 1945. The course was entitled "Thought and Reality" and years later he remarked on the receptiveness of his students and the encouragement it gave him to continue on the track he had begun.

In September there were about forty-five students coming; at Easter there were still forty-one. It seemed clear that I had a marketable product not only because of the notable perseverance of the class but also from the interest that lit up their faces and from such more palpable incidents as a girl marching in at the beginning of class, giving my desk a resounding whack with her hand, and saying, "I've got it." Those that have struggled with *Insight* will know what she meant.[5]

An incident such as this, recalled many years later, revealed to Lonergan the powerful effect of sharing with others the fruits of his own intellectual development. The fruit of this work was the publication in 1957 of *Insight: An Essay on Human Understanding.*

I worked at *Insight* from 1949 to 1953. During the first three years my intention was an exploration of methods generally in preparation for a study of the method of theology. But in 1952 it became clear that I was due to start teaching at the Gregorian University in Rome in 1953, so I changed my plan and decided to round off what I had done and publish it under the title of *Insight: A Study of Human Understanding.*

1. SOME MEMORIES

Of course, I knew none of this when in 1960 I first met Lonergan in Rome where he had been teaching since 1953. In the fall of 1962 and 1963 he was my professor of theology for two courses, one on the Trinity, "*De Deo Trino,*" the other on Christ, "*De Verbo Incarnato.*" There I listened as his pronounced English-Canadian twang combined with a classical Latin as he focused on shedding some light on the mysteries of the Trinity and the Incarnation.

The Gregorian was a dark stone building in the center of the city, intimidating, like many buildings in Rome, by its marble massiveness. In its great hall, the magna aula, about six hundred of us gathered daily, students from all over the world, to listen to our Jesuit lecturers. As a result, by tradition as well as by necessity, the only pedagogical method was the lecture. Years later Lonergan would refer to those teaching conditions as "impossible": so many young men from so many different countries listening to a professor lecturing about the Trinity in Latin!

Lonergan was not a *peritus*—an "expert" or invited theologian—at the Second Vatican Council. Still, perhaps more than many actually present at the Council, he was very aware of the massive forces that had brought about that great event. His reading was extensive, as even a cursory glance at the footnotes of his books attested. He even learned from his students!

For the first ten years I was there [in Rome] I lectured in alternate years on the In-

carnate Word and on the Trinity to both second and third year theologians. They
were about six hundred and fifty strong and between them, not individually but
distributively, they seemed to read everything. It was quite a challenge.[6]

And it was obvious that Lonergan was quite definitely "over the heads"
of most of us. On the one hand, the brightest students—and there were a
number—were convinced that "there was something there." They seemed to
be "caught" by something. But the rest of us were not sure what that "something" was. The name of his 700-page work, *Insight*, was on our horizon and
many of us at least owned our own copy. But in the midst of the many classroom and seminary demands few of us had broached it. One day I picked it
up to read and quickly got lost in the introduction! I put it away—not to be
picked up again for several years.

Besides, in October 1962 the Second Vatican Council began and it was easy
to get caught up in the excitement of Rome during those days. I also found
it quite demanding to battle through the intense Latin prose of Lonergan's
textbooks. That effort was valuable, because it at the least provided me with
some of the questions I brought to his classes. The Latin in the textbook was
often quite enigmatic and I found that if I listened carefully, he would often
provide words of explanation that would clarify his meaning. Something was
going on in my mind!

To a great extent, Lonergan did what any other Catholic theology professor
would have done: he provided us with the traditional historical background
for these ancient doctrines on Christ and the Trinity. But when it came to
the speculative meaning of these doctrines—a way of grasping what those
doctrines might mean in terms of my own life—I must confess that for the
most part he lost me. Lonergan once remarked that when someone is talking
"over your head," then that can be a sign that you have to change! You have
to undergo some kind of conversion.

> You can misunderstand because the author is talking over your head. And when
> he is talking over your head in a very radical fashion, then conversion becomes
> very relevant.[7]

Gradually, I realized that this was an issue for me.

But let me briefly present some memories of Lonergan from some other
students during those days in Rome. Tom Finucan from La Crosse, Wiscon-
sin, provided this recollection:

> My strongest memory would be an opening he often used for a lecture in the
> aula . . . *"hodie debemus tractare de rebus OMNINO complicatis . . . "* [Today
> we have to treat of some very complicated things.] Delivered in that wonder-
> fully deep, somewhat nasal style of his. His learning was obvious, deep, and

genuinely shared. For many of us, and I certainly include myself, he had us swimming in very deep water, which forced us to swim faster and think harder. I am grateful for his memory and his gifts . . .

Dave Adams from Kalamazoo, Michigan, wrote of him:

I just recall him as such a dear, gentle man, so very intelligent but so very patient with our undeveloped minds! He thought very logically and mathematically, one step at a time, and I found that if I paid very close attention, I could understand everything he was trying to explain. I always considered him to be the only person on earth who understood the working relationships operative in the Blessed Trinity—and I was very grateful he shared that "aliqua intelligentia" [some minimal understanding] (referred to in Vatican Council I) with us. I was also fascinated with the way he spoke—his face would remain somewhat motionless, while his jaw seemed to float up and down, but mostly back and forth! Watching his jaw during a lecture could nearly induce hypnosis!

George Saladna from Pittsburgh represented a very common experience.

My recollection of his class(es) is that no one seemed to know exactly what he was talking about, but for that very reason he must have been great. At least everyone who was in the know thought he was brilliant (which I do not doubt in the least). The big thing about him was his *Insight*, which we understood even less than his classes. Everyone relied on NOTES to help us through the classes and ESPECIALLY to prepare for finals on the Trinity. As I recall, everyone LOVED to imitate the way he talked and the gestures he made when he spoke.[8]

John Porter from Grand Rapids, Michigan, admired Father Lonergan as a priest, professor and scholar; nevertheless, he recalled the "crustier" side of his former professor.

I have some vivid memories of Father Lonergan. The first involved myself during the oral exam for the licentiate in theology. My four examiners were in order Fathers Zapelena, Lonergan, Liuma and Zielinski. I had been ill for a couple of months and had little opportunity to prepare for the exam. When my turn came Father Lonergan asked me to expound on the procession of the Holy Spirit in the Ante-Nicene and Post-Nicene Fathers. My mind went completely blank. He offered no help, he moved on not an inch. In fact he said nothing at all as we sat facing each other for the whole fifteen minutes. Without doubt it was the longest fifteen minutes of my life. Still the Holy Spirit did not abandon me entirely. I did receive the S.T.L. with an overall 7 out of a possible 10 on the oral exam.

Lonergan could at times be "testy"—he did not suffer fools lightly. I experienced that myself on one occasion! Still, I can also testify that he definitely mellowed with the years and became quite a kind responder to any and all questions.

Obviously, the set-up at the Gregorian was not pedagogically conducive and some students, such as the future world theologian, Hans Kung, recalled Lonergan's lectures as "boring."[9] So also the future well-known Oxford philosopher, Anthony Kenny, who was a student at the English College. He noted that Lonergan was not then the famous author he was to become and his lectures were not easy to follow. Nevertheless, Kenny was to become indebted to Lonergan's *Verbum: Word and Idea in Aquinas* for his understanding of the Saint Thomas. "I now admire that book greatly but at the time I did not fully appreciate his learning and originality."[10]

Consequently, at the time few could say that they really understood his thought, although a few were convinced there was "something there." Among those were two of my classmates, Joe Komonchak from New York and David Tracy from Bridgeport, both of whom later became well-known theologians. Komonchak gives the following testimony:

> To these contacts in classroom and in books I had the good fortune to be able to add more personal relations through Father Lonergan's willingness to receive David Tracy and myself for brief conversations in his room at the Gregorian. Here we would bring what we now regard as embarrassingly innocent question, to which Father Lonergan would respond patiently and generously, always taking us seriously even while prodding us beyond our starting points with deliberately enigmatic and elliptical answers. I will always remember how he watched us, waiting to see the light of insight show in our eyes. Sometimes he was even rewarded for his patience.[11]

Another student, Matt Torpey, a Trappist from Our Lady of the Holy Spirit monastery in Conyers, Georgia, studying philosophy at the Gregorian, told of once going to Lonergan's room for help on the history of philosophy. Lonergan, puffing on a meerschaum pipe, responded to him by saying: "Oh, you want the differential equation for the history of philosophy!" And then, as Matt sat there, Lonergan began shaving in preparation for class and at the same time outlining for him the key turning points in the history of philosophy: Plato, Aristotle, Augustine, Aquinas, Descartes, Newman, etc.

2. LONERGAN'S THEOLOGY

Lonergan once commented on the work of the nineteenth-century Catholic theologian, Mathias Scheeben, who wrote a great deal on the patristic understanding of the Church. Lonergan used the word "pathos" to describe Scheeben and by that he meant Scheeben's effect on others: the fact that he knew more than he was able to put into words. In *Insight* Lonergan touches more than once upon this apparently insoluble problem of communicating a major new insight. The words and thought-forms with which to express the new insight may simply not yet exist. They will be created only slowly and with the help of disciples as a new thought-world grows up around the insight. But at first the idea can be communicated only imperfectly, indirectly, obscurely. Quentin Quesnell applied this to Lonergan's Latin work.

> Now much of Lonergan's creative genius lies doubly buried in his Latin Scholastic works. It is hard for the average reader to believe that anyone with something new and important to say would go about writing it in Church Latin in a seminary textbook in the structured language of a medieval disputation. After all, we don't expect new automobiles to resemble a surrey with a fringe on top.[12]

This was Lonergan's situation while teaching theology in Rome. In spite of the Latin scholastic context, he was trying mightily to stretch that framework to express a new understanding. William Loewe put it this way:

> If these examples suggest that Lonergan was laboring mightily to cram alien material into the neo-Scholastic tract, the reason for this lies in the fact that his own aims were at cross-purposes with those which governed the genre within which he had to work. The Scholastic manual comprised a set of theses to be demonstrated, an operation geared to attaining certitude in the possession of truth. For Lonergan, however, the chief aim of systematic theology was not certitude but [an] understanding of what one knows by faith to be true . . . .[13]

Among Lonergan's favorite quotes from John Henry Newman was: "Ten thousand difficulties don't make one doubt."

> Newman's remark that ten thousand difficulties do not make a doubt has served me in good stead. It encouraged me to look difficulties squarely in the eye, while not letting them interfere with my vocation or my faith.[14]

Lonergan's effort was to recall theology to its proper goal of understanding by revitalizing the metaphysical context in which theology was conducted and by opening theology to modern science and modern historical scholarship. But in many ways he was pouring new wine into old wine skins. The entire situation was, as he himself remarked later, hopelessly behind the times, and its demands upon the theologian were impossible.

As I look back on it now, from the perspective of many years later, what strikes me most forcibly is that to have fully appreciated Lonergan's theology courses in 1962 and 1963 I needed first to have appreciated his *Insight: An Essay on Human Understanding*. For to fully appreciate Lonergan's theological analyses of God as the infinite act of knowing and loving, of the Trinitarian processions of the Word and Spirit, of the consciousness, knowledge and freedom of Jesus, of the development of Church teaching concerning Jesus—in order to fruitfully appreciate these and other points of theology, I needed to engage in the "intellectual therapy" that was the point of *Insight*—an intellectual therapy that he himself had undergone.

Now, after having engaged in that therapy for many years, I have come to a much deeper appreciation of what Lonergan meant in his books on Christ and on the Trinity. I am convinced of the treasures found in those Latin textbooks. "If today Lonergan's Latin texts lie buried amid the rubble of neo-Scholasticism, many a valuable insight lies buried with them."[15] Whole sections, paragraphs, lines, images, now jump off the page at me in a way that did not happen when I first struggled with those books in 1962 and 1963. At the time I struggled not only with his classical Latin, but even more with the question, "What is he getting at?"

Still, there were themes that stuck in my mind. There was first of all the distinction we mentioned above between certitude and understanding. Certitude adheres to the doctrines of the Church, the Church's judgments of faith concerning the mysteries of God, judgments to which I had given the assent of faith since my childhood. Theological understanding, on the other hand, seeks "some God-given insight" into how the mysteries could possibly be what they are. How could we possibly understand the life of the Trinity in a world of modern science, scholarship and philosophy?

Lonergan often quoted Augustine's phrase, "*Crede ut intelligas*"—"Believe in order that you may understand." And he was especially fond of quoting the text of the First Vatican Council: "Reason, illumined by faith, when it inquires diligently, piously, soberly, reaches with God's help some extremely fruitful understanding of the mysteries."[16] All of which implies a distinction—but not a separation—between the certitude that inheres in faith and the analogous knowledge attained through theological understanding.

Such theological knowledge is analogous, because God is incomprehensible. The excess of intelligibility that is the life of God can only be obscurely known by us, for

> . . . between the creator and the creature there cannot be acknowledged so great a likeness without at the same time acknowledging that between them there is an even greater unlikeness.
>
> And so, just as from the likeness a certain light arises, so from the greater unlikeness even greater darknesses arise.[17]

It reminded me of what struck Merton in Gilson's writings, "*Ipsa caligo summa est mentis illuminatio*"—the exceeding darkness is itself the enlightenment of the mind. Our theological knowledge is truly "through a glass darkly," partly because we do not even know ourselves clearly.

> We do not understand the infinite positively, but negatively. Our own rational and moral consciousness we rather live than clearly and distinctly understand. Which consciousness, if it is supposed to be the image of God, is indeed a very deficient image by means of which we are only able to conceive of divine consciousness analogically and imperfectly.[18]

Nevertheless, there is a role for human understanding as it seeks to come to "some God-given understanding" of these mysteries of faith. As he expresses the aim of his theological writings:

> Our present intention is neither to increase certitude concerning revealed truths, nor to confirm deductions from them, nor to more efficaciously refute the adversaries of Catholic truth. For just as the human person does not live by bread alone, so also knowledge does not live by certitude alone. And so, presupposing the firmest certitude of faith, presupposing the conclusions certainly deduced, presupposing the adversaries already refuted, we seek some understanding of the mystery.

The second point that struck me from his teachings was his emphasis on human consciousness. In each of his courses Lonergan applied "the psychological analogy," that is, his analysis of human consciousness, to understanding the mysteries of faith. Thus, in the course on Christology, *De Verbo Incarnato*, he employed the distinction between consciousness and knowledge to understanding the human knowledge in Christ.

Consciousness is not knowledge; it is, rather, "a concomitant awareness of self" present in certain acts, some of which are acts of knowing. It is presupposed to knowledge or the first step in knowing prior to the full flowering of knowledge in judgment. I remember a classmate demonstrating this distinction to me by walking across the room, illustrating by that the awareness of self implicit in his walking—prior to his putting it into words and affirming it.

In 1958 some of Lonergan's writings on the consciousness of Christ had come under attack by a certain Alfons Perego, a Jesuit at the Lateran University in Rome. In 1959 Lonergan replied to that attack with a strong response in the Jesuit journal, *Gregorianum*.

> As the position imputed to me, both in the presentation and in the critical evaluation, is one that I fail to distinguish from heresy, I feel called upon to supplement Fr. Perego's animadversions and, at the same time, to correct his imputation.[19]

Even though polemic was rarely characteristic of Lonergan's writings, his students enjoyed this kind of response. But what struck me from Lonergan's essay was a particularly succinct quote on consciousness from a French writer, Georges Van Riet, who referred to the thought of the existentialist, Jean Paul Sartre.

> In our opinion, every conscious activity is necessarily present to itself in an unreflected way, or, as Sartre writes it, is conscious (of) itself. What characterizes this consciousness (of) self is the fact that it is still unexpressed; it is presence to self, not knowledge of self; it does not use concepts, or judgments, or words; it is silent, it does not speak. From the moment it reflects, it speaks; to reflect is in fact to elucidate through expression; the fruit of reflection is the judgment. The paradox of human consciousness, which is incarnate and not angelic, is that even the elucidating act is unreflected for itself, conscious (of) self. It expresses something not reflected on, something lived or perceived, it does not express itself. Only a new act of reflection will elucidate it by giving it expression, but this new act will in its turn still be unreflected.[20]

So even contemporary atheists, such as Jean Paul Sartre, could help us in understanding ourselves! In a later work Lonergan would write on the importance of Catholics being able to read and profit from the works of non-Catholics.[21]

Besides a careful setting out of the Christian faith, then, there was in Lonergan a careful delineation of the human "inner world." It was only in terms of this inner world of the person that questions about the growing human understanding of Christ could be handled. In fact, some of my classmates who spent a great deal of time studying Lonergan's treatment of the consciousness of Christ seemed to be deeply moved by his articulation of the growing human knowledge of Jesus. That development included the influence of his parents and the Jewish community around him as he moved to a reflective self-knowledge in relation to his Father. It is that self-knowledge that is reflected in Jesus' acclamation, "Abba!"—"Dear Father!"

These distinctions between consciousness, understanding and self-knowledge allowed Lonergan to also analyze the complicated history of Christian theology. For example, the history of Christian thought on the way to the Council of Nicea's definition of the divinity Jesus is a long back and forth series of often conflicting viewpoints that, as Lonergan pointed out, often involved underlying conflicts on the meaning of "knowledge," "objectivity" and "reality." Over the years, within the community whose lives centered on the truth of Jesus, these errors tended to work themselves out. Inadequate and misleading expressions gradually were corrected and purified.

> [C]oncretely, a variety of incompatible concrete images gradually gave way to a privileged example drawn from human spiritual experience (knowing and lov-

ing). The truth that God is not a body—not in any sense—finally became more than words; and instead of somehow trying to imagine a three-in-one, thinkers settled on a rule of predication which was purely intelligible and which gave as little to imagination as do Maxwell's equations for the electro-magnetic field in the realm of physical science.[22]

The "rule of predication" that Christian thinkers settled upon to articulate that Jesus was on the same level as the Father was Athanasius' "All that is said of the Father is also said of the Son except that the Son is Son and not Father."

> Now such a determination of meaning is characteristically Hellenic. It is a matter of reflecting on propositions. It explains the word "consubstantial" by a second-level proposition to the effect that the Son is consubstantial with the Father, if and only what is true of the Father is also true of the Son, except that only the Father is Father.[23]

This is Athanasius "rule" for interpreting the term *homoousios—consubstantial*—which in popular parlance meant "of the same stuff" but which for Athanasius became a kind of technical term. I can still remember Lonergan in the midst of his Latin lecture emphatically quoting this phrase—"of the same stuff"—from G. Prestige's *God in Patristic Thought.* It was a delight to hear a phrase in English, but Lonergan's point was to distinguish this popular meaning from the highly intelligible, even quasi-theoretical meaning given it by Athanasius.[24]

The point seemed jejune to me at the time, too obvious to make such a fuss about, but to grasp it clearly one needed to have an intellectual conversion, a breakthrough to the virtualities of ourselves and the wonder of the theoretical. Lonergan constantly focused on such theoretical inter-relationships. Thus, in clarifying the ancient conciliar meaning of "person" and "nature" he wrote:

> While later developments put persons and natures in many further contexts, the context of Chalcedon needs no more than heuristic concepts. What is a person or hypostasis? It is in the Trinity what there are three of and in the Incarnation what there is one of. What is nature? In the Trinity it is what there is one of and in the Incarnation what there are two of.[25]

Lonergan delighted in such clarifications. But, as I would discover, such delight presupposed a breakthrough to one's own mind.

Another recurring theme in Lonergan's theology was that, since God is absolutely simple and unchanging, any activity of God *ad extra*, in the world, involves no change in God, but rather a change in the world. This is true, for example, in the "missions" of the Son and the Spirit in being sent into the world:

Since the reality of their being sent is their own eternal being (reality), it is obvious that any new reality implied in the sending is a new reality not in God, but
in us. We are changed when the Father and the Son send the Spirit. We begin to
love God and others in a new way. This change in us occurs because of God's
eternally loving and choosing the highest and the best and choosing that in our
time we might share it.

Again, the Father's sending his Son means that a human figure in history
became our key to knowing God as only God can know himself. That happens
because God eternally, perfectly does know himself and expresses himself to
himself and chooses that in time that expression might be shared with us.[26]

Obviously, this understanding of the divine missions has spiritual and as-
cetical implications:

The sendings of the Son and the Spirit open to us the relationships which the
Persons have with one another and invite us to share those relationships. God
loves us in the Spirit and loves us as he loves his own Son. And we reciprocate.
Our being redeemed and being graced are our sharing in God's knowing and
loving; created shares of the being of the Son and the Spirit are ours. This reality of being loved in the Spirit as the Son and in return loving God as children
is the way the divine Persons dwell in us—that is, as objects of our transformed
knowing and loving.

Such statements invite extended meditation and contemplation.

One further point: a further impression I took away from Lonergan's
courses. Throughout his treatise on the Trinity Lonergan writes of God as
Ipsum intelligere. I remember being somewhat puzzled by this emphasis on
intelligence, for in my neo-scholastic training God was "*Ipsum Esse subsistens*," that is, the fullness of "being"—subsistent being. Wasn't "being" so
much more important than "understanding?" Was not this Gilson's fear: that
being would become subordinate to thought? Why this emphasis on "understanding"—"*intelligere*?" This emphasis on God as *Ipsum intelligere* rather
than on God as *Ipsum esse subsistens* sounded a lot like "idealism" to me.

In fact, the word had gotten around that this was a criticism of Lonergan:
his seemingly single-minded emphasis on "understanding" seemed to pull
him too close to the idealist camp. I didn't know what to think of this accusa-
tion, but it was a worry that lodged in the back of my mind until I had to face
it head on when I wrestled with *Insight*.

Nevertheless, in spite of the wonderful teaching I now find in Lonergan's
theological works, I knew at the time that *I* didn't get it. What he wrote was
not clear to me. Not only was it hidden in "the decent obscurity of the Latin
language" and in the classicist thesis structure, but most fundamentally of all,
I didn't understand his basic point. In spite of the high esteem in which we

all held Lonergan, I know at the time that I didn't get it. Certainly there were clues. But I really didn't "get it."

A final point. As I mentioned previously, Lonergan obviously had read and was familiar with much contemporary thought and culture. He was familiar with the structures of modern science, structures which he invoked in his writings.[27] He had read and was reading the contemporary existentialist and phenomenological writers. At the same time, his writings witnessed to the past. Quotations from Aristotle and Aquinas laced his pages. There was, for example, Aristotle's mysterious dictum, "Sense in act is the sensible in act; intellect in act is the intelligible in act." So also he would quote Saint Thomas:

> Anyone can verify this in his own experience, that when he is trying to understand something, he forms some phantasms for himself by way of examples, and in these he as it were looks at what he wants to understand. It is for the same reason that when we want to have someone understand something, we offer him examples by means of which he may be able to form images for himself to aid his understanding.[28]

What did these lines mean? Was Lonergan actually saying that we "up to date" twentieth-century persons might really have something to learn from these ancient writers? Did we twentieth-century persons have to "reach up" to understand what Augustine and Aquinas had to say? Did they really have something to teach us? Wasn't the whole point of the Second Vatican Council that we might learn from the modern world and speak in the accents of the modern world? Was Lonergan really saying that we had something to learn from the classics? As he would write some years later:

> The major texts, the classics, in religion, letters, philosophy, theology, not only are beyond the initial horizon of their interpreters but also may demand an intellectual, moral, religious conversion of the interpreter over and above the broadening of his horizon. In this case the interpreter's initial knowledge of the object is just inadequate. He will come to know it only in so far as he pushes the self-correcting process of learning to a revolution in his own outlook. He can succeed in acquiring that habitual understanding of an author that spontaneously finds his wave-length and locks on to it, only after he has effected a radical change in himself.[29]

The question was whether these ancient writers have something to say to people today? Was their teaching really relevant to the questions people were asking today? What about Aristotle? Augustine? Aquinas? Did these folk really have something to say? Lonergan seemed to say they did. For me at the time that was still an open question.

NOTES

1. Bernard Lonergan, *Method in Theology*, 247.

2. William Shea, "Horizons on Bernard Lonergan," *Horizons* (Journal of College Theology Society) 15/1 (1988), 77.

3. Letter of Bernard Lonergan to Henry Keane, Provincial of the Vice-Province of Upper Canada written from the Gregorian University, Rome, July 20, 1938 (Lonergan Archives, Toronto). The North American College had begun to send its students to the Gregorian in 1930. Previously they had attended the College of the Propagation of the Faith.

4. *A Second Collection*, 267-268. For the most authoritative account of Lonergan's journey to the writing of *Insight*, see William Mathews, *Lonergan's Quest: A Study of Desire in the Authoring of Insight* (Toronto: University of Toronto Press, 2005).

5. *A Second Collection*, 268.

6. *A Second Collection*, 276.

7. Notes by Nicholas Graham from a discussion session at a workshop on method in theology, Regis College, Willowdale, Ontario, July 14, 1969.

8. Of course, a number of people "specialized" in imitating Lonergan's distinctive Canadian Latin drawl as he "explained" the mysteries of the faith in which, according to the theology of the North American College at that time, there are in the Trinity: "*Quinque notiones, quattuor relationes, tres personae, duae processiones, unus Deus et . . . nulla intelligentia.*" ["Five notions, four relations, three persons, two processions, one God—and no understanding!].

9. "I learn less from the Canadian Bernard Lonergan, well known in America; he leans toward philosophy and bores us with his dry traditional lectures on christology. In vain he tries to convince me in personal conversation that Thomas Aquinas anticipated Einstein's theory of relativity." Hans Kung, *My Struggle for Freedom* (Grand Rapids, MI: Eerdmans, 2003) 78.

10. Kenny, Anthony, *A Path From Rome* (Oxford: Oxford University Press, 1986) 77.

11. Joseph Komanchak, reminiscence quoted in *Compass: A Jesuit Journal*, published by the Upper Canada Province of the Society of Jesus, special issue on Bernard Lonergan, S.J., Spring 1985, 8.

12. Quentin Quesnell, "A Note on Scholasticism" in Vernon Gregson, ed., *The Desires of the Human Heart* (NY: Paulist Press, 1988) 149.

13. William P. Loewe, "Jesus, the Son of God," *The Desires of the Human Heart*, 185-186.

14. *A Second Collection*, 263.

15. Loewe, 186.

16. Denziger, H. and A. Schönnmetzer, *Enchiridion Symbolorum* (32nd ed.; Freiburg, 1963), 3016.

17. B. Lonergan, *De Deo Trino, Pars Systematica* (Rome: Typis Pontificiae Universitatis Gregorianae, 1964), 12.

18. *De Deo Trino, Pars Systematica*, 85.

19. "Christ as Subject," *CWL 4 Collection*, 153.

20. "Christ as Subject," *CWL 4 Collection*, 172-173.

21. See B. Lonergan, *CWL 10 Topics in Education*, 177-178: "The importance of the theory of philosophic differences is that, if one gets a sufficient grasp of it, one can read fruitfully all sorts of material without losing one's way. If one is limited in one's reading and inspiration exclusively to the works written by Catholics that have been approved as safe, one is cutting down enormously one's field of study, one's sources."

22. Quoted in Quentin Quesnell, *The Desires of the Human Heart*, 154. See references to Lonergan *De Deo Trino I*, 86 and numerous references to *Insight*.

23. *A Second Collection*, 23.

24. For an excellent and clear analysis of the whole trajectory of Lonergan's thought on Christ from his earliest writings, through his devotional and scholastic writings, to his later "existentialist" writings, see Frederick E. Crowe, *Christ and History: The Christology of Bernard Lonergan from 1935 to 1982* (Ottawa: Novalis, 2005).

25. *A Second Collection*, 259.

26. *Quesnell*, 155.

27. See *De Deo Trino, Pars analytica* (Romae: Gregorianae, 1961) 82: ". . . the terminal notion of consubstantiality not only transcends every image but also in a way all intelligibility grasped in the image. Just as the equations invented by Maxwell regarding the electro-magnetic field arise out of images that nevertheless have no image that corresponds to them, so also the rule posited by Athanasius only has reference to concepts and judgments. Athanasius' rule not only prescinds from images but also can't be grasped or understood in anything imaginable."

28. *Summa Theologiae* I, 84, 7.

29. *Method in Theology*, 161.

Chapter Four

Reading *Insight* 1964–1967

1. A DOCTORATE IN PHILOSOPHY

I was ordained to the priesthood on December 18, 1963, in Saint Ignatius Church in Rome by Archbishop Martin J. O'Connor, the Rector of the North American College. My parents and a number of relatives and friends traveled to Rome for the ordination. It was a joyous occasion that took place against the background of the catacombs, churches and classical monuments of the Eternal City.

Still, Vatican II was in session and the new topics unleashed by the Council were in the forefront of my mind. In particular, it was a time for thinking about "the Church in the world," "the Church of the poor" and issues of social and political justice. President Kennedy had just been assassinated the month before and his idea of the Peace Corps inspired me. I remember being touched to tears while reading Yves Congar's book, *The Church of the Poor*, and even more forcefully by the Lutheran, Dietrich Bonhoeffer's *Letters and Papers from Prison*. These were his writings as he awaited execution at the hands of the Nazis while asserting that Christ was to be found in the center of the world. I remember my tears as I stayed up all night reading that book and finishing it as dawn broke.

In that vein I spent the Easter vacation of 1964 with a couple of friends in a little shantytown on the outskirts of Naples. Our host was Father Mario Borelli, famous in the post-war years for living with the street urchins of the city. Never had I experienced such poverty, and never had I seen such joyful Christian witness. Many of the priests, sisters and young university students who served the poor there were influenced by the writings of Jacques Maritain and by the witness of the Little Sisters of Jesus and the spirituality of Charles De Foucauld. I was touched by something very authentic here: the

Church reaching out and "touching" the poor—and being touched by them.

I stayed on in Rome until July of 1964 to finish my licentiate in theology, a degree involving an examination on the four years of doctrinal and systematic theology. The exam lasted an hour and Lonergan was one of my four examiners. After struggling for what seemed like an eternity with my Latin explanations of the redemption, Lonergan asked me a final question to which I was to reply positively or negatively, "Sic? vel Non?" Yes or No?" he said in Latin as he held his hand over the bell. I gulped and took a guess: "Sic," I said. "Non!" he replied as his hand came down on the bell. My knees were shaking as I walked to the next examiner but I passed! with a decent "8" out of "10." I repeated this story to him years later, to his great delight!

That summer of 1964, after I returned from Europe, I remember a classmate and fellow "activist" saying something to me to the effect that he wasn't sure whether there had been anything at all worthwhile in our academic studies, but if there was, it lay in Lonergan's work. Fortunately, I was given the opportunity to search this out for myself.

After four years in Rome I returned home to New Jersey during the summer of 1964, a summer swelling with activism in the States. A number of my friends were involved in inner-city work, and I envied them. They were "doing something." After some weeks I had an interview with my bishop, Archbishop Thomas Boland, who told me he wanted me to teach at the seminary, "Darlington." "What would you prefer to teach?" he said, "philosophy or theology?" "Theology" I said immediately. "Well, we don't need anyone in theology right now—I'd like you to study philosophy." So much for collegiality!

It was painful to call my father and tell him I would be leaving home again to study in Rome for another three years. I remember very vividly laying on my bed that afternoon and wrestling with that decision. I was happy to be a priest; I was very excited about what was happening in the Church and in the world; I deeply wanted to get "out there" and begin to serve God's people. And now I was being asked to study what?—"PHILOSOPHY!"

First of all, what was "philosophy?" "Scholasticism?" I certainly had my doubts—and it was obvious that many other people did too, bishops among them. And I certainly wondered whether I was not compromising my principles by agreeing to this use of my time. Other priests I knew were already working in the inner-cities and the image of caring immediately for the poor seemed irresistible.

Nevertheless, I agreed to the study of philosophy. I returned to Rome on the ship, the "USS Constitution," in September of 1964. On the ship were many young people my age who each evening enjoyed getting together for "hootenannies," singing the "freedom songs" of the civil rights movement.

Sister Mary Luke Tobin of the Sisters of Loreto was on the ship, on her way to the Council as an "observer." It was a delight to talk with her and her companion about the prospects for the Council and the Church.

When I arrived in Rome to live and study at the Casa Santa Maria, the graduate house of the North American College, I found a very dynamic community of young priests. Some had already been out working in parishes for several years. One, Jim Doyle, a priest from Chicago, had spent some time with the Trappists, and gradually he became a very important mentor in my life. At "the Casa" we experienced more freedom and independence than we had as seminarians and at the same time we seemed to experience more community. Each evening a group of us would gather to pray together and to discuss the latest issues that were simmering in the church and the world. There I learned to drink scotch!

During my first year of graduate philosophy I had to take a number of courses in scholastic philosophy and none of my teachers inspired me. I became very "wary" of scholastic conceptualism that had no relationship to life. Still, I was expected to take the courses and pass a comprehensive exam in order to get my Licentiate degree in philosophy. It was the second such exam in the course of a year. The previous July I had finished months of rigorous study for the Licentiate in theology.

And I was tired. Tired of jumping through hoops and memorizing stuff about whose fundamental value I did not have basic convictions. Tired of so many "words" that seemed to be "out there." I have the vivid memory of walking near the Trevi Fountain one sunny but cold winter day and thinking to myself:

> I have to be careful I don't have a mental breakdown here. I have got to take charge of my life here. In fact, I am not going to attend one more class that I don't have to attend and don't want to attend. I am only going to listen to the professors who I think have something to say. I can't let a "system" determine my life and my mind. I have to take charge of my own life.

And that was a good decision. I believe I staved off mental fatigue and the possibility of a breakdown as I made the conscious decision to seek out the best intellectual fare I could find. The fear of a breakdown was not at all far-fetched, for some of my fellow students had to discontinue their studies because of the mental strain.

And yet, among a number of uninspiring teachers, there were a few who were noteworthy. One, the Englishman, Frederick Copleston, S.J., was known for his multi-volume *History of Philosophy*. I remember visiting him in his room at the Gregorian with another student and being intrigued as I watched him pull out tobacco and paper, role a cigarette by hand, and proceed

to smoke it. Spoiled American as I was, I had never seen someone rolling his
own cigarette!

Another, Fr. Peter Henrici, S.J., later named bishop in Switzerland, taught
an excellent course on the French philosopher, Maurice Blondel, and his seminal work, *L'Action*. Blondel's emphasis was on the pre-eminence of personal
decision-making and action in the life of the human person. We transcend
ourselves and we become ourselves by our decisions.

But there was one professor whose classes I never missed. The German
Jesuit, Johannes Lotz, had, along with Karl Rahner, studied under Martin Heidegger in Freiburg,. Lotz taught courses on Heidegger, on the existentialist
philosophers and on the philosophy of art. He was an excellent teacher, obviously in love with his subject, and obviously seeking to build bridges between
the scholasticism and the world of modern concerns. Later on I chose him for
my dissertation director, and it was a wise choice. He allowed me to follow
out my own interests in relating the study of Lonergan to the philosophy of
art of Susanne K. Langer.

In early 1965 Lonergan was still in Rome. About that time, however, he
was diagnosed with lung cancer and was forced to return to Canada to undergo a serious operation during which one lung was removed.[1] But before
he left Rome, I was fortunate to have a meeting with him to discuss a topic
for my doctoral dissertation. I was in search of a worthy topic and I made an
appointment to meet him in his room at the Gregorian to discuss some possibilities.

He was sitting in a cold and poorly lit room typical of the Jesuit quarters
at the Gregorian at the time. Before him was a manual typewriter that in my
mind I associated with the newspaper reporters of the 1930s. The whole scene
was most unpretentious, a word that captured for me the quality of his life.

Lonergan's typical advice to someone looking for a dissertation topic
was:

> Take a man—and ask "Why?" That is, do not try to do a "comparative" thesis
> between one person and another, for that really adds up to three theses: one
> on the first person, the second on the second, and the third on the comparison
> between them. Rather, seek to understand one person as well as you can on
> a well-defined topic. So-and-so on topic x, y, or z. Otherwise you will spend
> forever getting your tradesman's license. What the doctorate does is allow you
> to hang out your shingle.

I do not remember well all the details of our conversation that afternoon,
but from it came a decision to write a dissertation on the philosophy of art
of Susanne K Langer, an American philosopher whose work on aesthetic and
artistic meaning Lonergan refers to in *Insight*. Soon afterwards, Lonergan

returned to Canada for his lung operation and Father Lotz became my director, allowing me to find my own way into the thought of Langer, Lonergan, and myself.

In some ways I was hedging my bets. I aimed at keeping one foot in the narrowly experiential realm, the realm of symbols and feelings, the realm of the liturgy, while at the same time exploring Lonergan's work as a background. As time went on, I came to discover that that background was indispensable for understanding the foreground.

Langer was an American philosopher (1895-1985) who had studied under Alfred North Whitehead at Harvard. My early research consisted in exploring the origins of her thought in Anglo-American "logical" thought, for example, Bertrand Russell and Ludwig Wittgenstein, as well as in the German idealist philosophy of Ernst Cassirer. This gave me a background in her thought and allowed me to appreciate her very fine work on art in her early major works, *Philosophy in a New Key* (1941) and *Feeling and Form* (1952).

Through Langer's writings I began to became familiar with Anglo-American philosophy with its heavy emphasis on logic and the structures of language, as well as with the neo-Kantian philosophy of Ernst Cassirer. It was a good exercise for me to study Langer's writings on artistic consciousness while also intensely studying Lonergan's *Insight*. I was intent on seeing the connections—and there were many—between what Langer said about artistic consciousness and what Lonergan was saying.

At the same time there were differences. Not surprisingly, Langer basically came down on the side of modern "naturalism." As she once articulated her basic beliefs:

> That man is an animal I certainly believe; and also that he has no supernatural essence, "soul" or "mind-stuff," enclosed in his skin. He is an organism, his substance is chemical, and what he does, suffers, or knows, is just what this sort of chemical structure may do, suffer, or know. When the structure goes to pieces, it never does, suffers, or knows anything again.[2]

Nevertheless, in the beginning I overlooked this naturalist bias in her thought, and concentrated instead on all the fine and interesting things she was writing about aesthetic and artistic experience. Later on, while I was in the midst of writing my dissertation, she published the first volume of a three-volume work in which she would spell out more fully a biological naturalism. *Mind: An Essay on Human Feeling, Vol. I,* published in 1967, consisted in the reduction of all "higher" human activities to feelings and feelings to biological and electro-chemical events.[3] Such conclusions she considered "empirical," "rigorous thought," justified by the results of the empirical sciences.

Reading Langer's writings was an occasion of a real intellectual crisis during my time in Rome. She maintained clearly and seemingly "reasonable" positions that conflicted with my Christian faith and my religious commitments. In addition, on the level of my own personal life, this time was beginning to be one of crisis for me. The Council had ended and that ending had brought with it, unexpectedly, a period of disillusion for many of us who were young priests. Things in the Church had not suddenly changed. The old guard was still effectively in charge and the wheels of progress were grinding forward very slowly. In fact, as one person put it, "Every day we're taking one step backwards!" This seeming outer malaise was matched by inner crises in the lives of many of us. Some were already becoming so disillusioned that they left the priesthood. Even a bishop, Bishop James Shannon, from Minneapolis, who had spoken to us at the Casa during the Council, suddenly announced his intention to leave the ministry and to marry. All of this was unheard of in the traditional Catholicism to which I had been exposed and the situation was having its effect on me. An aura of crisis began to hang over the priesthood and over my life.

2. BEGINNING TO READ *INSIGHT*

Fortunately, as my period of doctoral study went on and I finished the required courses, I had much more time to follow out my own interests. I had an intense desire to get things straight. I had to read "the best stuff," even if there were no courses on it. And there weren't.

Again and again in discussions with people I trusted I would hear the advice, "If you really want to learn philosophy, if you want to get to the core of what it's about, study Lonergan." I heard that advice so often from so many respected people, that I couldn't ignore it. I decided, therefore, that I would study Lonergan in depth. I would go behind his theology. I would pick up *Insight*.

And yet, I must admit, I had a bias against Lonergan's stuff. Was this not "more of the same?" Was he not a "Thomist" in modern dress? Was he not hopelessly "intellectual," that is, "cold?" And what I really cared about were "feelings," that is, human warmth, human experience, human community. How could anyone so exigently intellectual speak to the cares of the human heart and the human family?

Nevertheless, relying on the advice of others, and with the hope that "there might be something there," I picked up *Insight*.[4] I spent a good part of one whole year working through that book. In a little room at the back of the library of the Casa Santa Maria, I spent day after day poring over *Insight*. I often remember studying as the lights dimmed in the early evening when

Rome's electric power was especially taxed, a fitting symbol, I thought, of the search for enlightenment.

I have a vivid memory of struggling and paining over *Insight*. Pages would go by with hardly a glimmer of understanding. Then, slowly, I began to discover connections. Flipping pages, I would compare later sections with earlier ones. I would spend hours going over just one short passage. Gradually, I began to feel a certain joy, a certain indefinable feeling of subtle elation as one insight led to another.

Just prior to embarking on the study of *Insight* I had been reading some works of contemporary psychology and was particularly intrigued by Carl Roger's book, *On Becoming a Person*. I was especially impressed by Roger's insistence on being "experiential" in one's efforts at self knowledge: letting one's words flow from one's feelings. And the Lord knew, I had a lot of feelings! I had feelings about the changes in the Church, about how "behind the times" we were, about conservatives who were living in a world that no longer existed, about the Church's mission to the world. I also had deeper and wilder feelings, feelings alluded to by Frances Thompson's poem, feelings of "vistaed hopes" and "chasmèd fears."

Carl Rogers aimed at refining the ability to identify levels of present feelings and at helping people to find the words to express those feelings. He spoke of "significant learnings," learnings that flowed out of experiences. There was a truth here I wanted to maintain. I remember saying to myself:

Lonergan can't contradict any of the truths I know—truths articulated by people like Rogers—truths I've been coming to through my own reading and reflection—or I'll know he's wrong. Anything he says will have to fit in with the truths I've already experientially appropriated or he won't be worth my while.

And I doubted he could do it. His work appeared so patently intellectual and all my leanings and the leanings of the culture around me were "experiential." And by that I understood chiefly the in's and out's of human feelings.

But strangely, as I studied and wrestled with *Insight*, there began to appear an experiential element. In fact, it began to appear that the whole aim of the work was the appropriation of human experience: not just the experience of feelings, but the appropriation of other dimensions of human experience as well, more subtle dimensions, such as the experience of human understanding. I remember formulating this to myself: "Lonergan is aiming at doing for human intellectual experience what Rogers is trying to do with feelings!"

Fortunately, at the time there were others in Rome, mostly at the North American College and the Casa Santa Maria, who were wrestling with the same book. Such community acted as a check on the adequacy and accuracy of my own understanding. Vinnie Murray, a seminarian from my own diocese in New Jersey, was part of an "*Insight* Group" at the North American College and my discussions with him helped to clear up some of my own misconceptions. One of the major leaders of the budding "Lonergan Movement" in those days was Fred Lawrence, presently Professor of Theology at Boston College and founder of the yearly "Lonergan Workshops." As Lonergan once said of these small learning communities:

> Everyone will have his own difficulties. There is an advantage, then, to having a seminar on the subject. It gives people a chance to talk these things out . . . to talk them out with others. There is a set of concrete opportunities provided by the seminar that cannot be provided by any mere book. The more you talk with another and throw things out, the more you probe, and the more you express yourself spontaneously, simply, and frankly, not holding back in fear of making mistakes, then the more quickly you arrive at the point where you get things cleared up.[5]

And indeed, the community that was studying Lonergan's *Insight* in those days continues today as there are "Lonergan Centers" in eight countries, a Lonergan journal, newsletter, various workshops, etc. Gradually, I moved from an adversarial relationship to *Insight* to the conviction that there was indeed "something there."

It was a big day when I finally finished reading *Insight* for the first time. I remember that day as a friend, Julian Miller, from Rockville Center, New York, and I took off on our Italian scooters—"Vespas"—on a ride out of the city, stopping every once in a while to rest and talk about *Insight*! Then began the process of going back over the book again and parts of it again and again—and asking myself whether I really understood it, and what in fact was I understanding?

3. SELF-APPROPRIATION AND TWO KINDS OF KNOWING

How does one write about a book? especially a book that has "changed one's life?" a book that has set in motion dynamics within one's own mind and heart that to this day have not stopped? As Jerome Miller has said of "a great work":

> To be under the sway of a great work does not only mean that one assents to a particular set of key propositions contained in it; it means that one is so deeply engaged by the way of thinking that animates it that one's own way of thinking is profoundly and permanently transformed. This can only be when we allow ourselves to enter inside the body of a work, instead of trying to seize on a list of theses that can be extracted from it. A great text is a world which

we can understand only if we inhabit and learn to feel at home in it. As this process progresses, we find that we cannot enter and leave the world of the text as casually as we pick up and put down the book; for our thinking gradually comes to be governed by the same throe of questioning which generated the text. This does not mean that we have mastered the text; it means, in fact, something nearly the opposite of this—that we are surrendering ourselves to the eros of inquiry which moves the text; and spending ourselves in service to it. To claim to have mastered a text would itself be proof that one had not understood it.[6]

Obviously I intend to present here some idea of the contents of *Insight*; but describing the contents is one thing; understanding the act of understanding the contents is another. Lonergan often described the aim of *Insight* as an invitation to "self-appropriation." In a series of lectures on *Insight* given in 1959 he described such self-appropriation by referring to Immanuel Kant's dictum that to be a philosopher, one cannot be just "the plaster cast of a man."

But why are we attempting self-appropriation? To use an expression borrowed from Kant last night, if one is to be a philosopher, one cannot be just "a plaster cast of a man." To deal with philosophical questions, one needs a point of reference, a basis that is one's own. Your interest may quite legitimately be to find out what Lonergan thinks and what Lonergan says, but I am not offering you that, or what anyone else thinks or says, as a basis. If a person is to be a philosopher, his thinking as a whole cannot depend upon someone else or something else. There has to be a basis within himself; he must have resources of his own to which he can appeal in the last resort.[7]

Lonergan's plea for "self-appropriation" implied, of course, that perhaps I did not, as of yet, know myself very well. I did not know myself adequately. It also implied that this whole process might be more difficult than I thought. Nevertheless, the process promised a "startling" enlightenment.

The book's "Table of Contents" was daunting. Let me list the chapters.

Part I: Insight as Activity
1. *Elements*
2. *Heuristic Structures of Empirical Method*
3. *The Canons of Empirical Method*
4. *The Complementarity of Classical and Statistical Investigations*
5. *Space and Time*
6. *Common Sense and Its Subject*
7. *Common Sense as Object*
8. *Things*
9. *The Notion of Judgment*
10. *Reflective Understanding*

In the preface to *Insight* Lonergan acknowledges that the above table of contents could indeed be intimidating!

> . . . I find it difficult to state in any brief and easy manner what the present book is about, how a single author can expect to treat the variety of topics listed in the table of contents, why he should attempt to do so in a single work, and what good he could hope to accomplish even were he to succeed in his odd undertaking. Still, a preface should provide at least a jejune and simplified answer to such questions, and perhaps I can make a beginning by saying that the aim of the work is to convey an insight into insight.[8]

An "insight into insight"—that's what this book is about. It's not about mathematics or science, although there are mathematical and scientific examples in the book. Rather it is about an insight into the insights of mathematicians, the insights of scientists, the insights of people of common sense, etc. In other words, the book is about "knowing." And even though the content of knowing "mocks encyclopedias and overflows libraries," still strategically chosen instances of knowing can reveal its basic structure.

The point of the book, then, is to go beyond the "scraps" of mathematics, science, common sense and metaphysics that are found in it to "the dynamic cognitional structure exemplified in knowing them." That dynamic cognitional structure is not something abstract, but rather "the personally appropriated structure of one's own experiencing, one's own intelligent inquiry and insights, one's own critical reflection and judging and deciding." *Insight*, then, points to a very personal, one could even say, very intimate act.

> The crucial issue is an experimental issue, and the experiment will be performed not publicly but privately. It will consist in one's own rational self-consciousness clearly and distinctly taking possession of itself as rational self-consciousness. Up to that decisive achievement all leads. From it all follows. No one else, no matter what his knowledge or his eloquence, no matter what his logical rigor

or his persuasiveness, can do it for you.[9]

As I mentioned, prior to reading *Insight* I had been reading Carl Roger's *On Becoming a Person*, a book that had emphasized the importance of "appropriating" one's feelings. Doing so, Rogers claimed, would result in "appropriated learnings," that is, learnings that came out of one's own life experience. Lonergan promised a similar experience.

> The present work is not to be read as though it described some distant region of the globe which the reader never visited, or some strange and mystical experience which the reader never shared. It is an account of knowledge. Though I cannot recall to each reader his personal experiences, he can do so for himself and thereby pluck my general phrases from the dim world of thought to set them in the pulsing flow of life.[10]

"The pulsing flow of life"—that's certainly what I was interested in. I began to think, "Perhaps this stuff is more related to 'real life' than I thought."

Okay, the point seemed clear. *Insight* is not about the abstract; it is about the concrete: getting in touch with and coming to know my own processes of knowing. But here is where Lonergan sounds a warning. This process of self-appropriation is not easy. In fact

> . . . the labor of self-appropriation cannot occur at a single leap. Essentially, it is a development of the subject and in the subject, and like all development it can be solid and fruitful only by being painstaking and slow.[11]

This I did not like to read. I was an impatient twenty-seven year old when I began the serious reading of *Insight*. I wanted to get to the heart of things. I had been reading and studying philosophy and theology for a number of years and here I was being told I should undertake a process that was said to be "painstaking and slow." How long would this painful process take? A year? A couple of years? Longer? Why? Why do it? Why undertake this arduous journey? And what was the cause of the arduousness of the journey?

Lonergan's response was that the pain of the journey was due to "a psychological problem" that somehow needed to be resolved. And I did not like to be told I had a psychological problem! On the other hand, beginning to realize one has a problem, is the first step to resolving it. Without this problem, Lonergan averred, he could set out quite clearly what he wanted to say about human knowing; nevertheless,

> . . . the hard fact is that the psychological problem exists, that there exist in man two diverse kinds of knowing, that they exist without differentiation and in an ambivalent confusion until they are distinguished explicitly and the implications of the distinction are drawn explicitly.[12]

The psychological problem, then, consists in the confusion of two different types of knowing: one, our strictly intellectual knowing; the other an amalgam of intellect and imagination. Throughout *Insight* Lonergan will, through numerous examples, illustrate these two kinds of knowing and the confusion that ensues when they are not clearly distinguished. That this process of clarification involves a significant "mental wrestling," then, is evident from what Lonergan would write some years later in *Method in Theology*:

> Our purpose is to bring to light the pattern within which these operations occur and, it happens, we cannot succeed without an exceptional amount of exertion and activity on the part of the reader. He will have to familiarize himself with our terminology. He will have to evoke the relevant operations in his own consciousness. He will have to discover in his own experience the dynamic relationships leading from one operation to the next. Otherwise he will find not merely this chapter but the whole book about as illuminating as a blind man finds a lecture on color.[13]

In a footnote to the above quote Lonergan distinguishes between a presentation of his theory "in the abstract" and the slow process of self-appropriation.

> Please observe that I am offering only a summary, that the summary can do no more than present a general idea, that the process of self-appropriation occurs only slowly, and usually, only through the struggle with some such book as *Insight*.[14]

4. "EXERCISES" AND THE PROMISE OF ENLIGHTENMENT

How then distinguish between these two kinds of knowing that, according to Lonergan, exist "in an ambivalent confusion" in ourselves? His answer: Take up strategically chosen "exercises" and analyze them.

> The first eight chapters of *Insight* are a series of five-finger exercises inviting the reader to discover in himself and for himself just what happens when he understands. My aim is to help people experience themselves understanding, advert to the experience, distinguish it from other experiences, name and identify it, and recognize it when it recurs. My aim, I surmise is parallel to Carl Rogers' aim of inducing his clients to advert to the feelings they experience but do not advert to, distinguish, name, identify, recognize.[15]

It is because of this confusion between two different kinds of knowing, that the early chapters of *Insight* make liberal use of "five finger exercises" from mathematics and empirical science. But as I can attest from my early childhood piano lessons with Sister Agnes Loyola, five-finger exercises can sometimes be very painful indeed! It had been some years since I had taken any courses in mathematics and science. So the early chapters of *Insight* were painful indeed. Just the sight of the differential equations struck terror! Nevertheless, Lonergan gives three reasons for his prominent use of mathematical and scientific examples. The first reason is clarity and exactitude. If you are seeking a clear and distinct apprehension of the activities that mark the different levels of consciousness, then you must prefer fields of intellectual endeavor in which the greatest care is devoted to exactitude.

> For this reason, then, I have felt obliged to begin my account of insight and its expansion with mathematical and scientific illustrations and, while I would grant that essentially the same activities can be illustrated from the ordinary use of intelligence that is named common sense, I also submit that it would be impossible for common sense to grasp and say what precisely common sense happens to illustrate.[16]

The second reason for invoking scientific examples is the criterion of the real implicit in scientific operations. It is this criterion that will address the confusion ordinarily involved in our human knowing of our human knowing. We will focus on this issue later on.

Finally, a third reason for the prominent use of scientific examples is that scientific method itself is just a specialized application of the object of Lonergan's interest, that is, "the dynamic structure immanent and recurrently operative in human cognitional activity."

The preface and the introduction, then, characterize the book as an invitation to "an insight into insight," that is, "the appropriation of our own rational self-consciousness." Because of a deep-seated psychological problem, however, a problem identified as the confusion between two different types of knowledge, the book involves "an arduous exploratory journey" through the fields of mathematics and science. The purpose of that journey is a personal development in the reader, a development that can be solid and fruitful only by being painstaking and slow.

Nevertheless, in spite of its radical intellectualism—or perhaps because of that—there is in the preface and the introduction to *Insight* an underlying passion. I caught some of that passion the first time I studied these pages. It came from the promise of an astounding development that would take place in the reader if he or she underwent the therapy outlined in *Insight*.

> But though the act is private, both its antecedents and its consequents have their public manifestation. There can be long series of marks on paper that communicate an invitation to know oneself in the tension of the duality of one's

own knowing; and among such series of marks with an invitatory meaning the present book would wish to be numbered. Nor need it remain a secret whether such invitations are helpful or, when helpful, accepted. Winter twilight cannot be mistaken for the summer noonday sun.[17]

At this point I had no idea what Lonergan was talking about; but I wanted to know. I wanted the experience he promised, an experience as distinctive as the summer noonday sun shining on an Italian hillside—an experience so different from that of winter twilight.

Of course, at this point, especially with his great emphasis on the importance of science, I assumed that Lonergan was talking of something totally over my head. Nevertheless, it was reassuring to read that he was referring to "a development that can begin in any sufficiently cultured consciousness." I assumed that, with my years of schooling behind me, I too might have a consciousness "sufficiently cultured" to begin that development.

Nevertheless, his aim was high indeed and, in words that I could scarcely comprehend, he describes the development he is seeking to engender as one "that heads through an understanding of all understanding to a basic understanding of all that can be understood."[18] In other words, it will be a subjective event that will imply an objective philosophy. That is, it will move from an understanding of understanding to an overall viewpoint or "vision" of what can be understood. This suggests a slogan; and he uses it to sum up the positive content of his work:

> Thoroughly understand what it is to understand, and not only will you understand the broad lines of all there is to be understood but also you will possess a fixed base, an invariant pattern, opening upon all further developments of understanding.[19]

This was extraordinary! In fact, it seemed crazy! In fact, one could at this point ask "Who in fact has the psychological problem—Lonergan or me?" How could "an insight into insight" have such extraordinary implications? But all Lonergan can do at this point is make a promise. For those who succeed in this challenge of self-appropriation, he promises a new vision, a new view, a new philosophy—beyond the other philosophies of the day.

> For the appropriation of one's own rational self-consciousness, which has been so stressed in this introduction, is not an end in itself but rather a beginning. It is a necessary beginning, for unless one breaks the duality in one's knowing, one doubts that understanding correctly is knowing. Under the pressure of that doubt, either one will sink into the bog of a knowing that is without understanding, or else one will cling to understanding but sacrifice knowing on the altar of an immanentism, an idealism, a relativism. From the horns of that dilemma one escapes only through the discovery—and one has not made it yet if one has

no clear memory of its startling strangeness—that there are two quite different realisms, that there is an incoherent realism, half animal and half human, that poses as a halfway house between materialism and idealism, and on the other hand that there is an intelligent and reasonable realism between which and materialism the halfway house is idealism.[20]

"Critical realism" is the philosophy. The way to that philosophy will be by making one's way through any inadequate realism and any other inadequate philosophy—materialism, idealism, relativism, etc. If one succeeds in making it through the thicket of these "counterpositions," what can one expect? As Lonergan put it, one can expect an experience of "startling strangeness."

As I read through the preface and the introduction to *Insight*, I kept asking myself, "What good is all this?" "Why bother with this stuff—especially if it involves a long and "arduous exploratory journey" through such areas as mathematics, science and philosophy? It was the temper of the times to ask such questions. (And perhaps our own times today?) How could this have anything to do with the lives of millions of suffering people "out there?" Wouldn't it be better to get "out there" and do something "practical"—something that would "really" affect people's lives, especially the lives of the poor?

Lonergan anticipated this question and his response consists in replying that if you truly want to be practical, then "Be intelligent!" Specifically, be intelligent about your own intelligence.

There remains the question, What practical good can come of this book? The answer is more forthright than might be expected, for insight is the source not only of theoretical knowledge but also of all its practical applications, and indeed of all intelligent activity. Insight into insight, then, will reveal what activity is intelligent, and insight into oversights will reveal what activity is unintelligent. But to be practical is to do the intelligent thing, and to be unpractical is to keep blundering about. It follows that insight into both insight and oversight is the very key to practicality.[21]

Since insight into insight is also the key to insight into oversight, to missing the point, to being in error, it is also the key to discerning progress and decline in history. Years later I would come across a quote from Lonergan where he says that if we really want to help the poor, we will spend our nights studying economics!

Cardinal Danielou speaks of the poor. It is a worthy topic, but I feel that the basic step in aiding them in a notable manner is a matter of spending one's nights and days in a deep and prolonged study of economic analysis.[22]

Let the following quote sum up what I learned from my first reading of the preface to *Insight* and what motivated me to keep reading the following

700 pages.

Unfortunately, as insight and oversight commonly are mated, so also are progress and decline. We reinforce our love of truth with a practicality that is equivalent to an obscurantism. We correct old evils with a passion that mars the new good. We are not pure. We compromise. We hope to muddle through. But the very advance of knowledge brings a power over nature and over men too vast and terrifying to be entrusted to the good intentions of unconsciously biased minds. We have to learn to distinguish sharply between progress and decline, learn to encourage progress without putting a premium upon decline, learn to remove the tumor of the flight from understanding without destroying the organs of intelligence.

No problem is at once more delicate and more profound, more practical and perhaps more pressing. How, indeed, is a mind to become conscious of its own bias when that bias springs from a communal flight from understanding and is supported by the whole texture of a civilization? How can new strength and vigor be imparted to the detached and disinterested desire to understand without the reinforcement acting as an added bias? How can human intelligence hope to deal with the unintelligible yet objective situations which the flight from understanding creates and expands and sustains? At least we can make a beginning by asking what precisely it is to understand, what are the dynamics of the flow of consciousness that favors insight, what are the interferences that favor oversight, what, finally, do the answers to such questions imply for the guidance of human thought and action.[23]

As would become evident as I read through *Insight*, the issue of self-appropriation was not just personal. It was also practical, social and cultural. In the original preface to the book Lonergan wrote of the massive disorientation attendant upon the twentieth century's inability to answer the question: "Who is the human person?"

In the midst of this widespread disorientation, man's problem of self-knowledge ceases to be simply the individual concern inculcated by the ancient sage. It takes on the dimensions of a social crisis. It can be read as the historical issue of the twentieth century.[24]

NOTES

1. William Mathews, S.J. has traced this period of Lonergan's life. See "A Biographical Perspective on Conversion and the Functional Specialties in Lonergan," *Method: Journal of Lonergan Studies*, Vol 16, no. 2 (Fall 1998), 133-160.

2. Susanne K. Langer, *Philosophy in a New Key* (New York: New American Library, 1948), 44.

3. See Richard M. Liddy, *Art and Feeling: An Analysis and Critique of the*

Philosophy of Art of Susanne K. Langer (Ann Arbor: University Microfilms, 1970). Also my review of Susanne K. Langer, *Mind: An Essay on Human Feeling, Vol I,* in *International Philosophical Quarterly,* Vol. 10, n.3 (1970), 481-484.

4. Some time ago I encountered a philosophy professor standing with two of his students. One I knew was struggling over *Insight.* As the two students walked away, the professor remarked to me that the other student had avoided picking up *Insight.* "It's all there," he said to me. "You either pick it up and start working through it or you avoid it. Ultimately, that's a very personal decision."

5. *CWL 5 Understanding and Being,* 18.

6. Jerome Miller, *In the Throe of Wonder,* (Albany, NY: State University of New York Press, 1992), 53.

7. *CWL 5 Understanding and Being,* 34-35.

8. *CWL 3 Insight,* 3 (ix). Numbers in parentheses are the pagination of the original version of *Insight.*

9. *CWL 3 Insight,* 13 (xviii).

10. *CWL 3, Insight,* 13 (xviii).

11. *CWL 3 Insight,* 17 (xxiii).

12. *CWL 3 Insight,* 17 (xxii).

13. *Method in Theology,* 7.

14. *Method in Theology,* 7. The question could be asked whether there are any other books like *Insight.*

15. "*Insight* Revisited," *A Second Collection,* 269.

16. *CWL 3 Insight,* 14-15 (xx).

17. *CWL 3 Insight,* 13 (xix).

18. *CWL 3 Insight,* 22 (xxviii).

19. *CWL 3 Insight,* 22 (xxviii).

20. *CWL 3 Insight,* 22 (xxviii).

21. *CWL 3 Insight,* 7-8 (xiii-xiv)

22. *CWL 17 Philosophical and Theological Papers 1965-1980,* 280.

23. *CWL 3 Insight,* 8-9 (xiv-xv).

24. Bernard Lonergan, "The Original Preface to *Insight,*" published in *Method: Journal of Lonergan Studies,* Vol. 3/1 (March 1985), 5.

Part II

READING *INSIGHT*

Chapter Five

Theoretical Insights

In the early pages of *Insight* Lonergan "describes" various insights. Always his aim is to have us become aware of insights happening in ourselves. He defines insight not as just any act of attention or advertence or memory but the supervening act of understanding.

> It is not any recondite intuition but the familiar event that occurs easily and frequently in the moderately intelligent, rarely and with difficulty only in the very stupid.[1]

On first reading this seemed a rather "undemocratic" definition of insight!—that which happens often in smart people and seldom in those that are not. And yet that certainly characterizes the act of "catching on," does it not?

So we are talking about something that on one level is very familiar to us. So familiar, in fact, that we might think it beneath us to pay much attention to it. Nevertheless, Lonergan recalls Descartes' advice on the importance of paying attention to basically very simple things.

> I thought it well to begin by recalling this conviction of a famous mathematician and philosopher, for our first task will be to attain familiarity with what is meant by insight, and the only way to achieve this end is, it seems, to attend very closely to a series of instances all of which are rather remarkable for their banality.[2]

But first he provides a dramatic instance of insight in the story of Archimedes rushing naked from the baths of Syracuse crying "Eureka!" "I've got it!" King Hiero had asked him to figure out whether his crown was made of pure gold or whether a dishonest goldsmith had crafted it with some baser metals.

Archimedes was wrestling with this problem when he visited the baths and there hit upon the solution—weigh the crown in water!

> Implicit in this directive were the principles of displacement and of specific gravity. With those principles of hydrostatics we are not directly concerned. For our objective is an insight into insight. Archimedes had his insight by thinking about the crown; we shall have ours by thinking about Archimedes.[3]

Lonergan highlights five characteristics of insight as exemplified in Archimedes:

1. it comes as a release to the tension of inquiry;
2. it comes suddenly and unexpectedly;
3. it is a function not of outer circumstances but of inner conditions;
4. it pivots between the concrete and the abstract; and
5. it passes into the habitual texture of one's mind.

First of all, it came as a release to the tension of inquiry. If Archimedes had not questioned, he would never have had the insight. His moment of enlightenment flowed from his questioning and from "the pure desire to know" beneath his questioning. In some of the most famous lines of *Insight* Lonergan describes this desire.

> Deep within us all, emergent when the noise of other appetites is stilled, there is a drive to know, to understand, to see why, to discover the reason, to find the cause, to explain. Just what is wanted, has many names. In what precisely it consists, is a matter of dispute. But the fact of inquiry is beyond all doubt. It can absorb a man. It can keep him for hours, day after day, year after year, in the narrow prison of his study or his laboratory. It can send him on dangerous voyages of exploration. It can withdraw him from other interests, other pursuits, other pleasures, other achievements. It can fill his waking thoughts, hide from him the world of ordinary affairs, invade the very fabric of his dreams. It can demand endless sacrifices that are made without regret though there is only the hope, never a certain promise, of success.[4]

Repeatedly in *Insight* Lonergan will return to this "pure, detached, disinterested desire to know." It is a desire that moves us beyond what we imagine things to be, beyond what we would like them to be, to what they are.

Secondly, Archimedes' insight came suddenly and unexpectedly. It came at a moment of relaxation. For some people insight might come after a good night's sleep. One's faculties are relaxed. One has put the problem away for a while. One returns to it. Eureka! The discovery is not the result of following a recipe, "the same old rules" or routines; it is rather, the source of new rules and new routines. When the question is posed, when the orientation of our consciousness is to understand, then we can relax. We can allow this underlying orientation to open up to us whatever we are seeking. Karl Jaspers, in an essay I read about the time I was reading *Insight* witnessed to this characteristic when he extolled the value of day-dreaming.

> Modest, seemingly accidental, occasions brought insights. Such work is, to be sure, work which requires planning and direction. It can, however, be successful only if something else is constantly effective: namely, dreaming. Often I gazed out on the scenery, up at the sky, the clouds; often I would sit or recline without doing anything. Only the calmness of meditation in the unconstrained flow of the imagination allows those impulses to become effective without which all work becomes endless, non-essential, and empty. It seems to me that for the man who does not daily dream a while, his star will grow dark, that star by which all our work and everyday existence may be guided.[5]

A third characteristic of Archimedes' insight is that it was a function, not of outer circumstances, but of inner conditions. Many people visited the baths of Syracuse and felt the relaxing waters there, but only Archimedes had the insight. This highlights the strange difference between insight and sensation. Unless you are blind, you only have to open your eyes to see. Insights, however, cannot be turned and off at will. To have an insight, you have to be in the process of learning or, at least, to reenact in oneself previous processes of learning. With insight, internal conditions are paramount.[6]

A fourth characteristic is that insight pivots between the abstract and the concrete. Archimedes had a concrete problem: to determine whether the king's crown was solid gold or not. He hit upon a concrete solution: weigh the crown in water. But what happened in between these two moments can be formulated only by the abstract equations representing the principles of displacement and specific gravity. Physics textbooks today, more than two millennia from the time of Archimedes' insight, still make reference to his discovery precisely because they revealed those abstract laws. Those laws still hold. Of course, they have been refined, clarified and set within the context of modern physics. Nevertheless, Archimedes' insight had a significance far beyond its origin and application to the king of Syracuse's crown. Because Archimedes' discovery can still speak to us today, it "pivots" between the abstract and the concrete.

> Because insights arise with reference to the concrete, mathematicians need pen and paper, teachers need black-boards, pupils have to perform experiments for themselves, doctors have to see their patients, trouble-shooters have to travel to the spot, people with a mechanical bent take things apart to see how they work. But because the significance and relevance of insight goes beyond any concrete

problem or application, men formulate abstract sciences with their numbers, symbols, their technical terms and formulae, their definitions, postulates and deductions. Thus, by its very nature, insight is the mediator, the hinge, the pivot. It is insight into the concrete world of sense and imagination. Yet what is known by insight, what insight adds to sensible and imagined presentations, finds its adequate expression only in the abstract and recondite formulations of the sciences.[7]

A fifth characteristic of insight is that it passes into the habitual texture of our minds. In order to solve his problem, Archimedes needed an instant of inspiration. But he needed no further inspiration when he went to offer the king his solution. He had crossed a divide. What previously had seemed so difficult now became incredibly simple and obvious. Moreover, it tended to remain simple and obvious. However difficult the first occurrence of an insight may be, subsequent repetitions occur almost at will. It is this characteristic of insight that constitutes the possibility of human learning. We are able to add insight to insight inasmuch as the new does not banish the old but complements it, refines it and completes it.

> [I]nasmuch as the subject to be learnt involves the acquisition of a whole series of insights, the process of learning is marked by an initial darkness in which one gropes about insecurely, in which one cannot see where one is going, in which one cannot grasp what all the fuss is about; and only gradually, as one begins to catch on, does the initial darkness yield to a subsequent period of increasing light, confidence, interest, absorption.[8]

This was my experience in reading *Insight*. At first I groped around insecurely, not sure where I was going—perhaps as the reader of this book. But gradually, things began to change.

And at the end of the first chapter Lonergan makes the point that the important issue here is not the particular examples he uses, but rather the insight into insight. "It follows that for the story of Archimedes the reader will profitably substitute some less resounding yet more helpful experience of his own."[9] Thus, as I read and re-read this first chapter of *Insight* I constantly asked myself: "Am I having insights?" "What are they like?" "Do they resemble Lonergan's descriptions?" Vaguely I became aware that I was indeed having insights—especially, as I was reading *Insight*.

1. THE CIRCLE AS PARADIGMATIC EXAMPLE

My intention is not to repeat *Insight*, but just to point out what struck me when I first read the book, such as the "exercises" that constitute the first part of the book. Among these exercises the foremost was the insight into the circle.[10] Many of us when we were in high school memorized the definition of a circle, rooted in Euclid's *Elements*, as "a locus of coplanar points equidistant from a center." But what we did not learn was the precise difference between repeating that definition as a parrot and uttering it intelligently. That is Lonergan's point. Why these words? Why not some others? Lonergan performs a mental experiment, an exercise, taking us through a scenario for Euclid's discovery. Elements of his scenario are, of course, imaginative, but Lonergan's aim is to help us focus on how the definition arose. His aim is to help us come to understand the elements involved in our own understanding of a circle.

Obviously, Euclid must have been interested in the shapes of things: triangles, squares, circles, etc. Perhaps his questions were initially pragmatic, for example, what role do certain shaped things—e.g. circular wheels—play in bringing about certain effects, such as the transportation of goods? But his questioning obviously led him beyond such immediately practical considerations to eventually asking something like "What is roundness?" or "Why is this wheel round?" In later philosophical language, he was seeking "the formal cause" of a circle, that is, "What makes a circle a circle?"

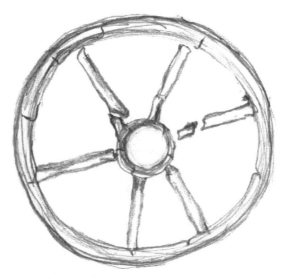

Now initially someone might have answered by immediately responding, "The wheel is round because the spokes are all equal." And to this Euclid might well have responded that in this particular case that might be so, but it is not necessarily the case. After all, one spoke might be longer than another; one might go further into the hub; another might go deeper into the rim, etc.

Still, perhaps the suggestion of equal spokes might have provided a clue and Euclid might have said something like this to himself:

> Let's suppose a perfect wheel, that is, a perfect circle. Let's imagine the hub of the wheel becoming merely a point; let the spokes (let's call them "radii") and the rim (the "circumference") thin out into lines. Then, if all the spokes are exactly equal, the rim has to be perfectly round. Conversely, if any of the spokes are unequal, then the wheel cannot be perfectly round.

Something like this must have gone on in Euclid for something similar must go on in the mind of anyone who comes to understand a circle.

Lonergan makes a number of observations on this simple insight and his first observation is that "*points and lines cannot be imagined.*"

> One can imagine an extremely small dot. But no matter how small a dot may be, still it has magnitude. To reach a point, all magnitude must vanish, and with all magnitude there vanishes the dot as well. One can imagine an extremely fine thread. But no matter how fine a thread may be, still it has breadth and depth as well as length. Remove from the image all breadth and depth, and there vanishes all length as well.[11]

Secondly, points and lines are concepts. Human intelligence creates concepts just by supposing, thinking, formulating. Human intelligence can do such things: it can "suppose." It can create concepts, even of the unimaginable. And following out the clue on the equality of the spokes, the human person can push that clue for all it's worth.

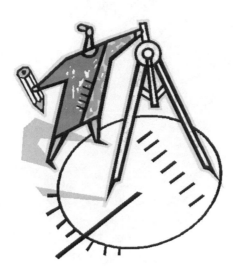

As long as the hub has any magnitude, the spokes can be sunk into it unequally. As long as the spokes have any thickness, the wheel can be flat at their ends. So let's suppose a point without magnitude, and lines without thickness to obtain a curve that would be perfectly, necessarily round.

> Just as imagination is the playground of our desires and fears, so conception is the playground of our intelligence. Just as imagination can create objects never seen or heard or felt, so too can conception create objects that cannot even be imagined. How? By supposing. The imagined dot has magnitude as well as position, but the geometer says, "Let us suppose it only has position." The imagined line has breadth as well as length, but the geometer says, "Let us suppose it has only length."

What human intelligence grasps in the imagined equal radii is the *necessity* of a perfect circle as well as the *impossibility* of having a circle without equal radii. And just as points and lines cannot be imagined, neither can "necessity" and "impossibility" be imagined.

Still, imagination was necessary. "Eliminate the image of the center, the radii, the curve, and by the same stroke there vanishes all grasp of necessary or of impossible roundness." [12] But it is the grasp, the insight, the understanding—equivalent terms for Lonergan—that makes all the difference in the world. This is the difference between repeating the definition as a parrot and uttering it intelligently. If one utters it intelligently, then one can change the words and even make up a new definition for oneself. [13]

And the whole process is initiated by questioning. For it is the prior questioning that brings imagining and supposing into the mutual relationship that issues in the cry, "I've got it!" "Eureka!"

> By their co-operation, by successive adjustments, question and insight, image and concept, present a solid front. The answer is a patterned set of concepts. The image strains to approximate to the concepts. The concepts, by added conceptual determinations, can express their differences from the merely approximate image. The pivot between images and concepts is the insight. And setting the standard which insight, images and concepts must meet is the question, the desire to know, that could have kept the process in motion by further queries, had its requirements not been satisfied. [14]

The process of the genesis of the definition of the circle, then, involves at least the following conscious activities linked to one another:

concepts	("inner words" e.g. *radii*, *center*, etc.)
insight	(the grasp—the "aha!" experience)
questioning	(initiating and inspiring the whole process)
imagining	(striving to keep up with questioning)
sensitive experiencing	(for example, the ox-cart wheels)

The outcome of the whole process finds expression in words and concepts. Concepts and words "consolidate" our understanding and it is by means of words and concepts that we communicate with others. But words and concepts can be "static." Because we have words and concepts, we can tend to think we understand. But understanding is *pre-conceptual, pre-verbal.* To "get it," that is, to have an insight into insight—to focus on what Lonergan is talking about—you have to experience yourself "getting it," and come to understand that experience correctly.

Lonergan elsewhere adds refinements to this analysis of the insight into the circle. For example, a diagram on a globe might have points equidistant to the center of the globe and yet not be a circle. Hence, the word "co-planar" needs to be added to the formulation of the insight. Further refinements need to be made in terms of later types of geometry in which the intelligibility of a circle can be expressed in purely formal ways, such as $(x^2 + y^2) = r^2$ without reference to diagrams.[15]

Still, Lonergan's basic point is that there is a pattern in the elements that go into having an insight: that is, the activities of experiencing, imagining, questioning, understanding, conceiving or "formulating."

2. EXPLANATORY UNDERSTANDING

Lonergan notes that the definition of a circle arrived at in this way is an explanatory definition as distinct from a nominal definition. A nominal definition concerns the correct use of words, such as a definition of a circle as "a perfectly round plane curve." We are normally pretty good at nominal definitions because, within limits, we know how to use words about the things around us. Socrates' dialogue partners were pretty good at nominal definitions for they knew how to use words; but they were not able to explain what the words meant.

On the contrary, a definition of a circle that includes the necessity of equal radii is an explanatory definition: it presupposes an insight into the object that is a circle. In such a definition each of the concepts is implicitly defined by its relation to each of the other concepts in the definition. That is, "center" is defined in terms of "circumference" and "radii"; and a "radius" takes its definition from its relationship of equality to the center and the circumference.

> Let us say, then, that for every basic insight there is a circle of terms and relations, such that the terms fix the relations, the relations fix the terms, and the insight fixes both. If one grasps the necessary and sufficient conditions for the perfect roundness of this imagined plane curve, then one grasps not only the circle but also the point, the line, the circumference, the radii, the plane, and equality.[16]

In other words, through such explanatory understanding a whole set of terms falls into place. Such explanation is central for Lonergan. It is the focal point of science. Every science begins descriptively, that is, describing the relationships of things to our senses; but eventually it becomes explanatory, that is, it relates things to one another in an explanatory scheme. Thus, the periodic table in chemistry relates the chemical elements to each other in an overall explanatory schema. So also, the evolutionary chart in biological science relates various living species to each other in a total genetic and developmental viewpoint. In Lonergan's later book, *Method in Theology*, he writes of this world of explanations as "the world of theory." Just as geometric definitions transcend the images of ox cart wheels, so the world of theory transcends the ordinary language of common sense.

Lonergan's own "theory" of the structure of our human knowing will be an explanatory understanding: it will begin from description and then move on to explanation. That explanatory understanding will involve at least the terms we have been using to evoke an insight into insight: sensitive experiencing, imagining, questioning, understanding, conceiving or formulating. All of these terms are defined and theoretically understood by their relationships to each other. Experiencing and imagining are what are presupposed to human questioning and are raised to a higher level through human questioning. Questioning presupposes experience and imagination and leads to understanding or insight. Understanding or insight presupposes experiencing, imagining and questioning and finds formulation in concepts.

A refinement: I remember David Tracy saying to me one evening in 1966: "Now I understand what 'abstraction' is all about! It's not an impoverished replica of the real. It's an enrichment. It's grasping what's important as important, what's relevant as relevant." Thus, in the example of the circle, what is grasped as important is the equality of the radii. All else—the size of the circle, the color it is drawn and symbolized with—all this pertains to what Lonergan calls "the empirical residue": what is left over on the empirical level when one has grasped the form of a thing. In the empirical sciences the individuality of things as well as the particularity of times and places pertains to the empirical residue. This notion will reappear in the chapter on metaphysics.

3. THE "LAW" OF FALLING BODIES

Lonergan once remarked that the important thing in understanding the early chapters of *Insight* with their heavy focus on scientific understanding was not to become a physicist, but rather to attain some understanding of "the general orientation of the scientific mind."

> I think a philosopher does need some grasp of the general orientation of the scientific mind; he has to be able to understand the type of thinking the sci-

entist does; he has to know something about heuristic structures and higher viewpoints. At least that is a minimum requirement. I do not think he needs detailed knowledge in the various scientific fields or an ability to discuss them in detail.[17]

We will illustrate this paragraph in the pages that follow. The general orientation of the scientific mind can be illustrated from a work that Lonergan often referred to and that I read during the time I was first struggling with *Insight*: Herbert Butterfield's *The History of the Scientific Revolution*. For me this was a significant historical introduction to the meaning of modern science. Butterfield emphasizes the fact that prior to the scientific revolution in the seventeenth century what was lacking was neither an intense interest in learning about the facts of nature, nor observations, nor experiences. Rather, what was lacking was a whole new way of looking at things.

> . . . We shall find that in both celestial and terrestrial physics . . . change is brought about, not by new observations or additional evidence in the first instance, but by transpositions that were taking place inside the minds of the scientists themselves.[18]

It was a question of handling the same data as before, but placing these data in a new framework, a new system of relations:

> In fact the modern law of inertia is not something you would discover by mere photographic methods of observation—it required a different kind of thinking-cap, a transposition in the mind of the scientist himself.[19]

What then, was this "new thinking cap" that turned out to be remarkably successful in uncovering nature's secrets? It consisted in the use of mathematics in the investigation of nature:

> . . . nothing could have been more important than the growing tendency to geometrise or mathematise a problem. Nothing is more effective, after people have long been debating and wrangling and churning the air, than the appearance of a person who draws a line on the blackboard, which with the help of a little geometry solves the whole problem in an instant.[20]

Butterfield quotes an unknown author to the effect that "the application of algebraic methods to the geometric field was the greatest single step ever made in the progress of the exact sciences."[21]

> . . . the problem of gravitation would never have been solved—the whole Newtonian synthesis would never have been achieved—without first, the analytical geometry of René Descartes and, secondly, the infinitesimal calculus of Newton

and Leibniz. . . . Without the achievements of the mathematicians the scientific revolution as we know it, would have been impossible.[22]

We might note here Lonergan's remark in chapter one of *Insight* that just as explanatory insight led to explanatory concepts (radii, circumference, etc.), so also it led to new types of mathematical symbolism, or imaginative presentations, in which insight could grasp new levels of intelligibility. Imagination, under the influence of questioning, cooperates in this process to the extent that it allows for ever more apt "heuristic symbolisms," that is, symbolisms that aid our discovery. "Heuristic" is cognate to "Eureka!" ("I've found it!") and denotes that which helps us to make discoveries, to understand. Thus, the discovery of the Arabic numerical system greatly enhanced the possibility for new discoveries. "It is easy enough to take the square root of 1764. It is another matter to take the square root of MDCCLXIV."[23] Finding an apt symbolism allows the mind to concentrate on what is important. As Alfred North Whitehead noted, writing of the enormous importance of a good mathematical notation:

> By relieving the brain of all unnecessary work, a good notation sets it free to concentrate on more advanced problems, and in effect increases the mental power of the race. . . . It is a profoundly erroneous truism, repeated by all copy-books and by eminent people when they are making speeches, that we should cultivate the habit of thinking about what we are doing. The precise opposite is the case. Civilization advances by extending the number of important operations which we can perform without thinking about them. [24]

Because of this "mathematization" of science, the resort to experiment now came to have direction and empirical observations came at last to be organized to some purpose. But why? Why was this move so successful? Lonergan answers this question in the second chapter of *Insight* by stating that insight in empirical science is similar to insight in mathematics in that it seeks "an immanent intelligibility."

> Just as we ruled out of consideration the purpose of cartwheels, the materials from which they are made, the wheelwrights that make them, and the tools that wheelwrights use, so also Galileo was uninterested in the final cause of falling, he drew no distinction between the different materials that fall, he made no effort to determine what agencies produce a fall.[25]

Furthermore, the significance of the use of mathematics in science is that it enables the researcher to seek the intelligibility of things in their relationships to each other and not just in their relationships to our concerns. Just as in understanding the definition of a circle, we started from a clue, the equality of the spokes,

. . . so too Galileo supposed that some correlation was to be found between the measurable aspects of falling bodies. Indeed, he began by showing the error in the ancient Aristotelian correlation that bodies fell according to their weight. Then he turned his attention to two measurable aspects immanent in every fall; the body traverses a determinate distance; it does so in a determinate interval of time. By a series of experiments he provided himself with the requisite data and obtained the desired measurements. Then he discovered that the measurements would satisfy a general rule: the distance traversed is proportional to the time squared.[26]

That Galileo's insight captured some inner character of the universe is evident from the fact that the law of falling bodies "is a correlation that has been verified directly and indirectly for over four centuries." Furthermore, just as the definition of a circle involved unimaginable points and lines, so something similar happens when we formulate the law of falling bodies: it holds in a vacuum. But to actually realize a perfect vacuum is impossible. What can be established empirically is that the more closely one approximates the conditions of a vacuum, the more accurate the law of falling bodies is found to be. In a real sense, the use of mathematics in empirical science enables the scientist to transcend representative imagination, that is, images rooted in our own ordinary common sense frameworks. This was the significance of Galileo's measuring and correlating.

A theme sounded in the introduction to *Insight* is re-emerging: there exist two types of knowing: one theoretical, transcending imagination: the other wrapped up in representative imagination.

4. THE HEURISTIC STRUCTURES OF SCIENCE

The second thing that a philosopher should know about modern science is "something about heuristic structures." A heuristic structure is a methodical and fruitful way of asking questions. It is a way of questioning well. The word, method, comes from the Greek words, "*meta*" and "*hodos*," which together mean: proceeding according to a certain way or path. A methodical heuristic structure, then, is a definite way of proceeding in order to increase one's chances of finding answers in a particular area. That is why the word "heuristic" is used: it is cognate to Archimedes' cry, "Eureka!" "I've found it!"

The scientific method is a particularly prominent way in which human beings have gradually refined their way of asking questions and thereby successfully arriving at answers. In the second chapter of *Insight* Lonergan analyzes the classical and statistical heuristic structures of scientific method. His point is to analyze what scientists concretely do as they dynamically seek insight. He was fond of quoting Einstein's dictum that it was more important to pay attention to what scientists do than to what they say.[27]

> Scientists achieve understanding, but they do so only at the end of an inquiry. Moreover, their inquiry is methodical, and method consists in ordering means to achieve an end. But how can means be ordered to an end when the end is knowledge and the knowledge is not yet acquired? The answer to this puzzle is the heuristic structure. Name the unknown. Work out its properties. Use the properties to direct, order, guide the inquiry.[28]

Lonergan illustrates a heuristic structure by using a simple problem from algebra. "If the clock on the wall now reads three o'clock, how do you determine when exactly the minute hand will catch up with the hour hand?" Well, to solve the problem, you first name the unknown, "Let x be the time you're looking for." This act of "naming the unknown," the use of such a symbol as "x," has turned out to be a particularly fruitful moment in the development of human knowing.

Secondly, you name as many of the characteristics of that "x" as you can. For one thing, the hour hand will have a fifteen minute head start. In addition, the ratio of the hour hand in relation to the speed of the minute hand will be 1/12. It is on the basis of these pieces of information about x that you can concretely determine its value. Invoking one's high school algebra, one can determine that if the clock on the wall reads 3 o'clock, the minute hand will catch up with the hour hand at 16 and 4/11 minutes after 3. Try it!

Now something similar can be found in the procedures of classical science. Empirical scientists asked the question: what is the "nature of" heat, the "nature of" light, the "nature of" change, etc. And just as the mathematician can first name his unknown, an "x," then determine its properties and thus come to know it, so the empirical inquirer can name his unknown, the "nature of. . . ," because it will be what he will know when he understands.

What are the characteristics of the x, "the nature of light. . . ," for example, that he seeks to understand? Preliminary classifications begin with similarities of things in their relationships to us: "it shines"; "it has this color," "it smells like this," etc. These are the descriptions from which science begins. But the scientist does not stop there:

> There also are the similarities of things in their relations to one another. Thus, they may be found together or apart. They may increase or decrease concomitantly. They may have similar antecedents or consequents. They may be similar in their proportions to one another, and such proportions may form series of relationships, such as exist between the elements in the periodic table of chemistry or between the successive forms of life in the theory of evolution.[29]

Hence, the empirical inquirer will say that he is not merely seeking the "nature of," but more precisely, "the unspecified correlation to be specified," "the undetermined function to be determined."

> . . . and now the task of specifying or determining is carried out by measuring, by tabulating measurements, by reaching an insight into the tabulated measurements, and by expressing that insight through some general correlation or function that, if verified, will define a limit on which converge the relations between all subsequent appropriate measurements.[30]

It is precisely because of such mathematical techniques that Galileo in his discovery of such correlations as "the law of falling bodies" differed from his predecessors.

> The Aristotelians were content to talk about the nature of light, the nature of heat, etc. Galileo inaugurated modern science by insisting that the nature of weight was not enough; from sensible similarity, which resides in the relations of things to our senses, one must proceed to relations that hold directly between things themselves.[31]

Thus, a piece of metal might "feel" cooler than a piece of wood, but they can both be the same temperature. In science, relationships to our feelings give way to relationships between things themselves.

Galileo's introduction of mathematical techniques into empirical inquiry represented a "conversion" in the minds of scientists. This classical heuristic structure characterized succeeding scientists in the line of Galileo, Newton, Clerk-Maxwell and even Einstein. That conversion was an epochal event in the history of the human family.

Distinct from such classical science, the emergence of quantum mechanics in the twentieth century highlighted the birth of another major scientific method, that is, *statistical heuristic structure.*

> Either intelligence anticipates the discovery of functional relations on which relations between measurements will converge, or else it anticipates the discovery of probabilities from which relative actual frequencies may diverge though only randomly. The latter alternative has a fairly clear claim to the name 'statistical.' The former alternative is not limited to Newtonian mechanics, and in the opinion of many does not regard quantum mechanics. It is a mode of inquiry common to Galileo, Newton, Clerk-Maxwell, and Einstein; it is as familiar to the chemist as to the physicist; it long was considered the unique mode of scientific investigation; it has been the principal source of the high repute of science. In such a work as the present no one, I trust, will be misled if so classical a procedure is named 'classical.'[32]

Statistical heuristic structure aims at determining the probability of events, that is, ideal frequencies from which actual frequencies diverge in a non-systematic manner. If actual frequencies diverge systematically from ideal probable frequencies, one would conclude to the presence of a "systematic" influence.

> While classical science aims at determining functions and correlations under the proviso, "other things being equal," statistical science aims at determining concretely how often other things are equal and what are the probabilities of the occurrences of events. Hence while classical conclusions are concerned with what would be if other things were equal, statistical conclusions directly regard such aggregates of events as the sequences of occasions on which a coin is tossed or dice are cast, the sequence of situations created by the mobility of molecules in a gas, the sequences of generations in which babies are born, the young marry, the old die.[33]

Statistical inquiry is not concerned with the intelligibly grouped events of systematic process, but rather with coincidental aggregates of events.

> There are no statistics on the phases of the moon or on the transit of Venus, and there are no random differences in ordinary astronomical tables. . . . It remains, then, that the object of statistical inquiry is the coincidental aggregate of events, that is, the aggregate of events that has some unity by spatial juxtaposition or by temporal succession or by both but lacks unity on the level of insight and of intelligible relation. In other words, statistical inquiry is concerned with non-systematic process.[34]

Lonergan goes into extensive analyses of the complementarity of classical and statistical heuristic structures as methods for understanding our universe. But what was the "vision" of the universe emerging from these two complementary ways of investigating reality?

5. "EMERGENT PROBABILITY"

In chapter one Lonergan calls attention to "higher viewpoints" in mathematics. For example, arithmetic provides the images in which insight grasps the possibility of a higher-level intelligibility found in the rules and operations of algebra. Similarly, algebra provides the images in which the calculus can be grasped.

Higher viewpoints are also operative in the empirical sciences as insight grasps in the images of a lower level—physics, for example—a higher-level intelligibility which de facto we call the science of chemistry. The possibility of higher-level intelligibilities derives from the combination of classical and statistical heuristic structures in the understanding of each level.

In chapter four of *Insight* Lonergan focuses on the complementarity of classical and statistical heuristic structures and on the "worldview" that emerges from the fact that humans seek the intelligibility of the universe through both of these procedures. That world-view Lonergan calls emergent probability. As classical and statistical heuristic structures, so also the world-view of emergent probability emerges from an insight into insight. Thus, insight into the concrete heuristic structures of empirical science reveals a world process characterized by both classical scientific "laws" as well as the statistical techniques of extremely large numbers and long intervals of time.

> Strangely enough, world process in its concrete historical unfolding rather conspicuously makes a large and generous use of the statistical techniques of large numbers and long intervals of time; it exhibits not a rigid but a fluid stability; it brings forth novelty and development; it makes false starts and suffers breakdowns. It would seem, then, that an understanding of the concrete unfolding of the world process will not be based exclusively on classical laws, however exactly and completely known, but in a fundamental manner will appeal to statistical laws.[35]

Classical science alone, when it was the only recognized kind of science, spawned a mechanistic and reductionist view of the universe. This can be seen even in Galileo's own interpretation of his discoveries. The world of common sense was "merely appearance." What was "really real" were the imaginable atoms and their elements moving about in an imaginable space-time. The classical exposition of such a mechanistic view found expression in the nineteenth century physicist, Laplace, who claimed that, given full knowledge of the positions of all the elements in the universe, all the past and future events of the universe would be totally predictable. (And when asked "What about God?" he replied, "I have no need of that hypothesis.")

But scientific development itself has undercut the presuppositions of such mechanistic determinism. What is obvious in the concrete operations of scientists are statistical ways of questioning: that is, determining probabilities of events from which concrete events diverge but they do so non-systematically. In addition, according to Lonergan, the acknowledgment of the integral role of statistical ways of understanding also promotes an understanding of the interrelationships of the various sciences to each other. For certainly this is a major question regarding our knowing: How is one area of knowing related to another? Is knowledge just a series of disparate fields? Is chemistry unrelated to physics? And how is biology related to these other two? And how are all three related to the world of human psychology? To "consciousness?"

Acknowledging not just classical heuristic structures, but also statistical structures can answer these questions as well. For by acknowledging the role of statistical science one allows for the possibility of the higher systematization of what from a lower point of view would be merely coincidental. Thus, from the viewpoint of physics, the classical laws that constitute the periodic table in chemistry are merely coincidental. The periodic table in chemistry cannot be "explained" from the viewpoint of physics alone. On the other hand, if one admits the possibility of higher viewpoints that systematize what from a lower viewpoint is merely coincidental, one acknowledges the possibility of a specifically higher viewpoint of chemistry.

Similarly, what from the viewpoint of chemistry is merely coincidental, can from the viewpoint of the evolutionary chart be understood as the emergence of the higher forms or inter-dependent "schemes of recurrence" that we know as biological and sentient life. Lonergan gives as illustrations of such schemes the planetary system, the circulation of water over the surface of the earth, the nitrogen cycle familiar to biologists, the routines of animal life, the repetitive economic rhythms of production and exchange.[36] In all of these at least two elements are at work: first, a certain scheme or set of routines that can be understood through classical science; second, the probability of that scheme or set of routines being realized and understood through statistical methods. Abstractly, the scheme itself is a combination of classical laws. Concretely, schemes begin, continue, and cease to function in accord with statistical probabilities.[37]

A major significance of Lonergan's study of classical and statistical heuristic structures and their coalescence into the world view of emergent probability is precisely that it allows for the emergence of human understanding—including the scientist's own understanding. Such understanding is rooted in the ability to "ask questions" about the physical, chemical and biological conditions for the emergence of human questioning. Thus, through the very activity of empirical scientists the multi-leveled being of this world becomes "luminous."

That is why, as I wrestled with these early chapters of *Insight,* I so much began to enjoy "reading around in science." For the human act of understanding, so conspicuous in the dynamisms of science, far from being reducible to underlying levels, exhibits an extraordinary transcendence and freedom from these underlying levels. It was a remarkable discovery when, contrary to all mechanistic assumptions, Wolfgang Köhler, a Gestalt psychologist in the 1920's, declared that the human person was the only animal with free imagination. That freedom, though conditioned by underlying levels, can also be the subtle companion of the human spirit of inquiry as it explores the universe. Also in the 1920s Hans Berger highlighted the physiological differences between ordinary consciousness, internally focused states, drowsiness, and deep sleep.[38] It was because of these correlations that Lonergan was once asked about "the biological bases of thought." The question implied a mechanistic and materialistic view of the universe and Lonergan answered with an interesting analogy:

> The biological basis of thought, I should say, is like the rubber-tire basis of the motor car. It conditions and sets limits to functioning, but under the conditions and within the limits the driver directs operations.[39]

The worldview of emergent probability, which Lonergan found implied in the classical and heuristic structures of scientists, envisions the emergence, according to statistical schedules, of higher levels from lower levels. As higher forms emerge, they re-arrange what is coincidental from a lower point of view into systematic "schemes of recurrence." Chemical forms, or schemes of recurrence, systematize into molecules coincidental manifolds of atomic and sub-atomic elements. Biological forms systematize chemical. Sensitive forms systematize coincidental manifolds of biological forms. Finally, intellectual forms systematize what from the viewpoint of sensitive psychology is merely coincidental.

For example, these black marks on a white piece of paper are not just random physical-chemical markings resulting from the sensitive psychological activities involved in my writing and your reading. They are words filled with meaning—meaning achieved through the specifically human intellectual activities of questioning and understanding. Thus, many levels of activities are involved:

$$\textit{intellectual activities—insights}$$
$$\textit{psychological}$$
$$\textit{biological}$$
$$\textit{chemical}$$
$$\textit{physical}$$

In addition, intelligence is the source of ever-new systematizations. Every new science, every new form of civilization and culture, is the emergence of a new "form," a new level of reality, in the universe, this time created by human intelligence. As one goes up the scale of levels of reality, there is an ever-increasing freedom from underlying levels. Plants evidence significant schemes of recurrence beyond inorganic life. Animals evidence the tremendous freedom that comes from local motion within an environment. Human intelligence evidences the freedom to ask questions about the universe. Each level is conditioned by the lower levels at the same time as there is an increasing freedom. Typing on this computer involves the laws of physics, bio-chemistry, the sensitive-psychological routines of moving one's fingers and, most significantly, the expression of human meanings.

As I studied *Insight* I was led to seek out books on mathematics and physics, to attend lectures on quantum mechanics and relativity theory. I will always remain a layman in these areas, but I became more and more confident
that I could discern what the scientists were doing—often as distinct from
what they said they were doing.

6. THE "ALREADY OUT THERE NOW REAL"

In the course of clarifying his own view of the universe that emerges from
acknowledging both classical and statistical heuristic structures, Lonergan
contrasts it with Galileo's worldview.

> Galileo discovered our law of falling bodies, but he failed to recognize its ab-
> stractness. Correctly, he grasped that explanation lies beyond description, that
> the relations of things to our senses must be transcended, that the relations of
> things to one another must be grasped, and that a geometrization of nature is the
> key tool in performing this task.
>
> Still, Galileo did not cast his methodological discoveries in the foregoing
> terms. Instead of speaking of the relations of things to our senses, he spoke of
> the merely apparent secondary qualities of things. Instead of speaking of the
> relations of things to one another, he spoke of their real and objective primary
> qualities, and these he conceived as the mathematical dimensions of matter in
> motion.[40]

In other words, Galileo made tremendous scientific discoveries; at the
same time, he thought that his scientific discoveries were of the "really real"
concrete world. He thought of the classical "laws" he had discovered, not as
abstractions statistically united to the concrete, but as concrete themselves.
He was guilty of what Alfred North Whitehead called "the fallacy of misplaced concreteness." From this there easily followed a mechanistic view of
the universe.[41]

Lonergan's critique of mechanistic determinism and its reductionism is always a function of his refusal to reduce understanding to imagination. Throughout *Insight* the distinction between insight and imagination remains constant.
Thus, in the concrete practice of scientists there is a world of difference between
a "systematic unification" of physical laws and an "imaginative synthesis."

> As systematic unification does not include imaginative synthesis, so it does not
> even guarantee its possibility. It is true enough that images are necessary for the
> emergence of insights, but images may be not representative but symbolic, not
> pictures of the visible universe but mathematical notations on pieces of paper.[42]

The point is that we cannot reach a representative image of what scientific reality "looks like." Scientific explanation of its very essence transcends imaginative representation: it relates things to each other in their systematic correlations and not to our visual imagination.

Lonergan analyzes the various "canons" or guiding principles implicit in scientific consciousness that keep science on the track of explanatory understanding. One such canon, the canon of parsimony, forbids the empirical scientist from affirming what, as an empirical scientist, he does not know.[43] This has a relevance to the human tendency to try to visually imagine the objects of his science. Such was Eddington's tendency as he sought to distinguish the desk he was writing on, hard, palpable, colored, from what his physics told him of the composition of his desk: the manifold of colorless "wavicles" so minute that the desk was mostly empty space.[44] On the contrary,

> The canon of parsimony excludes any problem concerning the picture of objects too small to be sensed. For the image as image can be verified only by the occurrence of the corresponding sensation. Thus, the visual image of a small ball can be verified only by seeing a small ball, and the visual image of a wave can be verified only by seeing a wave. When the sensations neither occur nor can occur, all that can be verified are certain equations and the terms implicitly defined by such equations.[45]

Empirical science grasps in heuristic imaginative presentations the "conjugate forms" emergent in empirical potentialities and statistically verified in events. The progress of empirical science is from description, that is, the relationships of things to us and to our senses, to explanation, the relationships of things among themselves.

Things and Bodies

Lonergan begins the eighth chapter of *Insight* by the laconic statement: "So far we have been dodging the question, 'What is a thing?'" and to answer this question he identifies a quite distinct type of insight. This is the kind of insight that grasps a unity-identity-whole. The possibility of moving from description to explanation implies the possibility of grasping "things," that is, "unities-identities-wholes" in which both descriptive and explanatory attributes or "conjugates" can be verified. It is understanding's ability to grasp "things" that makes it possible to go from description to explanation and from scientific explanation back to the concrete implementation of scientific insights. "Things" are what you get at by asking and answering questions. To get at "things" you have to use all your cognitive operations—not just sensing and imagination.

The "body out there," however, to which we are physically related, includes our accustomed feelings and habitual imaginary constructs, especially the habitual feeling that we know things merely by seeing them. A "body" in this sense is the correlative of our "extroverted biological consciousness." It is, as Lonergan says elsewhere, "the sure and firm-set earth on which I tread."[46] It is the sensible environment that is already constituted as the objective of biological desires and fears. It is "out there," full of sensuous dangers and opportunities. It is as "real" as a saucer of milk is real for a kitten while a painting of a saucer of milk, still less, the chemical analysis of milk, is not real.

> By a "body" is meant primarily a focal point of extroverted biological anticipation and attention. It is an "already out there now real," where these terms have their meanings fixed solely by elements within sensitive experience and so without any use of intelligent and reasonable questions and answers.[47]

And yet human understanding can grasp dimensions of reality far beyond the possibilities of a kitten. A chemical analysis of milk can grasp real dimensions of milk that can have profound and far-reaching implications for the human family. The practice of the sciences illustrates that human understanding can penetrate to the "inwardness" of things—to use another image—far beyond what we can know by sensation and imagination.

There are, then, as Lonergan promised to illustrate in the introduction to *Insight*, two kinds of human knowing. One we share with the higher animals, the other distinctively human. The second adds understanding and, as we shall see, judgment, to human sensation and representative imagination.

> The problem set by the two types of knowing is, then, not a problem of elimination but a problem of critical distinction. For the difficulty lies, not in either type of knowing by itself, but in the confusion that arises when one shifts unconsciously from one type to the other. Animals have no epistemological problems. Neither do scientists as long as they stick to their task of observing, forming hypotheses, and verifying. The perennial source of nonsense is that, after the scientist has verified his hypothesis, he is likely to go a little further and tell the layman what, approximately, scientific reality looks like![48]

Such is the origin of the "cover story" that has accompanied the successes of the natural sciences during the last few centuries. Mechanistic reductionism interpreted the sciences as giving us pictures of the "already out there now real" atoms and sub-atomic elements. But the deepest significance of Einstein's relativity theory and Heisenberg's quantum physics is that an explanatory account of space and time transcends any imaginative construct we can invent.

For Lonergan a conversion is needed here, even in the minds of scientists: from what they think they know to what they truly know. Hence the significance of the powerful passage from the introduction to *Insight*:

St Augustine of Hippo narrates that it took him years to make the discovery that the name "real" might have a different connotation from the name "body." Or, to bring the point nearer home, one might say that it has taken modern science four centuries to make the discovery that the objects of its inquiry need not be imaginable entities moving through imaginable processes in an imaginable space-time. The fact that a Plato attempted to communicate through his dialogues, the fact that an Augustine eventually learnt from the writers whom, rather generically, he refers to as Platonists, has lost its antique flavor and its apparent irrelevance to the modern mind. Even before Einstein and Heisenberg it was clear enough that the world described by scientists was strangely different from the world depicted by artists and inhabited by men of common sense. But it was left to twentieth-century physicists to envisage the possibility that the objects of their science were to be reached only by severing the umbilical cord that tied them to the maternal imagination of man.[49]

What I learned about science from wrestling with the early chapters in *Insight* I learned mostly by *believing* others. But it was a controlled belief. I had had some familiarity with scientific procedures from high school and college courses. And as I wrestled with these chapters, I "read around" in scientific writing and discovered a remarkable convergence with Lonergan's thought. Nor was his analysis totally foreign to me—it was not about the other side of the moon. Scientists seek understanding. I was seeking to understand understanding. Our goals were similar.

Lonergan's analysis of scientific activity uncovered the same basic elements as were evident in the first chapter of *Insight*. Only now these elements were seen to be operative in a more dynamic way: they were elements in the heuristic structures of science. At this point we might diagram this parallel between mathematical and scientific activities; for both are evidence of what Lonergan will refer to as "the invariant structure" of the human mind.

MATHEMATICAL ACTIVITY	SCIENTIFIC ACTIVITY
verification	*verification*
explanatory definition	*hypothesis*
insight	*discovery*
questioning	*heuristic structures*
imagination	*imagination*
"paper and pencil"	*empirical data*

While there is some sensitive activity in mathematics—they use pencils and paper—as well as a process of verification, these latter activities are much more prominent in the dynamic activities of empirical science. Lonergan's emphasis is that in both processes there is a basically similar structure, a structure rooted in questioning and centered on the dynamic activity of insight or discovery.

As I finished studying these early chapters of *Insight*, I certainly had questions. And I came back to these questions again and again.

* *Are concepts really distinct from images?*
* *Couldn't concepts just be highly refined images?*
* *Is Lonergan's analysis of the "circle of terms" needed to understand the act of understanding correct?*
* *Can't questioning and insight be collapsed into feeling and imagination?*

I raised these questions and many others as I worked through *Insight*. They were my questions and I was seeking a very personal act through which all the pieces of the puzzle might come together.

NOTES

1. *CWL 3 Insight*, 3 (ix).
2. *CWL 3 Insight*, 27 (3).
3. *CWL 3 Insight*, 27-28 (3). Alfred North Whitehead once commented on Archimedes' discovery: "Hiero sent the crown to Archimedes and asked him to test it. In these days an indefinite number of chemical tests would be available. But then Archimedes had to think out the matter afresh. The solution flashed upon him as he lay in his bath. He jumped up and ran through the streets to the palace, shouting Eureka! Eureka! (I have found it, I have found it.) This day, if we knew which it was, ought to be celebrated as the birthday of mathematical physics. . . . Archimedes had in truth made a great discovery. He saw that a body when immersed in water is pressed upwards by the surrounding water with a resultant force equal to the weight of the water it displaces. This law can be proved theoretically from the mathematical principles of hydrostatics and can also be verified experimentally." *Introduction to Mathematics* (NY: Oxford University Press, 1958), 24-25.
4. *CWL 3 Insight*, 28-29 (4).
5. Karl Jaspers, "Autobiographical Writings," *Library of Great Philosophers, Vol. IX, Karl Jaspers,* ed. Paul Arthur Schilpp (Chicago: Opencourt Publishing Co., 1957, augmented 1981), 37.
6. *CWL 3 Insight,* 29 (5). See also, "Cognitional Structure," *Collection,* 209.
7. *CWL 3 Insight,* 30 (6).
8. *CWL 3 Insight,* 31 (6).
9. *CWL 3 Insight,* 55 (31). Terry J. Tekippe provides a number of descriptions of insight in his book, *What is Lonergan Up to in Insight?* (Collegeville, MN: Liturgical Press, 1996).
10. The circle was perhaps Lonergan's favorite example for illustrating insight: see *CWL 2 Verbum: Word and Idea in Aquinas,* ed. Frederick E. Crowe and Robert M. Doran (Toronto: University of Toronto Press, 1997), 27-29; *CWL 5 Understanding*

and Being, 45-49; *CWL 4 Collection*, 96-98.

11. *CWL 3 Insight*, 32 (7).

12. *CWL 3 Insight*, 33 (9).

13. See *CWL 5 Understanding and Being*, 24: "You see, then, in the concrete instance what is universally true. But you cannot see, imagine, a must. You understand that it must, and this understanding with respect to diagrams, with respect to images, is insight."

14. *CWL 3 Insight*, 34-35 (10).

15. "Euclid says he is proving everything from his definitions, axioms, postulates, but he really is not. He uses casual insights as he goes along. . . . To do geometry the way Euclid did it, you have to be having insights as you go along. Because Euclid uses casual insights, he illustrates very clearly the occurrence of insight." *CWL 5 Understanding and Being*, 25-26. On other possible definitions of a circle in terms of coordinate geometry, see Joseph Flanagan, *Quest for Self-Knowledge* (Toronto: University of Toronto Press, 1997), 18-23.

16. *CWL 3 Insight*, 36 (12). Lonergan gives further illustrations and analyses of insight in *Understanding and Being*, 21-52.

17. *CWL 5 Understanding and Being*, 98.

18. Herbert Butterfield, *The Origins of Modern Science* (NY: The Free Press, 1957), 13.

19. Butterfield, *The Origins of Modern Science*, 16-17.

20. Butterfield, *The Origins of Modern Science*, 25-26.

21. Butterfield, *The Origins of Modern Science,* 102.

22. Butterfield, *The Origins of Modern Science*, 101.

23. *CWL 3 Insight*, 42 (17).

24. A.N. Whitehead, *Introduction to Mathematics*, 39, 41-42.

25. *CWL 3 Insight*, 57 (33).

26. *CWL 3 Insight*, 58 (33-34).

27. Albert Einstein, *Essays in Science* (NY: Philosophical Library, 1934) 12.

28. *CWL 3 Insight*, 67-68 (44).

29. *CWL 3 Insight*, 61-62 (37).

30. *CWL 3 Insight*, 68 (44).

31. *CWL 3 Insight*, 62 (38).

32. *CWL 3 Insight*, 91 (68).

33. *CWL 3 Insight*, 76 (53)

34. *CWL 3 Insight*, 79 (56).

35. *CWL 3 Insight*, 115 (91-92)

36. *CWL 3 Insight*, 141 (118).

37. *CWL 3 Insight*, 140-141 (117).

38. Quoted in Lonergan, *A Third Collection*, 65, with a reference to William Johnston, *Silent Music: The Science of Meditation* (NY: Harper & Row, 1974) 32.

39. *A Second Collection*, 35.

40. *CWL 3 Insight*, 152-153.(130)

41. *CWL 3 Insight*, 153-154. (130-131).

42. *CWL 3 Insight*, 116 (93)

43. *CWL 3 Insight*, 102 ff. (78ff).

44. *Method in Theology*, 84, 258, 274.

45. *CWL 3 Insight*, 123 (99).

46. *CWL 2 Verbum: Word and Idea in Aquinas*, 20.

47. *CWL 3 Insight*, 279 (254).

48. *CWL 3 Insight*, 278 (253)

49. *CWL 3 Insight*, 15 (xx-xxi).

Chapter Six

Common Sense Insights

There is intelligence in the home and in friendship, in conversation and in sport, in the arts and in entertainment. In every case the man or woman of intelligence is marked by a greater readiness in catching on, in getting the point, in seeing the issue, in grasping implications, in acquiring know-how. In their speech and action the same characteristics can be discerned, as were set forth in describing the act that released Archimedes' "Eureka!" For insight is ever the same, and even its most modest achievements are rendered conspicuous by the contrasting, if reassuring, occurrence of examples of obtuseness and stupidity.[1]

1. THE NATURE OF COMMON SENSE

After hundreds of pages of "exercises" in scientific understanding, I suddenly found myself in quite interesting material: common sense living. After plowing through *Insight*'s early chapters on science, I found these chapters to be riveting. I began to feel I was on my own turf—for was I not an expert in "ordinary" understanding? Certainly, I would not have been studying philosophy if I had not had a few insights along the way.

Still, it is not easy to get a hold of "ordinary" understanding. Besides a descriptive account of understanding, one needs a theory, a method, by means of which one can discern the elements of ordinary understanding. One needs a "pincers" with which to hold it. That "pincers" was the theory brought from the previous chapters: the explanatory account of understanding. That is why Lonergan puts off the analysis of common sense understanding to chapters six and seven of *Insight*. Having highlighted the elements and dynamism of explanatory understanding in the early chapters, he is now able, with the help of that analysis, to circle back and analyze that ordinary exercise of our understanding called "common sense."

Lonergan begins by noting that intelligence is present in all of human life. It is not limited to mathematicians and scientists. One can see it in the wonder of children as they learn how to do things, adapt to situations, catch on. Insight follows on insight as they learn the shortcomings of previous answers and new clusters of insights enable them to speak and to act in new ways.

> Just as the mathematician advances from images through insights and formulations to symbols that stimulate further insights, just as the scientist advances from data through insights and formulations to experiments that stimulate further insights, so too *the spontaneous and self-correcting process of learning* is a circuit in which insights reveal their shortcomings by putting forth deeds or words or thoughts, and through that revelation prompt the further questions that lead to complementary insights.[2]

This "self-correcting process of learning" is one of key mantras of *Insight*. It is spontaneously shared with others through language.

> . . . for by speech and, still more, by example, there is effected a sustained communication that at once disseminates and tests and improves every advance to make the achievement of each successive generation the starting point of the next.[3]

Later on Lonergan will analyze "belief," our basic acquiescence in trusting the insights of others. This development "from above downwards" as he would come to call it, begins with the child trusting his parents and his community as he begins to open up his mind to the world. He will gradually complement this development with his own development "from below upwards," his own acquisition of knowledge through the dynamism of his own experiencing, imagining, questioning, understanding, etc.

Lonergan defines common sense as "an incomplete set of insights having to do with the concrete and particular." The set of insights is incomplete because in each new situation it needs to be completed by at least one more insight into that new situation.

> Common sense is more at home in doing than in speaking, and its speaking is apt to be terse and elliptical, or else metaphorical if not fanciful. It is a development of intelligence that is prior to the systematic mode of differentiated consciousness. Common sense does not argue from principles but attends to proverbs, i.e. brief bits of advice that are worth attending to when the occasion arises. It does not define terms, but along with the analysts, knows when terms are used appropriately. It is a specialization of intelligence in the realm of the particular and the concrete.[4]

In addition, common sense develops differently in different places and towns, in different age groups, in different social strata.

At once it adapts individuals in every walk of life to the work they have chosen or the lot that has befallen them and, no less, it generates all those minute differences of viewpoint and mentality that separate men and women, old and young, town and country until in the limit, one reaches the cumulative differences and mutual incomprehension of different strata of society, different nations, different civilizations, and different epochs of human history.[5]

Common sense is a genuine development of human intelligence. Even scientists need common sense in order to apply their methods properly to their particular investigations. Even logicians needs common sense if they are to grasp what the content of their propositions really mean.

2. PATTERNS OF EXPERIENCE

It is here that Lonergan emphasizes the changes that common sense understanding introduces into a person by detailing the various "patterns" in which human consciousness can flow: biological, aesthetic, intellectual, dramatic. Elsewhere, in a religious and theological context, he will add the "mystical" or religious pattern of consciousness. A common dimension of all these patterns is that they change us: they open us up to new dimensions of our own being and new dimensions of reality.

Besides the spontaneous rhythms of biological consciousness and the tendency to "fight and flight" that comes with it, there are the other patterns that shape our selves. When I play golf I focus on the ball in such a way as to bring all the dimensions of my body together into hitting it correctly, I am "in the zone": a different dimension than ordinary consciousness. So also, when contemplating a beautiful sunset, something is going on in me, my consciousness, my care, so that my inner being flows in a different way. Such is the aesthetic pattern of consciousness—the aesthetic zone.

So also, as I was studying *Insight* every day, caught up in trying to decipher what it meant, my consciousness was caught up in the intellectual pattern of experience.

To the liveliness of youth, study is hard. But in the seasoned mathematician, sensitive process easily contracts to an unruffled sequence of symbolic notations and schematic images. In the trained observer, outer sense forgets its primitive biological functions to take on a selective alertness that keeps pace with the refinements of elaborate and subtle classifications. In the theorist intent upon a problem, even the subconscious goes to work to yield at unexpected moments the suggestive images of clues and missing links, of patterns and perspectives, that evoke the desiderated insight and the delighted cry "Eureka!"[6]

I too had tasted what Lonergan was describing. I too was tasting how difficult fidelity to this pattern could be.

No doubt, the frequency, intensity, duration, and purity of the intellectual pattern of experience are subject to great variation. For they depend upon native aptitude, upon training, upon age and development, upon external circumstance, upon the chance that confronts one with problems and that supplies at least the intermittent opportunity to work towards their solution. To be talented is to find that one's experience slips easily into the intellectual pattern, that one's sensitive spontaneity responds quickly and precisely to the exigencies of mind. Insights come readily. Exact formulation follows promptly. Outer sense pounces upon significant detail. Memory tosses out immediately the contrary instance. Imagination devises at once the contrary possibility.

Still, even with talent, knowledge makes a slow, if not a bloody entrance. To learn thoroughly is a vast undertaking that calls for relentless perseverance. To strike out on a new line and become more than a weekend celebrity calls for years in which one's living is more or less constantly absorbed in the effort to understand, in which one's understanding gradually works round and up a spiral of viewpoints with each complementing its predecessor and only the last embracing the whole field to be mastered.[7]

3. PRACTICAL COMMON SENSE AND CULTURE

But what I was also trying to understand now was "practical" common sense, that is, the common sense that "creates worlds." For the orientation of common sense understanding is practical. It seeks knowledge, not for the sake of knowledge—for the sake of the pure desire to know—but to use knowledge in making and doing. Such making and doing involve a transformation both of the human person and of his environment. In an article written in the early 1960s, "The Dimensions of Meaning," Lonergan describes this practical and creative character of human common sense.

The pioneers in this country found shore and heartland, mountains and plains, but they have covered it with cities, laced it with roads, exploited it with their industries, till the world man has made stands between us and a prior world of nature. Yet the whole of that added, man-made, artificial world is the cumulative, now planned, now chaotic product of human acts of meaning.[8]

Thus, common sense understanding constitutes the various levels of common human meaning that separate us from brute nature. The streets I walk on, the cars and trucks that travel on them, the buildings in which I live and work—all are the result of human acts of understanding that have transformed nature into a human world.

Lonergan's analysis of common sense as shared meaning sheds light on human community and "power" within community. For he points out that the source of power is cooperation and, while the exercise of power resides in "the word of authority," the real carrier of power is the community, that is, the accepted common meanings residing in the community.

In *Insight* Lonergan spells out this development from human needs to the division of labor spawned by primitive and developing technology. And as intelligence gives rise to technology, so also it gives rise to the division of labor that is the economy and to the political realm, a specialization of intelligence that consists in persuading the different parts of the economic system to cooperate with each other. Most people get ideas, but the ideas reside in different minds, and the different minds do not quite agree. "Of itself, communication only reveals the disparity. What is wanted is persuasion, and the most effective persuader becomes a leader, a chief, a politician, a statesman."[9]

In a section on the dynamic structure of common sense as object, Lonergan writes that such practical common sense falls under the same rule of emergent probability that governs the underlying physical, chemical and biological levels, but it does so in a new way: As humans develop, the probability of appropriate constellations of material circumstances becomes less important and more importance attaches to the probabilities of the occurrence of insight, communication, persuasion, agreement, decision.[10]

Thus, the practical common sense of a group, like all common sense, is an incomplete set of insights that is ever to be completed differently in each concrete situation. Nor does it exist entire in the mind of any one man. It is parceled out among many, to provide each with an understanding of his role and task, to make every person an expert in his own field, and no one an expert in another's.

> So it is that to understand the working of even a static social structure, one must inquire from many men in many walks of life, and as best one can, discover the functional unity that organically binds together the endlessly varied pieces of an enormous jigsaw puzzle.[11]

In all of this Lonergan emphasizes the duality of the human person's relationship to the community: that is, the duality of "intersubjective spontaneity" on the one hand and intelligent common sense on the other.

> Thus, primitive community is intersubjective. Its schemes of recurrence are simple prolongations of pre-human attainment, too obvious to be discussed or criticized, too closely linked with elementary processes to be distinguished sharply from them. The bond of mother and child, man and wife, father and

son, reaches into a past of ancestors to give meaning and cohesion to the clan or tribe or nation. A sense of belonging together provides the dynamic premise for common enterprise, for mutual aid and succor, for the sympathy that augments joys and divides sorrows. Even after civilization is attained, intersubjective community survives in the family with its circle of relatives and its accretion of friends, in customs and folk ways, in basic arts and crafts and skills, in language and song and dance, and most concretely of all in the inner psychology and radiating influence of women.[12]

But quite distinct from such intersubjective and "radiating" spontaneity, another "notion of the good" emerges for human beings and that is "the good of order." It is rooted in human intelligence.

Though civil community has its obscure origins in human intersubjectivity, though it develops imperceptibly, though it decks itself out with more primitive attractions, still it is a new creation. The time comes when men begin to ask about the difference between *physis* and *nomos*, between nature and convention. There arises the need of the apologue to explain to the different classes of society that together they form a functional unity and that no group should complain of its lot any more than a man's feet, which do all the walking, complain of his mouth, which does all the eating.

The question may be evaded, and the apologue may convince, but the fact is that human society has shifted away from its initial basis in intersubjectivity and has attempted a more grandiose undertaking. The discoveries of practical intelligence, which once were an incidental addition to the spontaneous fabric of human living, now penetrate and overwhelm its every aspect. For just as technology and capital formation interpose their schemes of recurrence between man and the rhythms of nature, so economics and politics are vast structures of interdependence invented by practical intelligence for the mastery not of nature but of man.

Lonergan defines this new notion of "the good of order":

In primitive society it is possible to identify the good simply with the object of desire; but in civil community there has to be acknowledged a further component, which we propose to name the good of order. It consists in an intelligible pattern of relationships that condition the fulfillment of each man's desires by his contributions to the fulfillment of the desires of others, and similarly protect each from the object of his fears in the measure he contributes to warding off the objects feared by others.[13]

The smooth functioning of the "good of order" gives rise to an increase in the standard of living. On the other hand, it is the breakdown of this good of order that is at the source of economic disaster and political disarray.

4. THE BIASES OF COMMON SENSE

But common sense has its negative side as well and this is a theme Lonergan will return to again and again.

Indeed the supreme canon of common sense is the restriction of further questions to the concrete and particular, the immediate and practical. To advance in common sense is to restrain the omnivorous drive of inquiring intelligence and to brush aside as irrelevant, if not silly, any question whose answer would not make an immediate palpable difference.

Just as the scientist rises in stern protest against the introduction into his field of metaphysical questions that do not satisfy his canon of selection, so the man of common sense (and nothing else) is ever on guard against all theory, ever blandly asking the proponent of ideas what difference they would make and, if the answer is less vivid than an advertisement, then solely concerned with thinking up an excuse for getting rid of the fellow. After all, men of common sense are busy. They have the world's work to do.[14]

Because of this duality of intelligence and intersubjectivity, there arises "the tension of community."

Intersubjective spontaneity and intelligently devised social order have their ground in a duality immanent in man himself. As intelligent, man is the originator and sponsor of the social systems within which, as an individual, he desires and labors, enjoys and suffers. As intelligent, man is a legislator, but as an individual, he is subject to his own laws.[15]

Perhaps in untroubled times these two principles can live in mutual accord, but in troubled times, there is need for new insights.

As the serenity of the good old days rests on an integration of common sense and human feeling, so the troubled times of crisis demand the discovery and communication of new insights and a consequent adaptation of spontaneous attitudes.[16]

Unfortunately, common sense does not know how to do this.

Common sense knows, but it does not know what it knows nor how it knows nor how to correct and complement its own inadequacies. Only the blind and destructive blows inevitable in even a partial breakdown of social order can impress on practical common sense that there are limits to its competence and that, if it would master the new situation, it must first consent to learn.

In a section on "The Dialectic of Community" Lonergan writes of the structure of this often conflicting relationship between human intersubjectiv-

ity and intelligently devised social order. It is in this context that he treats of
the biases of our ordinary common sense intelligence: the individual, group
and general "blind spots" that darken the social and cultural functioning of
human intelligence. There is the bias of the dramatic subject that psychologists study, the hidden resistance to self-knowledge, to trying to spot one's
own blind spots within the drama of human living. Individual bias, normally
called selfishness or egoism, uses intelligence to circumvent the just and reasonable demands of one's community.

> Egoism, then, is an incomplete development of intelligence. It arises above a
> merely inherited mentality. It has the boldness to strike out and think for itself.
> But it fails to pivot from the initial and preliminary motivation, provided by
> desires and fears, to the self-abnegation involved in allowing complete free play
> to intelligent inquiry.[17]

The cool schemer, the shrewd calculator, the hard-headed self-seeker, is usually a very intelligent person. But by a conscious self-orientation he sizes up the
social order, ferrets out its weak points and loop-holes, and discovers ways of
getting access to its rewards while evading its responsibilities. Nevertheless,

> . . . prior to the criteria of truth invented by philosophers, there is the dynamic
> criterion of the further question immanent in intelligence itself. The egoist's
> uneasy conscience is his awareness of his sin against the light. Operative in him,
> there is the Eros of the mind, the desire and drive to understand; he knows its
> value, for he gives it free rein where his own interests are concerned; yet he also
> repudiates its mastery, for he will not grant serious consideration to its further
> relevant questions.[18]

Reading this provided an "examination of consciousness" for me. Did I
myself allow that free rein to the spirit of inquiry? Really? I was aware that
at times I did not.
   Then there is group bias expressed in such phrases as "My country right or
wrong, but my country." While individual bias has to overcome normal community feelings, group bias finds itself supported by such feelings.

> Just as the individual egoist puts further questions up to a point, but desists
> before reaching conclusions incompatible with his egoism, so also the group is
> prone to have a blind spot for the insights that reveal its well-being to be exces-
> sive or its usefulness at an end.[19]

Group bias is responsible for the conflicts between groups, between the
have's and the have-not's, the privileged and the oppressed. There results the
distortion of the social process.

The sins of group bias may be secret and almost unconscious. But what originally was a neglected possibility, in time becomes a grotesquely distorted reality.[20]

Such bias gives rise to group conflict—what Lonergan calls "the shorter cycle" of human conflict. "The have-not's" replace "the have's" in the halls of power. Eventually, however, such a back-and forth cycle makes it evident that all groups are subject to a bias against intelligence as such, a general bias responsible for the "longer cycle" of human decline.

Every specialist runs the risk of turning his specialty into a bias by failing to recognize and appreciate the significance of other fields. Common sense almost invariably makes that mistake; for it is incapable of analyzing itself, incapable of making the discovery that it too is a specialized development of human knowledge, incapable of coming to grasp that its peculiar danger is to extend its legitimate concern for the concrete and the immediately practical into disregard of larger issues and indifference to long-term results.[21]

Such bias finds expression in the ancient saying, "Whom the gods destroy they first make blind." But whether the general bias finds expression in myths or in advertising symbols or in consciously articulated philosophies, it makes the human family its captive. Its essence lies in not giving intelligence its free scope, in subordinating it to short-term "practical" or "realistic" ends. Only intelligence wedded to power is respected. Writing soon after World War II, while Stalin still held power in Russia, Lonergan noted:

The helplessness of tolerance to provide coherent solutions to social problems called forth the totalitarian, who takes the narrow and complacent practicality of common sense and elevates it to the role of a complete and exclusive viewpoint. On the totalitarian view every type of intellectual independence, whether personal, cultural, scientific, philosophic, or religious, has no better basis than non-conscious myth. The time has come for the conscious myth that will secure man's total subordination to the requirements of reality. Reality is the economic development, the military equipment, and the political dominance of the all-inclusive state.[22]

The general bias of common sense leads to the acceptance of the deteriorating social situation as it is. And as it is, it is unintelligible. It includes "the social surd": the situation exists, it is real, but it does not make sense. It is not understandable. In such a situation to be "realistic" or to be "pragmatic" means to continue the absurdity. The general bias is the failure of common sense to learn that it needs to learn, that it needs a higher viewpoint. That higher viewpoint is a theory of human history that is critical, that is able to distinguish progress from decline.

The needed higher viewpoint is the discovery, the logical expansion and the
recognition of the principle that intelligence contains its own immanent norms
and that those norms are equipped with sanctions that man does not have to
invent or impose.[23]

Lonergan calls this needed higher viewpoint "*cosmopolis,*" a heuristic term
designating the anticipated liberation of human community from bias.

What is necessary is a *cosmopolis* that is neither class nor state, that stands
above all their claims, that cuts them down to size, that is founded on the native
detachment and disinterestedness of every intelligence, that commands man's
first allegiance, that is too universal to be bribed, too impalpable to be forced,
too effective to be ignored.[24]

Such a *cosmopolis* will be effective through a critical culture that will be
able to speak to the human heart as well as to human intelligence.

It invites the vast potentialities and pent-up energies of our time to contribute
to their solution by developing an art and a literature, a theater and a broadcast-
ing, a journalism and a history, a school and a university, a personal depth and
a public opinion, that through appreciation and criticism give men of common
sense the opportunity and help they need and desire to correct the general bias
of their common sense.[25]

How to do this? Ah, that's the rub.

For the most part, the origin of chapter seven of *Insight* on practical common sense can be traced to Lonergan's studies in the ideology-torn Europe of
the 1930s. All these ideologies were rooted in the nineteenth-century ideologies of mechanistic determinism, the liberal "automatic progress" and various
nationalist ideologies. The massive bloodshed of the twentieth century can be
traced to this string of false philosophies and cultural visions.

Thus the heritage of intellectual vacuity and social chaos given by the nineteenth
century to the twentieth is the real reason why the twentieth century is such a
mess.[26]

It was in interaction with all such ideologies that the young Lonergan came
to see the need for a "return to reason" with its own built-in norms and sanctions. Such reason had to be in dialogue with all of reason's expressions in the
twentieth century: with the empirical and human sciences, with scholarship,
with philosophy, and especially with the philosophy of history. This was the
program of *Insight.*

Elsewhere Lonergan paid tribute to Pierre Teilhard de Chardin for speaking
to this human need for a vision of history that could touch both the minds and
hearts of people at the end of the twentieth century.

. . . what moves men is the good, and good in the concrete. . . . If at one time law was in the forefront of human development . . . still, at the present time it would seem that the immediate carrier of human aspiration is the more concrete apprehension of the human good effected through such theories of history as the liberal doctrine of progress, the Marxist doctrine of dialectical materialism and, most recently, Teilhard de Chardin's identification of *cosmogenesis, anthropogenesis,* and *christogenesis.*[27]

The Christian doctrine of the Word of God finds insertion into the emergence of the natural world and the human world of communities seeking the meaning of their existence. Early in his life Lonergan found a great deal of inspiration in Saint Paul's doctrine in his Letter to the Ephesians: namely, the Father's plan that "the universe, all in heaven and on earth, might be brought into unity in Christ." This seemed to be the ultimate thrust of *Insight,* to link all that the sciences can teach us, and all that the humanities and human sciences can teach us, into a unity. A religious sister once told me that as she studied chapter seven of *Insight,* she found herself in tears. I can believe it; this chapter opens up an awesome vision of human history.

NOTES

1. *CWL 3 Insight,* 196 (173).
2. *CWL 3 Insight,* 197 (174) my emphases.
3. *CWL 3 Insight,* 198 (175).
4. *"Insight* Revisited," *A Second Collection,* 270. This is one of Lonergan's few direct remarks on the prominent philosophical stream of linguistic analysis. For fuller comments on that stream, see *Method in Theology* 253-257.
5. *CWL 3 Insight,* 203 (180).
6. *CWL 3 Insight,* 209 (186).
7. *CWL 3 Insight,* 209-210 (186).
8. *CWL 4 Collection,* 233.
9. *CWL 3 Insight,* 234 (210).
10. *CWL 3 Insight,* 236 (209).
11. *CWL 3 Insight,* 237 (211)
12. *CWL 3 Insight,* 237-238 (212).
13. *CWL 3 Insight,* 238 (213).
14. *CWL 3 Insight,* 201-202 (178).
15. *CWL 3 Insight,* 239-240 (214).
16. *CWL 3 Insight,* 241 (216).
17. *CWL 3 Insight,* 245-246 (220).
18. *CWL 3 Insight,* 247 (221-222).
19. *CWL 3 Insight,* 248 (223).
20. *CWL 3 Insight,* 250 (224).

21. *CWL 3 Insight*, 251 (226).

22. *CWL 3 Insight*, 256-257 (231-232).

23. *CWL 3 Insight*, 259 (234).

24. *CWL 3 Insight*, 263 (238).

25. *CWL 3 Insight*, 266 (241).

26. "Philosophy of History," (unpublished notes from the mid-1930s in the archives of the Lonergan Research Institute in Toronto) 93.

27. *A Second Collection*, 6-7. See also 93: "So a contemporary humanism is dynamic. It holds forth not an ideal of fixity but a program of change. It was or is the automatic progress of the liberal, the dialectical materialism of the Marxist, the identification of *cosmogenesis* and *christogenesis* by Pierre Teilhard de Chardin."

Chapter Seven

Reflective Insights

1. JUDGMENT

It was during the school year of 1964 and I remember standing in the hallway of the North American College talking with my classmate, David Tracy. We were discussing Father Lonergan's class on the Trinity and particularly his notion of an "intelligible emanation"—in Latin an "*emanatio intelligibilis.*" That notion spoke to the question, what happens when we make a judgment? I remember him putting it to me this way:

> You know, in a detective story, when you have a question, such as "Did the butler do it?" and all the evidence points in the direction of the butler and you've checked to see if the evidence might have been planted, etc., and you've asked all the reasonable questions—why then it is just foolish not to make the judgment, "The butler did it!"
>
> The "intellectual emanation" in this case is what happens inside you, in your mind, as you realize the rational necessity of saying "Yes! That's it!" That "Yes!" comes from having caught on, having grasped the sufficiency of the evidence. If you make a judgment before having grasped the sufficiency of the evidence, you're pre-judging, you're quite literally "prejudiced"—you've judged too quickly. If, on the other hand, you have all the evidence and have asked all the relevant questions and you still don't make the judgment, then you're just being silly or foolish or diffident. For the sufficient evidence for making the judgment is staring you right in the face. That "rational necessity" of making a judgment—different from all other processes in nature—is what Lonergan means by an "intellectual emanation."

That little conversation came back to me as I plowed through chapters nine and ten of *Insight*, the chapters on reflecting and judging. Chapter nine, "The

Notion of Judgment," is the shortest the book. Perhaps that is because judgment is the result of our intellectual processes and we are much more aware of the results of our mental processes—such as concepts, words and judgments—then we are of the processes by which we arrive at those results.

Lonergan begins by relating judgment to 1) propositions, 2) questions and 3) personal commitment. 1) Propositions are distinguished from utterances and sentences. If one person says, "*Der König ist tot,*" and another person says, "The king is dead," then there are two utterances and two sentences but only one proposition.[1] Now with regard to such propositions there can be two distinct mental attitudes: one can consider them as "an object of thought," the content of an act of conceiving or defining; or one can agree or disagree with them: they can be the content of an act of judging.

> In writing *Insight* I said what I thought was true, but in reading *Insight* a person does not say after every sentence, "It is true." One has to come to make one's own judgments on the matter. The eight hundred pages of propositions are just objects of thought until such time as one sees reason to agree with them.[2]

Evidently, I eventually came to the judgment agreeing with the contents of *Insight.* One characteristic, then, of the act of judgment is that it transforms a proposition from an object of thought into an object of knowledge. The level of thinking heads for objects of thought; but the level of judgment heads for objects of knowledge.

2) In addition, Lonergan relates judging to questioning. Taking a clue from Aristotle, he divides questioning into two main classes.[3] There are questions for reflection and they can be answered by a "Yes" or a "No." And there are questions for intelligence that cannot be answered by a "Yes" or a "No."

> Thus, one may ask, "Is there a logarithm of the square root of minus one?" This is a question for reflection. It is answered correctly by saying "Yes." On the other hand, though it would be a mistake to answer "No," still that answer would make sense. But if one asks, "What is the logarithm of the square root of minus one?" there is no sense in answering either yes or no. The question is not for reflection but for intelligence.[4]

Questions for intelligence correspond to the attitude of the inquiring mind, the second level of consciousness; questions for reflection correspond to the critical mind: "Is it so or isn't it?"

3) Finally, Lonergan relates the notion of judgment to personal commitment. He quotes de la Rochefoucauld's maxim, "Everyone complains of his memory but no one of his judgment." He explains this by saying that memory does not lie directly under one's personal power while judgment does. You do not have to say yes or no; you can say, "I don't know." You do

not have to say "It certainly is so"; you can say, "It probably is so" or "It is possibly so."

> All the alternatives relevant to human weakness, ignorance, and tardiness are provided for, and it is your rationality that is involved in picking out the right one. Judgment is something that is entirely yours; it is an element in personal commitment in an extremely pure state. Because it is so personal, so much an expression of one's own reasonableness apart from any constraint, because all alternatives are provided for, it is entirely one's own responsibility.[5]

As one moves from experience to understanding to judging, then, the element of personal responsibility increases.

Lonergan then relates judgment to the general structure of our process of knowing. So far *Insight* has focused on understanding. But understanding presupposes something to be understood and thus the level of understanding both presupposes and completes the level of experience. On the other hand, this level of understanding itself is presupposed by and completed by another level, the level of reflecting and judging.

> It is on this third level that there emerge the notions of truth and falsity, of certitude and the probability that is not a frequency but a quality of judgment. It is within this third level that there is involved the personal commitment that makes one responsible for one's judgments. It is from this third level that come utterances to express one's affirming or denying, assenting or dissenting, agreeing or disagreeing.[6]

Lonergan represents the three levels of the knowing process schematically, each level having basically three elements: what is presupposed, an activity, and an expression of that activity.

1. Data, Perceptual Images	Free Images	Utterances
2. Questions for Intelligence	Insights	Formulations
3. Questions for Reflection	Reflective Understanding	Judgment

As in any "theory," these nine terms are related to each other and to the whole of the theory. All these elements coalesce into a single knowing through relationships of presupposition and completion.

> Questions for intelligence presuppose something to be understood, and that something is supplied by the initial level. Understanding grasps in given or imagined presentations an intelligible form emergent in the presentations. Conception formulates the grasped idea along with what is essential to the idea in the presentations. Reflection asks whether such understanding and formulation are correct. Judgment answers that they are or are not.[7]

Thus, the process is cumulative: later steps presuppose earlier contributions and add to them. But what precisely does judgment add? Lonergan distinguishes between the proper and borrowed content of judgment. The proper content of the judgment is its specific contribution to the cognitional process: the "Yes" or the "No." Elsewhere he calls this proper content a "positing" of what is understood. Judgment is not a synthesis of mental contents: it is a positing of that synthesis. A theory, an hypothesis, a proposition, a definition, already contains a synthesis.[8] Judgment does not add a further synthesis; it simply posits the synthesis. Distinguishing his thought from Plato, Lonergan writes:

> Corresponding to judgment there is not a synthesis of Forms but the absolute of fact. Platonism is magnificent in its devotion to the pure desire to know. But its failure to grasp the nature of judgment resulted in a deviation from the concrete universe of fact to an ideal heaven.[9]

There is, then, in judgment a certain absoluteness that is at the root of its "public" character.

> . . . there is to the judgment an element of absoluteness. If it is true that on this day at this hour and moment I am talking to you, then eternally it could never have been and never will be true that I am not on this day at this hour and moment talking to you. There is an element of the absolute that appears in the truth of the judgment. But if we regard truth as a quality of the judgment, then since human judgments are not eternal, there is no human eternal truth. Whatever we say about that, still there is an element of the absolute in the judgment that is illustrated by the statement, If Caesar did cross the Rubicon at such and such a time, then eternally no one could say that he would not and be truthful, and no one could say that he did not and be truthful.[10]

On the other hand, the "borrowed" content of judgment is either direct or indirect. The direct borrowed content is found in the question to which one answers "Yes" or "No." On the other hand, there is the indirect borrowed content that emerges in the reflective act linking question and answer, that claims the "Yes" or "No" to be true, and indeed, either certainly or only probably true.

> Thus, the direct borrowed content of the judgment, I am writing, is the question, Am I writing? The proper content of that judgment is the answer, Yes, I am. The indirect borrowed content of the same judgment is the implicit meaning "It certainly is true that I am writing."[11]

In other words, as Cardinal Newman pointed out in the *Grammar of Assent*, in the unfolding of the reflective process there is a sense in which *"I know that I know."* Lonergan echoed this in his *Verbum* articles, which I also began to read at this time:

> . . . while the direct act of understanding generates in definition the expression of the intelligibility of a phantasm, the reflective act generates in judgment the expression of consciously possessed truth through which reality is both known and known to be known.[12]

The final section of chapter nine outlines the contextual aspect of judgment, that is, each single judgment we make is only an incremental addition to numerous other judgments that make up the fabric of our minds. In *Method in Theology* Lonergan will speak of this accumulation of habitual judgments as forming the "horizon" of our mind. Such an horizon governs the direction of our attention, guides our formulations, and influences the acceptance or rejection of new judgments. It is also the source of a dialectical process that goes on within us as some judgments are found to conflict with others. That battle was going on within me as I read *Insight*:

> Is Lonergan correct here? What about those other truths which I know to be correct? How do these fit together? Is he correct and some of my habitual judgments incorrect?

2. REFLECTIVE UNDERSTANDING

Lonergan then turns to a more subtle dimension in making a judgment, the process to judgment, that is, the reflective act of understanding whereby we grasp the grounds for making a judgment. What he asks for in chapter ten is "a prolonged effort at introspective analysis" whereby we can say what exactly happens in us when we make the judgment, "The butler did it!" For to make a judgment without that reflective grasp—that *"emanatio intelligibilis"*—is merely to guess; it is to be presumptuous. On the other hand, once that grasp has occurred, to refuse to judge is silly.[13]

His question, then, concerns what precisely is meant by the "sufficiency of the evidence" for making a prospective judgment. What precisely is meant by expressions such as "weighing the evidence" or "marshaling the evidence?" And it is here that he introduces the notion of *"the virtually unconditioned."* He distinguishes the virtually unconditioned from the formally unconditioned. The formally unconditioned has no conditions whatsoever and such, in the Christian tradition, is God. According to Saint Thomas, God is the absolutely necessary being.

The virtually unconditioned, on the other hand, has conditions, but the conditions de facto are fulfilled. The virtually unconditioned, then, involves three elements:

1) *a conditioned*—for example, "The White House is in Washington, D.C."
2) *a link* between the conditioned and the conditions: "It is true that the White House is in Washington, D.C. if I have seen the White House there; if my senses are in order and I am not hallucinating; etc. and
3) *the conditions are fulfilled.*

Hence a prospective judgment will be virtually unconditioned if 1) it is conditioned; 2) its conditions are known, and 3) the conditions are fulfilled. Lonergan explains how these three elements come together in an act of reflective understanding.

> By the mere fact that a question for reflection has been put, the prospective judgment is a conditioned: it stands in need of evidence sufficient for reasonable pronouncement. The function of reflective understanding is to meet the question for reflection by transforming the prospective judgment from the status of a conditioned to the status of a virtually unconditioned; and reflective understanding effects this transformation by grasping the conditions of the conditioned and their fulfillment.[14]

Lonergan illustrates this general scheme in the form of deductive inference where both A and B stand for one or more propositions: "*If A, then B. But A. Therefore B.*" For instance: "*If X is material and alive, X is mortal. But people are material and alive. Therefore, people are mortal.*"

The conclusion is a conditioned, for an argument is needed to establish it. The major premise links the conditioned to its conditions. The minor premise presents the fulfillment of the conditions. The point, then, of the form of deductive inference is to exhibit a conclusion as virtually unconditioned. Reflective insight grasps the pattern, and by rational compulsion, an "*emanatio intelligibilis,*" there follows the judgment.[15]

"A rational compulsion"—that is what Lonergan is trying to get us in touch with. The form of deductive inference is only a clear expression of reflective insight itself.

> Before the link between conditioned and conditions appears in the act of judgment, it existed in a more rudimentary state within cognitional process itself. Before the fulfillment of conditions appears in another act of judgment, it too was present in a more rudimentary state within cognitional process. The remarkable fact about reflective insight is that it can make use of those more rudimentary elements in cognitional process to reach the virtually unconditioned.[16]

Lonergan gives a number of other examples of the act of reflective insight in more complex cases. There are, for example, concrete judgments of fact.

> Suppose a man to return from work to his tidy home and to find the windows smashed, smoke in the air, and water on the floor. Suppose him to make the extremely restrained judgment of fact "Something happened." The question is, not whether he was right, but how he reached his affirmation.[17]

The conditioned is the judgment, "Something happened." The fulfilling conditions will be two sets of data: 1) the remembered data of his home as he left it in the morning; and 2) the present data of his home as he finds it in the evening. Both of these fulfilling conditions are found on the level of empirical presentations. They are not insights or judgments. The link between the conditioned and the fulfilling conditions is a structure immanent within cognitional process which is called "knowing change." Both common sense and science illustrate this structure, but the structure exists prior to the expressions.

> Now in the particular instance under consideration, the weary worker not only experiences present data and recalls different data but by direct insights he refers both sets of data to the same set of things, which he calls his home. The direct insight, however, fulfils a double function. Not merely are two fields of individual data referred to one identical set of things but a second level of cognitional process is added to a first. The two together contain a specific structure of that process, which we may name the notion of knowing change. Just as knowing a thing consists in grasping an intelligible unity-identity-whole in individual data, so knowing change consists in grasping the same identity or identities at different times in different individual data. If the same thing exhibits different individual data at different times, it has changed. If there occurs a change, something has happened. But these are statements. If they are affirmed, they are judgments. But prior to being either statements or judgments, they exist as unanalyzed structures or procedures immanent and operative within cognitional process. It is such a structure that links the conditioned with the fulfilling conditions in the concrete judgment of fact.[18]

So three elements have been assembled:

1. On the level of presentations there are two sets of data.
2. On the level of intelligence there is an insight referring both sets to the same thing. When both sets are taken together, there is involved the notion of "knowing change."
3. Reflective understanding grasps all three as a virtually unconditioned to ground the judgment, "Something happened."

Lonergan notes that this very simple judgment provides the model for the analysis of more complex judgments of fact.

> The fulfilling conditions may be any combination of data from the memories of a long life, and their acquisition may have involved exceptional powers of observation. The cognitional structure may suppose the cumulative development of understanding exemplified by the man of experience, the specialist, the expert. Both complex data and a complex structure may combine to yield a virtually unconditioned that introspective analysis could hardly hope to reproduce accurately and convincingly. But the general nature of the concrete judgment of fact would remain the same as in the simple case we considered.[19]

This was Newman's point in the *Grammar of Assent* where he asserts that it would be very difficult to analyze all that goes into a farmer's judgment, "It will probably rain tomorrow," for such a judgment presupposes years of experiences, insights and judgments about connections between various natural events. Still, such judgment could very well express the authentic dynamism of the farmer's intelligence and reasonableness.

One of Lonergan's signature aphorisms, pronounced with his own peculiar Canadian twang, was, "Bright ideas are a dime a dozen; what matters is 'are they correct?'" How tell the difference between a mere bright idea and one that hits things off correctly? Thus, the man returning to his home might have said, "There's been a fire." Since there is no longer a fire, how did he arrive at that insight and that judgment?

Lonergan answers by noting that insights not only arise in response to questions, but they also give rise to further questions. These questions may stick to the original issue or they may go on to raise distinct issues: "What started the fire?" "Where is my wife?" This raising of distinct issues might come about merely because one's attention was drawn to these other issues. Or, perhaps the initial issue has been exhausted and there are no further questions to be raised. To analyze this, Lonergan distinguishes between *vulnerable* and *invulnerable insights*.

> Insights are vulnerable when there are further questions to be asked on the same issue. For the further questions lead to further insights that certainly complement the initial insight, that to a greater or less extent modify its expression and implications, that perhaps lead to an entirely new slant on the issue. But when there are no further questions, the insight is invulnerable. For it is only through further questions that there arise the further insights that complement, modify, or revise the initial approach and explanation.[20]

Prior to the distinction between correct and mistaken insights, then, there is "an operational distinction" between invulnerable and vulnerable insights.

When an insight meets the issue squarely, when it hits the bull's eye, when it settles the matter, there are no further questions to be asked, and so there are no further insights to challenge the initial position. But when the issue is not met squarely, there are further questions that would reveal the unsatisfactoriness of the insight and would evoke the further insights that put a new light on the matter.

There is a law immanent in cognitional process, then, that an insight into a concrete situation is correct when there are no further pertinent questions. When there are no further relevant questions to be raised concerning a judgment, that judgment is a conditioned whose conditions de facto have been fulfilled.

Lonergan adds that it is not enough to say that the conditions have been fulfilled when no further questions occur to me. I just might not have any curiosity; or I might be distracted. In that case I might very well be making a rash judgment. Or, there might in fact be no further relevant questions and I might still suffer from indecision. How strike the balance between these two: rashness and indecision?

In the first place, then, one has to give the further questions a chance to arise. The seed of intellectual curiosity has to grow into a rugged tree to hold its own against the desires and fears, conations and appetites, drives and interests, that inhabit the heart of man. Moreover, every insight has its retinue of presuppositions, implications, and applications. One has to take the steps needed for that retinue to come to light.[21]

Is that not what a "retreat" is about—giving ourselves the opportunity to allow "all the relevant questions" to arise? Is that not what study is about? Is that not what "the intellectual pattern of experience" is about? In a way similar to the way in which a scientist puts his insights to the test, something equivalent has to be sought in ordinary living: "by intellectual alertness, by taking one's time, by talking things over, by putting viewpoints to the test of action."

For behind the theory of correct insights, there is the theory of correct problems. How figure out what questions to ask? Does not good judgment about any issue depend on the previous acquisition of a large number of other insights? It is precisely to break this apparent vicious circle that Lonergan introduces the notion of "*the self-correcting process of learning*." He calls attention to the process of growth from childhood to the "age of reason" and also the law's determination of the age of maturity (eighteen? twenty-one?) to illustrate our growing ability to make responsible judgments.

So it is the process of learning that breaks the vicious circle. Judgment on the correctness of insights supposes the prior acquisition of a large number of correct insights. But the prior insights are not correct because we judge them to be correct. They occur within a self-correcting process in which the shortcomings of each insight provoke further questions to yield complementary insights. [22]

This self-correcting process of learning tends to a limit. We become familiar with concrete situations and we know what to expect. When the unexpected occurs, we can spot just what happens and why. Or, if the totally unexpected takes place, we know enough to begin again the process of learning. [23]

Furthermore, in lines reminiscent of Jung's characterization of different "personality types," Lonergan acknowledges the role of *temperament*:

> For unless a special effort is made to cope with temperament itself, the rash man continues to presume too quickly that he has nothing more to learn, and the indecisive man continues to suspect that deeper depths of shadowy possibilities threaten to invalidate what he knows quite well.

Elsewhere, he calls the person of rash temperament a "scatterbrain" and the indecisive person "scrupulous." And in *Understanding and Being* he speaks of "psychic disturbances" interfering with good judgment.

> Again, psychic disturbances can eclipse judgment, for the level of judgment is a much more delicate level, one on which the balance of control is much more difficult. And one reaches in psychosis the impossibility of judging. One uses here what are called "reality tests"—really tests of the possibility of judging.[24]

He illustrates the "delicate" character of judging by referring to St. Thomas.

> In short, a man may be rich, over rich, in insights, but the control needed for judgment may be lacking. One needs for judgment a fuller control of all faculties than one needs for insight. The control of judgment requires the poise of consciousness and the control over sensitive presentations and images that can be disturbed in the human makeup. If that control is disturbed, judgment is disturbed. St. Thomas says that we can syllogize in our dreams, but when we wake up we find that we have made some mistake. Syllogizing in one's sleep is on the level of insight, finding the mistake upon waking up is on the level of judgment. While insights are not excluded by the fact that one is dreaming, the intellectual element is not dominant at all; the dream is disconnected, and lower factors have control.

Did I have questions about these early chapters? I certainly did and I came back to them again and again. I mentioned previously some of my recurring questions: Is it true that concepts are really distinct from images?

Couldn't concepts just be highly refined images? And is Lonergan's analysis of the "circle of terms" needed to understand the simple act of understanding correct? And can't questioning and insight be collapsed into feeling and imagination?—as is the presumption in much contemporary thought about consciousness?

I raised these and many other questions as I read through *Insight*. They were my questions and I was seeking a very personal act through which all the pieces of the puzzle might come together.

NOTES

1. *CWL 3 Insight*, 296 (271).
2. *CWL 5 Understanding and Being*, 110.
3. Cf. Aristotle's *Posterior Analytics*. References given in *Verbum*, 12-16.
4. *CWL 3 Insight*, 297 (272).
5. *CWL 5 Understanding and Being*, 113.
6. *CWL 3 Insight*, 298-299 (273).
7. *CWL 3 Insight*, 300 (275).
8. *CWL 5 Understanding and Being*, 114; cf. *Verbum*, 48-59.
9. *CWL 3 Insight*, 390 (366).
10. *CWL 5 Understanding and Being*, 117.
11. *CWL 3 Insight*, 301 (275-276).
12. *Verbum*, 47-48. See Newman, *Grammar of Assent*, 188 f., on complex assent in which "we not only know, but we know that we know."
13. *CWL 3 Insight*, 304 (279).
14. *CWL 3 Insight*, 305 (280).
15. *CWL 3 Insight*, 306 (281).
16. *CWL 3 Insight*, 306 (281).
17. *CWL 3 Insight*, 306-307 (281).
18. *CWL 3 Insight*, 307-308 (282).
19. *CWL 3 Insight*, 308 (283).
20. *CWL 3 Insight*, 309 (284).
21. *CWL 3 Insight*, 310 (285).
22. *CWL 3 Insight*, 311 (286).
23. *CWL 3 InsightInsight*, 311-312 (286-287).
24. *CWL 5 Understanding and Being*, 123.

Chapter Eight

The Self-affirmation of the Knower

Acts of understanding are much rarer than acts of experiencing, and acts of judging are much rarer than acts of understanding. We need a flow of experiences to have a single insight, and a flow of insights to have a single judgment. But rational reflection is the key level, and this is the level that comes to the fore in philosophy. . . .[1]

1. CONSCIOUSNESS

But how is it that I can come to know—"from the inside"—my own experiencing, understanding and judging? How is it that I have such immediate access to these acts, an access I do not have to my blood circulating or my hair growing? It is precisely because experience, understanding and judging are "conscious," that I can come to understand them and know them as constituting the structure of my human knowing.

But what is consciousness? It is a notion that perplexes many today—so that some even deny consciousness, calling it an "epiphenomenon" or an illusion. In *Insight*, however, Lonergan is careful to specify what he means by consciousness and what he does not mean. Most of all, he is careful to purify the notion of intuitionist and visual connotations.

People are apt to think of knowing by imagining a man taking a look at something, and further, they are apt to think of consciousness by imagining themselves looking into themselves."[2]

Not only does the person in the street tend to think of consciousness as some kind of an "inner look," but many philosophers do as well.[3] But just as it is possible to understand understanding as transcending visual representa-

127

tion, so also it is possible to understand consciousness as something other than an inner type of looking. For Lonergan consciousness is *an awareness immanent in cognitional acts.* Later on he will extend this awareness to other acts as well—acts of evaluating, deciding and acting—but here his focus on the acts employed in trying to understand understanding.

All through the previous chapters he has presupposed the distinction between act and content: that is, between seeing and color, or between hearing and sound, or between insight and idea. Now he asserts that to affirm consciousness is to affirm that cognitional process is not merely a procession of contents but also a succession of conscious acts.

> It is to affirm that the acts differ radically from such unconscious acts as the metabolism of one's cells, the maintenance of one's organs, the multitudinous biological processes that one learns about through the study of contemporary medical science. Both kinds of acts occur, but the biological occur outside consciousness, and the cognitional occur within consciousness. Seeing is not merely a response to the stimulus of color and shape; it is a response that consists in becoming aware of color and shape.[4]

By the conscious act is not meant a deliberate act, for we are conscious of acts without debating whether we will perform them. Nor is a conscious act an act to which one attends, for even though consciousness can be heightened by shifting attention from the content to the act, consciousness is not constituted by that shift of attention. It is a quality immanent in certain kinds of acts "and without it the acts would be as unconscious as the growth of one's beard." Nor by a conscious act is meant an act that is somehow isolated for inspection, "nor that one grasps its function in cognitional process, nor that one can assign it a name, nor that one can distinguish it from other acts, nor that one is certain of its occurrence."

Lonergan's point is that by consciousness he means a self-awareness immanent in certain acts. Here his emphasis is on cognitional acts and he focuses on three different kinds of consciousness corresponding to three different kinds of cognitional acts: empirical, intelligent and rational. On a first level there is an empirical consciousness characteristic of sensing, perceiving, imagining. As the content of these acts is merely presented or represented, so the awareness immanent in the acts lies in "the mere givenness" of the acts.

But there is also an intelligent consciousness characteristic of inquiry, insight, and formulation. On this level cognitional process not merely strives for and reaches the intelligible, but in doing so it exhibits its intelligence; it operates intelligently. It is the awareness of the striving to understand and of what is satisfied by understanding, of what formulates the understood not as a schoolboy repeating by rote a definition, but as one that grasps why that definition hits things off.[5] He describes this level of intellectual consciousness.

Again, if at moments I can slip into a lotus land in which mere presentations and representations arc juxtaposed or successive, still that is not my normal state. The Humean world of mere impressions comes to me as a puzzle to be pieced together. I want to understand, to grasp intelligible unities and relations, to know what's up and where I stand. Praise of the scientific spirit that inquires, that masters, that controls, is not without an echo, a deep resonance within me, for in my more modest way I too inquire and catch on, see the thing to do and see that it is properly done. But what are these but variations on the more basic expression that I am intelligently conscious, that the awareness characteristic of cognitional acts on the second level is an active contributing to the intelligibility of its products?[6]

Finally, on a third level of judgment, there is rational consciousness.

It is the emergence and the effective operation of a single law of utmost generality, the law of sufficient reason, where the sufficient reason is the unconditioned. It emerges as a demand for the unconditioned and a refusal to assent unreservedly on any lesser ground. It advances to grasp of the unconditioned. It terminates in the rational compulsion by which grasp of the unconditioned commands assent.[7]

He describes this level of rational consciousness:

It is repugnant to me to place astrology and astronomy, alchemy and chemistry, legend and history, hypothesis and fact, on exactly the same footing. I am not content with theories, however brilliantly coherent, but insist on raising the further question, Are they true? What is that repugnance, that discontent, that insistence? They are just so many variations on the more basic expression that I am rationally conscious, that I demand sufficient reason, that I find it in the unconditioned, that I assent unreservedly to nothing less, that such demanding, finding, self-committing occur, not like the growth of my hair, but within a field of consciousness or awareness.[8]

As I read these paragraphs, I said to myself, "He's describing me!" Lonergan then goes on to make the point that there is a unity in consciousness. Just as various cognitional acts coalesce around different dimensions of one content of knowing, so there is a unity among the various cognitional acts. Not only is there a similarity between my seeing and your hearing, inasmuch as both acts are conscious; there also is an identity involved when my seeing and my hearing or your seeing and your hearing are compared.[9] This identity extends all along the line to all the cognitional acts.

Indeed, consciousness is much more obviously of this unity in diverse acts than of the diverse acts, for it is within the unity that the acts are found and distinguished, and it is to the unity that we appeal when we talk about a single field of consciousness and draw a distinction between conscious acts occurring within the field and unconscious acts occurring outside it.

Postmodern thought often so emphasizes the diversity of personal stories that it tends to deny the "self," the "I"—there are only particular stories that you and I play out. Lonergan's assertion is that prior to any story and grounding the unity of the stories, there is the unity of the conscious agent, one's self.

By this, of course, I do not mean that it is the object of some inward look.

What is meant is that a single agent is involved in many acts, that it is an abstraction to speak of the acts as conscious, that, concretely, consciousness pertains to the acting agent.[10]

Consciousness, therefore, is the quality of *identity* immanent in the diverse cognitional acts. But such an account of consciousness is not itself consciousness. The account supposes consciousness as its data, but giving the account is one's affirmation of what one has understood in the data of consciousness.

2. THE SELF-AFFIRMATION OF THE KNOWER

. . . from a logical viewpoint the first judgment that occurs in the whole work is the judgment of self-affirmation in the eleventh chapter.[11]

But was all of this true? Was it true that the structure of knowing involves experiencing, understanding and judging as explained in *Insight*? Perhaps it was true that knowing consisted in the acts I had come to recognize, identify and distinguish in the previous ten chapters of *Insight*. But then again, perhaps I was mistaken?

Chapter eleven is the central chapter in *Insight*. The previous ten chapters lead up to it and the following chapters flow from it. In its essence it invites the reader to ask, "Am *I* a knower in the sense outlined so far in this book?" The chapter focuses on bringing the reader to acknowledge the inevitability of employing this structure in knowing one's own knowing.

The question is, "Am I a knower?" Each person must ask this question for himself or herself, but to ask the question is already to be rationally conscious. For it is a question that asks for a "Yes" or "No" answer and asking the question means entering into "the dynamic state in which dissatisfaction with mere theory manifests itself in a demand for fact." Furthermore, in some way I know what the question means.

What do I mean by "I?" The answer is difficult to formulate, but strangely, in some obscure fashion, I know very well what it means without formulation and by that obscure yet familiar awareness, I find fault with various formulations of what is meant by "I." In other words, "I" has a rudimentary meaning from consciousness, and it envisages neither the multiplicity nor the diversity of contents and conscious acts but rather the unity that goes along with them. But if "I" has some such rudimentary meaning from consciousness, then consciousness supplies the fulfillment of one element in the conditions for affirming that I am a knower.[12]

In other words, my consciousness itself supplies the condition for affirming a unity and identity in diverse acts. What about the acts that we have previously discriminated within consciousness? Do I perform the cognitional acts that characterize this unity and identity? Does consciousness supply the fulfillment of these conditions for affirming "I am a knower in the sense explained above?"

Do I see, or am I blind? Do I hear, or am I deaf? Do I try to understand, or is the distinction between intelligence and stupidity no more applicable to me than to a stone? Have I any experience of insight, or is the story of Archimedes as strange to me as the account of Plotinus' vision of the One? Do I conceive, think, consider, suppose, define, formulate, or is my talking like the talking of a parrot?

I reflect, for I ask whether I am a knower. Do I grasp the unconditioned, if not in other instances, then in this one? If I grasped the unconditioned, would I not be under the rational compulsion of affirming that I am a knower and so, either affirm it, or else find some loop-hole, some weakness, some incoherence, in this account of the genesis of self-affirmation?[13]

Each one has to answer these questions for himself or herself. As Newman pointed out in the *Grammar of Assent*, the ultimate court of appeal for the knowledge of human mentality is our own knowledge of ourselves. "In these provinces of inquiry egotism is true modesty."[14] Lonergan makes a similar point in the section entitled "self-affirmation as immanent law."

Am I a knower? The answer yes is coherent, for if I am a knower, I can know that fact. But the answer no is incoherent, for if I am not a knower, how could the question be raised and answered by me? No less, the hedging answer "I do not know" is incoherent. For if I know that I do not know, then I am a knower; and if I do not know that I do not know, then I should not answer.

Aristotle's response to the skeptic, the one who is not sure that he knows, was to get him to speak: that is, to lead him to implicitly refute the content of his statement by his own practice. The only coherent performance for the genuine skeptic is the silence of the vegetable. Lonergan takes the same tactic.

Am I a knower? If I am not, then I know nothing. My only course is silence. My only course is not the excused and explained silence of the skeptic, but the complete silence of the animal that offers neither excuse nor explanation for its complacent absorption in merely sensitive routines. For if I know nothing, I do not know excuses for not knowing. If I know nothing, then I cannot know the explanation of my ignorance.

Lonergan applies this implicit contradiction to the Freudian who would assert that all thought is just a by-product of the unconscious.

If enthusiasm for the achievement of Freud were to lead me to affirm that all thought and affirmation is just a byproduct of the libido, then since I have admitted no exceptions, this very assertion of mine would have to be mere assertion from a suspect source. If second thoughts lead me to acknowledge an exception, they lead me to acknowledge the necessary presuppositions of the exception. By the time that list has been drawn up and accepted, I am no longer a skeptic.

The contradiction to be pointed out, then, is not just between self-contradictory statements, but rather between those statements and *the natural spontaneities and inevitabilities* that go with making any statements.

Why is it that one can count on his being nonplussed by self-contradiction? It is because he is conscious, empirically, intelligently, and rationally. It is because he has no choice in the matter. It is because extreme ingenuity is needed for him not to betray his real nature. It is because, were his ingenuity successful, the only result would be that he had revealed himself an idiot and lost all claim to be heard.[15]

This is what Newman meant when he said that "my first elementary duty is resignation to the laws of nature . . . which are identical with myself."[16] Here Lonergan connects this dynamic structure of our consciousness with *natural law*. I cannot escape sensation. I can exercise a selective control over what I sense, but the choice I cannot make is to sense nothing. Similarly, I cannot escape asking questions.

Spontaneously I fall victim to the wonder that Aristotle named the beginning of all science and philosophy. I try to understand. I enter, without questioning, the dynamic state that is revealed in questions for intelligence.

I can ridicule intelligence; I can reduce its use to a minimum; but I cannot eliminate it.

I can question everything else, but to question questioning is self-destructive. I might call upon intelligence for the conception of a plan to escape intelligence, but the effort to escape would only reveal my present involvement, and strangely enough, I would want to go about the business intelligently, and I would want to claim that escaping was the intelligent thing to do.

Similarly, as I cannot be content with "the cinematographic flow of presentations and representations," so I cannot be content with the level of inquiry and understanding.

> I may say I want not the quarry but the chase, but I am careful to restrict my chasing to fields where the quarry lies. If, above all, I want to understand, still I want to understand the facts. Inevitably, the achievement of understanding, however stupendous, only gives rise to the further question, Is it so? Inevitably, the progress of understanding is interrupted by the check of judgment. Intelligence may be a thoroughbred exulting in the race; but there is a rider on its back; and without the rider the best of horses is a poor bet.[17]

Here Lonergan focuses on "*fact*," for it is fact that he is after—the fact that combines "the concreteness of experience, the determinateness of accurate intelligence, and the absoluteness of rational judgment." Such is the natural objective of human cognitional process. And such fact is in the realm of the unimaginable.

> When quantum mechanics and relativity posit the unimaginable in a four-dimensional manifold, they bring to light the not too surprising fact that scientific intelligence and verifying judgment go beyond the realm of imagination to the realm of fact.

Later on he will analyze the philosophical implications of that "realm of fact." Now, in some of his most beautiful words, he simply says:

> Our present concern is that we are committed to fact. We are committed, not by knowing what it is and that it is worth while, but by an inability to avoid experience, by the subtle conquest in us of the *eros* that would understand, by the inevitable aftermath of that sweet adventure when a rationality identical with us demands the absolute, refuses unreserved assent to less than the unconditioned, and when that is attained, imposes upon us a commitment in which we bow to an immanent *Anankê*.[18]

Lonergan's words here are passionate: "the subtle conquest in us of the *eros* that would understand." To be obedient to the structure of our own being is our destiny. If the rational spirit can criticize the achievement of science, it cannot criticize itself without self-destruction. "It" is what does the criticizing and from within its own immanent norms. The ultimate issue is one of pragmatic involvement with the facts of my own being. One cannot seek any deeper foundations.

> The ultimate basis of our knowing is not necessity but contingent fact, and the fact is established, not prior to our engagement in knowing, but simultaneously

with it. The skeptic, then, is not involved in a conflict with absolute necessity. He might not be; he might not be a knower. Contradiction arises when he utilizes cognitional process to deny it.[19]

Lonergan expressed this same issue a few years later:

> . . . does this many-leveled subject exist? Each man has to answer that question for himself. But I do not think the answers are in doubt. Not even behaviorists claim that they are unaware whether or not they see or hear, taste or touch. Not even positivists preface their lectures and their books with the frank avowal that never in their lives did they have the experience of understanding anything whatever. Not even relativists claim that never in their lives did they have the experience of making a rational judgment. Not even determinists claim that never in their lives did they have the experience of making a responsible choice. There exist subjects that are empirically, intellectually, rationally, morally conscious. Not all know themselves as such, for consciousness is not human knowing but only a potential component in the structured whole that is human knowing. But all can know themselves as such, for they have only to attend to what they are already conscious of, and understand what they attend to, and pass judgment on the correctness of their understanding.[20]

3. DESCRIPTION AND EXPLANATION

Lonergan then asks an important question: Has all this about the self-affirmation of the knower been just descriptive knowledge or does it enter into the realm of explanation?

> Is the self-affirmation that has been outlined descriptive of the thing-for-us or explanatory of the thing-itself? We have spoken of natural inevitabilities and spontaneities. But did we speak of these as they are themselves or as they are for us?[21]

His answer is "both." Just as in the natural sciences one moves from descriptive categories that relate things to ourselves to explanatory categories that relate things to each other, so in the process of self-affirmation one moves from the description of experiencing, understanding and judging to an explanatory understanding of these elements in their relationships to each other.

But this process of achieving the explanatory self-affirmation of the knower differs in one major respect from the process of reaching an explanatory understanding of something in nature. For in the case of self-affirmation we enjoy an immediate access to what we are trying to understand, that is, our own selves. On the other hand, the scientific explanation of nature based on sense experience can reduce the element of hypothesis to a minimum, but it cannot avoid it entirely. An empirical hypothesis always involves an element of the provisional in choosing a particular set of primitive terms and relations with which to frame one's hypothesis. Explanation on the basis of consciousness, however, can escape entirely the merely supposed, the merely postulated, the merely inferred.

> I do not mean, of course, that such explanation is not to be reached through the series of revisions involved in the self-correcting process of learning. Nor do I mean that, once explanation is reached, there remains no possibility of the minor revisions that leave basic lines intact but attain a greater exactitude and a greater fullness of detail. Again, I am not contending here and now that human nature and so human knowledge are immutable, that there could not arise a new nature and a new knowledge to which present theory would not be applicable. What is excluded is the radical revision that involves a shift in the fundamental terms and relations of the explanatory account of the human knowledge underlying existing common sense, mathematics and empirical science.[22]

In *Understanding and Being* Lonergan brings out the foundational character of this process:

> . . . in our account of the knower, the subject is not something hypothetical. The subject is the "I" that says, "I am a knower." Insight is not simply an hypothesis. A behaviorist or a certain type of linguistic analyst may say that intelligence, insight, has a meaning insofar as there are modes of behavior that show a man to be intelligent. If that were the only evidence, insight would be a hypothetical entity used to account for that type of behavior. But if, in your presence to yourself within your own consciousness, you are aware that there occur jumps, that periods of darkness are followed by periods of increasing light, catching on, understanding things and seeing how they hold together, then insight is not simply a hypothetical entity but something that is verified in your experience.[23]

Consequently, this account of the process of self-affirmation has the advantages of both the descriptive and the explanatory approaches.

> It has all the advantages of the concreteness of the descriptive type insofar as the elements and the unity are verifiable in consciousness. It has all the advantages of the explanatory type insofar as the different elements are of their very nature interdependently linked together in the process.[24]

4. CONTRAST WITH OTHER ANALYSES

The impossibility of the revision of such an account is evident from the very notion of a revision. For revision, appeals to new data, claims a new under-

standing of the data, and points to a probable verification of the new theory.
But in our case

> . . . a reviser cannot appeal to data to deny data, to his new insights to deny
> insight, to his new formulation to deny formulation, to his reflective grasp to
> deny reflective grasp.[25]

In other words, one's attempt to refute this explanation of the knowing subject as experiencing, understanding and judging will in fact, in *performance*,
involve experiencing, understanding and judging.

As I mentioned in chapter one, when I was a young student first studying
Neo-scholastic philosophy, our major adversary was Immanuel Kant. Kant
held that we could not really know "things in themselves" because we have
no intellectual intuition—*Anschauung*—that connects our minds directly with
things. Rather, all our knowledge is mediated by the *a priori* forms of space
and time and the categories of understanding. Our method of refuting Kant,
largely influenced by Etienne Gilson, was to assert that "there was so!" a direct intellectual intuition of being. Ours was a dogmatic realism, an "intuitionism" that implied that intellectual knowledge was similar to sense experience.
There are things "out there." I am "over here." Obviously I know things "out
there" because I can see them, touch them, etc. That's all there is to it. No need
to examine concretely the processes of human knowing in science, scholarship
and common sense. Such an analysis might weaken your realism, which is
so important for Christianity's vindication of the validity of human knowing.
Suffice it to assert a realism of human knowing and let it go at that.

Lonergan's analysis obviously represented another position. Not only is
there a dimension of human knowing that does indeed involve seeing and
touching objects "out there," but there are two other dimensions of full human
knowing that are quite different from such sensitive experience. There is understanding and there is judging. Because neither understanding nor judging
"resembles" sensitive intuition, there is no reason to deny the basic validity
of the human knowing that issues in judgment.

> Moreover—and this is the essential difference—the process of checking reveals
> in human knowledge, beyond experience and understanding, a third, distinct,
> constitutive level that is both self-authenticating and decisive. It is self-authen-
> ticating: rational reflection demands and reflective understanding grasps a virtu-
> ally unconditioned; and once that grasp has occurred, one cannot be reasonable
> and yet fail to pass judgment. Again, the third level is alone decisive: until I
> judge, I am merely thinking; once I judge, I know; as insight draws the definite
> object of thought from the hazy object of experience, so judgment selects the
> objects of thought that are objects of knowledge.[26]

As Lonergan will point out in numerous places, the one criterion of the validity of human knowing is rational judgment—the act conspicuously misconstrued by Kant.

> Now because the third level is self-authenticating, reason and its ideal, the unconditioned, cannot be left in the dubious and merely supervisory role assigned them by Kant. Because it is constitutive and alone decisive, the one criterion in our knowledge is rational judgment; and this rules out the vestigial empiricism so often denounced in Kantian thought.

Kantian theory has no room for a consciousness of the generative principles of the categories Kant extols. On the other hand, if the Kantian philosopher praises intelligent curiosity and the critical spirit, "then he is on his way to acknowledge the generative principles both of the categories Kant knew and of the categories Kant did not know."[27]

If Kantian thought was one major adversary of my youth, relativist thought has become much more prevalent in recent years. The postmodern unease with the totalitarian pretensions of modern science and universalist ideologies has resulted in the recognition of numerous worlds or "universes of discourse" that are valid within certain limited areas or communities. But postmoderns are very wary of speaking of "truth." In fact, they would generally proscribe talk about truth altogether. Perhaps it is a future ideal, but the obvious limitations of every present point of view cautions us against any absolute assertions. Lonergan's response to relativism is to call attention to the nature of human judgment.

> . . . a judgment is a limited commitment; so far from resting on knowledge of the universe, it is to the effect that, no matter what the rest of the universe may prove to be, at least this is so. I may not be able to settle borderline instances in which one might dispute whether the name "typewriter" would be appropriate. But at least I can settle definitively that this is a typewriter. I may not be able to clarify the meaning of "is," but it is sufficient for present purposes to know the difference between "is" and "is not;" and that, I know. I am not very articulate when it comes to explaining the meaning of "this," but if you prefer to use "that," it will make no difference provided we both see what we are talking about. You warn me that I have made mistakes in the past. But your warning is meaningless if I am making a further mistake in recognizing a past mistake as a mistake.[28]

I ended up reading this chapter with two questions on my mind: First, can I really arrive at *convictions,* that is, grounded judgments about the very structure of my self? The chapter sounded quite authentic, but was it true?

Secondly, if I can arrive at such convictions, what follows from them?

NOTES

1. *CWL 10 Topics in Education*, 178.
2. *CWL 3 Insight*, 344 (320).
3. It is because of the absurdity of this position that some cognitive scientists have recently taken to denying the existence of consciousness at all. See Daniel Dennett, *Consciousness Explained* (Boston: Little, Brown, 1991) and *Breaking the Spell: Religion as a Natural Phenomenon* (Penguin, 2006). Dennett considers our ordinary idea of consciousness to be that of a "little man," a "homunculus," peering out onto the world outside. As a result, he and other cognitive scientists deny such appearances of consciousness in favor of "what science says," the really real neuro-biological activity. On this see the new *Journal of Consciousness Studies: Controversies in Science and the Humanities* where these issues are explicitly debated.
4. *CWL 3 Insight*, 344-345 (320-321).
5. *CWL 3 Insight,* 346 (322).
6. *CWL 3 Insight,* 348 (324).
7. *CWL 3 Insight*, 346 (322).
8. *CWL 3 Insight*, 348 323-324).
9. *CWL 3 Insight*, 349 (325).
10. *CWL 3 Insight*, 350 (326).
11. *CWL 3 Insight*, 17 (xxii).
12. *CWL 3 Insight*, 352 (328).
13. *CWL 3 Insight*, 352-353 (328).
14. J. H. Newman, *A Grammar of Assent* (London: Longmans, Green, & Co., 1913) 384.
15. *CWL 3 Insight*, 354 (329-330).
16. Newman, *A Grammar of Assent*, 347.
17. *CWL 3 Insight*, 355 (330-331).
18. *CWL 3 Insight*, 355-356 (331).
19. *CWL 3 Insight*, 356-357 (332).
20. *CWL 4 Collection*, 227.
21. *CWL 3 Insight*, 357 (332-333).
22. *CWL 3 Insight*, 359 (335).
23. *CWL 5 Understanding and Being*, 142.
24. *CWL 5 Understanding and Being,* 142-143.
25. *CWL 3 Insight*, 360 (336).
26. *CWL 3 Insight*, 364 (340).
27. *CWL 3 Insight*, 365 (341).
28. *CWL 3 Insight*, 368 (344).

Chapter Nine

Being and Objectivity

What in the world is "being?" I had used the term in discussing Thomistic metaphysics, but with the onslaught of historical consciousness and existential philosophy, it seemed very much like a term out of another world, a world gone forever.

Yet here was Lonergan in chapter twelve of *Insight* saying that being was a valid and useful term, a term rich in meaning. For the whole meaning of the chapter was that being was the object of our pure desire to know, what we were heading for in our process of understanding and judging. In fact, the pure desire to know could be called "the notion of being," that is, the unlimited anticipation that sparks our search for knowledge. Prior to any concepts, prior to any judgments, there is in us the notion of being, the unknown "*x*" that our questioning heads for and that we progressively fill out by our understandings and correct judgments.

In other words, to use a term Lonergan will often employ after *Insight*, our questioning, understanding and judging takes place within the horizon of being. When we seek to understand, we are seeking to understand being. When we reflect on our understanding and seek to judge correctly, we are seeking to understand being correctly. We do not seek merely the satisfaction of our own activities of understanding and judging. We are seeking to transcend ourselves, that is, to attain being. As Lonergan himself introduced the issue in an article from the early 1960s:

> At this point one may ask why knowing should result from the performance of such immanent activities as experiencing, understanding, and judging. This brings us to the epistemological theorem, namely, that knowledge in the proper sense is knowledge of reality or, more fully, that knowledge is intrinsically objective, that objectivity is the intrinsic relation of knowing to being, and that being and reality are identical.[1]

139

In other words, after spending eleven chapters on the activities of the subject, the question arises: What is this all about? Is all this mental activity—experiencing, imagining, perceiving, questioning, understanding, etc.—is all this
"inner" activity just "inner?" Does all this mental activity—sometimes intricate, refined and exigent as in the case of science—have anything to do with
"the real world?" Put crudely, Does what goes on *in* me relate to reality?

Lonergan's answer in chapter twelve of *Insight* is: "What goes on in me—
and you—is in order to know the real world—or, to use the heuristic term,
to know 'being.'" Experiencing, questioning, understanding, formulating,
reflecting, judging—all function in order to know what is.

1. THE NOTION OF BEING

As I mentioned, at the time I was reading *Insight* I was very leery of such
a "scholastic-sounding" word as "being." It reeked of mystification, of
"mystery-mongering," a game-playing with technical-sounding terms to fool
people into thinking you know more than you do. Some philosophers were
reminding people of the "bewitching" power of words—how they can intimi-
date us into thinking they mean more than they mean. They can lull us into
thinking that by such words we know more than we actually know.

And yet as I read this chapter I came to realize that by "being" Lonergan
meant something very simple and yet very foundational. "Being" is that
which our questioning intends. And since our questioning is radically unrestricted, rooted as it is in the pure desire to know, being is all that all that our
questioning intends. It is "that which is totally universal and totally concrete":
the "all": "everything about everything." But how do we get at "everything
about everything?" We obviously don't know everything about everything.

Lonergan answers: we get at it *heuristically*, that is, we give the unknown
a name—in this case "being"—and we work out its characteristics. And the
first characteristic of being is that *it is what we are heading for as we ask
questions*. We don't know being immediately; we come to know it by means
of questioning. It is the objective of the pure desire to know. Lonergan speaks
of this "notion of being" as implicit in our questioning.

> Just as the notion of the intelligible is involved in the actual functioning of intel-
> ligence, just as the notion of the grounded is involved in the actual functioning
> of reasonableness, so the notion of being is involved in the unrestricted drive of
> inquiring intelligence and reflecting reasonableness.[2]

The notion of being, implicit in our spirit as we raise questions, heads us
toward being. It is prior to all acts of understanding, all concepts, all judg-

ments. But it drives us to understand and to judge correctly.

> It is to be known, not by the misleading analogy of other desire, but by giving free rein to intelligent and rational consciousness. It is, indeed, impalpable but also it is powerful. It pulls man out of the solid routine of perception and conation, instinct and habit, doing and enjoying. It holds him with the fascination of problems. It engages him in the quest of solutions.[3]

The pure desire to know, which welled up in me in Rome as I struggled with *Insight*, is not strictly for cognitional acts and for the satisfaction these acts give their subject, but rather for cognitional contents, for what is to be known.

> But as pure desire, as cool, disinterested, detached, it is not for cognitional acts and the satisfaction they give their subject, but for cognitional contents, for what is to be known. The satisfaction of mistaken understanding, provided one does not know it as mistaken, can equal the satisfaction of correct understanding. Yet the pure desire scorns the former and prizes the latter; it prizes it, then, as dissimilar to the former; it prizes it not because it yields satisfaction but because its content is correct. The objective of the pure desire is the content of knowing rather than the act.[4]

This certainly is an "intellectualist" stance. Feelings and emotions take second place to correct understanding. The notion of being heads us toward correct judgment and indeed, the totality of correct judgments. This, then, is another characteristic of being: it is *what is to be known by the totality of true judgments*. It is all-inclusive. Apart from being there is nothing. It is completely concrete and completely universal. It is the unrestricted goal towards which the notion of being implicit in our pure questioning heads.

> Every doubt that the pure desire is unrestricted serves only to prove that it is unrestricted. If you ask whether **X** might not lie beyond its range, the fact that you ask proves that **X** lies within its range.[5]

Of course, besides the underlying notion of being that heads for knowledge of everything about everything, there are also concepts of being and philosophical articulations of being. These are strategic sets of judgments that define the general character of being. Such sets of judgments about the nature of being would be the various philosophies: for example, that being is material and nothing but material; or being is "appearance" and nothing but appearance. Lonergan's option is that being reflects the structure of our self as we head toward knowing everything about everything. The implications of this he will bring out in his chapters on metaphysics.

And so the notion of being is the heuristic anticipation of the unrestricted goal towards which all our knowing heads. Our hearing concerns the limited realm of objects that are sounds; our seeing concerns the limited realm that are sights. But the pure desire to know is unrestricted.[6] It is opposed to any obscurantism which would brush questions aside in principle. "The radical meaning of obscurantism is implicitly or explicitly holding the thesis that the range of our knowledge, the range of our desire to know, is limited."[7]

Lonergan speaks of the "notion" of being precisely because it is intellectually and rationally *conscious* and, as such, anticipates all intelligibility. It is not mere emptiness as a box is empty. Nor is it like a stomach growling for food.

> [T]he desire to know is not unconscious, as is the fetal eye, nor empirically conscious, as is hunger, nor a consequence of intellectual knowledge, as are deliberation and choice. The desire to know is conscious intelligently and rationally; it is inquiring intelligence and reflecting reasonableness.[8]

Lonergan says that the notion of being is all-pervasive because it underpins all cognitional contents; it penetrates them all; it constitutes them as cognitional. It *underpins* all cognitional contents, for without the pure desire to know we would remain in an animal's habitat of purely sensitive living. What breaks that circle and thereby underpins even the empirical component in our knowing is the pure desire to know unfolding through experience and understanding to true judgments.

The notion of being also *penetrates* all cognitional contents, for it is the supreme heuristic notion. Prior to every cognitional content, there is the notion of the "to be known" through that content.

> As each content emerges, the "to-be-known through that content" passes without residue into the "known through that content." Some blank in universal anticipation is filled in, not merely to end that element of anticipation, but also to make the filler a part of the anticipated. Hence, prior to all answers, the notion of being is the notion of the totality to be known through all answers.[9]

Thirdly, the notion of being *constitutes all contents as cognitional.*

> Experience is for inquiring into being. Intelligence is for thinking out being. But by judgment being is known, and in judgment what is known is known as being. Hence knowing is knowing being, yet the known is never mere being, just as judgment is never a mere yes apart from any question that "yes" answers.

All of which relates to the old philosophical question whether everything in our knowledge depends on our experience. For certainly I was trained in the old Thomist maxim, *Nihil in intellectu quod non prius fuerit in sensibus:*

"There is nothing in the intellect which was not first in the senses." That is, except for the intellect itself, that pure transparency that sets up the criteria that moves you through the different stages of knowing towards the knowledge of everything about everything.

2. OBJECTIVITY

In his 1973 article, "*Insight* Revisited" Lonergan wrote that the problem tackled in the book was complex indeed. At its root was a question of psychological fact:

> Human intellect does not intuit essences. It grasps in simplifying images intelligible possibilities that may prove to be relevant to an understanding of the data. However, naive realists cannot remain naive realists and at the same time acknowledge the psychological facts. For them knowing is a matter of taking a good look; objectivity is a matter of seeing just what is there to be seen. For them my account of human understanding would appear to present intelligence as merely subjective and so imply an empiricism and, if they managed to get beyond empiricism, they would find themselves mere idealists. Accordingly, besides convincing people of the precise manner in which human understanding operates and develops, I also had to persuade them to drop intuitionist assumptions and come to understand the discursive character of human knowledge. Besides the world of immediacy alone known to the infant, there is also the world mediated by meaning into which the infant gradually moves. The former is Kant's world in which our only intuitions are sensitive. The latter is the world of critical realism in which the objects are intended when we question and are known when the questions are answered correctly.[10]

It is only within the horizon of being, operative "behind the scenes" of all our questioning, understanding and judging, that we can come to some adequate understanding of the meaning of "objectivity." If you ask most people what they mean by objectivity, they will say something like "What's out there" and they will probably point beyond themselves to the surrounding environment. Lonergan's point on objectivity in *Insight* is that this common sense notion of objectivity is radically inadequate and that only on the foundation of the notion of being as actually operative in our knowing can we come to an adequate account of objectivity.

How, for example, do scientists come to an "objective" account of their theories? How do interpreters come to an "objective" account of the meaning of ancient texts? Certainly, not just by looking or touching things "out there" or the black marks on white pieces of paper. The things and instruments scientists deal with and the texts interpreters deal with come to be known objectively to the extent that these searchers not only look and touch, but even more importantly, to the extent that they ask all the relevant questions and seek to understand correctly.

> Such prerequisites for genuine objectivity add two other elements to the experiential requirements most people identify with objectivity. Not only is there an empirical element necessary for being objective, but there are also normative and absolute requirements for being objective.

Accordingly, in chapter thirteen of *Insight* Lonergan distinguishes a principal notion of objectivity and three partial notions. The principal notion of objectivity takes place within the human person's growing knowledge of being. It is contained within a patterned context of judgments which serve as implicit definitions of the terms "object," and "subject."

> For one may define as *object* any A, B, C, D, . . . where, in turn, A, B, C, D, . . . are defined by the correctness of the set of judgments
>   A is; B is; C is; D is; . . .
>   A is neither B nor C nor D nor . . .
>   *B* is neither *C* nor *D* nor . . .
>   C is neither D nor . . .
> Again, one may define a *subject* as any object, say A, where it is true that A affirms himself as a knower in the sense explained in the chapter on self-affirmation.

In other words, the terms "object" and "subject" can be defined implicitly within a set of true judgments about objects, one of which is also a subject.

> The bare essentials of this notion of objectivity are reached if we add to the judgments already discussed—I am a knower, This is a typewriter—the further judgment that I am not this typewriter. An indefinite number of further objects may be added by making the additional appropriate positive and negative judgments. Finally, insofar as one can intelligently grasp and reasonably affirm the existence of other knowers besides oneself, one can add to the list the objects that also are subjects.[11]

A set of judgments, then, is needed to articulate the principal meaning of objectivity. This is obviously a more complex notion of objectivity than the common sense notion of objectivity as taking a good look at what is "out there." Since this way of defining the principal notion of objectivity employs "the somewhat recondite art of implicit definition," its meaning tends to be missed by people who would prefer to locate the principal notion of objectivity in one particular element of the knowing process, particularly the experiential element.

. . . people are apt to jump to the conclusion that so evident a matter as the existence of objects and subjects must rest on something as obvious and conspicuous as the experiential aspect of objectivity.[12]

Objectivity, then, can only be understood within being. "In brief, there is objectivity if there are distinct beings, some of which both know themselves and know others as others."[13] Objectivity in its principal sense then is a determination *within being* as the notion of being becomes differentiated by judgments about objects and subjects.

It follows, then, that there cannot be a subject that stands outside being and looks at it.

The subject has to be before he can look; and once he is, then he is not outside being but either the whole of it or some part. If he is the whole of it, then he is the sole object. If he is only a part, then he has to begin by knowing a multiplicity of parts (A is; B is; A is not B;) and add the one part that knows others ("I" am A).

The principal notion of objectivity illuminates the meaning of the expression, "going beyond oneself," which is used to describe the quality by which, through knowledge, we transcend ourselves. Here again it is obvious that a purification of our thinking about our own thinking is needed to properly conceive the objectivity of our knowing.

This is wild stuff. It is not very difficult, but it is wild. For constantly we use the words "objective" and "subjective." Most of the time we put a premium on being objective to the detriment of being subjective—although in the 1960s there was a change of fortune in the use of these terms. Lonergan seemed to be bringing out the positive side of both terms while at the same time highlighting misunderstandings in their use. And he was doing so in a "controlled" way, a way controlled by our own self-knowledge.

3. EXPERIENTIAL, NORMATIVE AND ABSOLUTE OBJECTIVITY

Within this principal notion of objectivity, there are partial notions of objectivity as experiential, normative and absolute. Experiential objectivity is provided by the data as given. It is appealed to when people are intent on finding out "the bare data" on a problem or when the teacher exhorts the student to "pay attention."

But experiential objectivity is not the only dimension of objectivity to be attended to, for there is also normative objectivity rooted in the intrinsic demands of intelligence and reasonableness. Such normative objectivity finds formulation in logic and methods or in the teacher's insistence that the student "use your head!" If you want to get somewhere, this is the way to go! This is the method to use!

Finally, absolute objectivity is rooted in the grasp of the virtually unconditioned. This third type of objectivity comes to the fore when we judge, when we distinguish sharply between what we feel, what we imagine, what seems to be so and, on the other hand, what is so.[14] I might have wanted things to be one way, but I came to judge they were not.

The experiential aspect of objectivity, then, is the objectivity of the given apart from all questioning.[15] The normative aspect of objectivity is the objectivity "opposed to the subjectivity of wishful thinking, of rash or excessively cautious judgments, of allowing joy or sadness, hope or fear, love or detestation, to interfere with the proper march of cognitional process.[16] In very powerful sentences Lonergan explains the absolute aspect of objectivity.

> Because the content of the judgment is an absolute, it is withdrawn from relativity to the subject that utters it, the place in which he utters it, the time at which he utters it. Caesar's crossing the Rubicon was a contingent event occurring at a particular place and time. But a true affirmation of that event is of an eternal, immutable, definitive validity. For if it is true that he did cross, then no one whatever at any place or time can truly deny that he did.[17]

By its absolute objectivity our knowledge acquires its public character: it is withdrawn from relativity to its source and becomes accessible to others. It is formulated in the logical principles of identity and contradiction. "The principle of identity is the immutable and definitive validity of the true. The principle of contradiction is the exclusiveness of that validity. It is, and what is opposed to it, is not."[18] As we often say in our conversation, "It either is or it isn't!"

4. OBJECTIVITY AND THE PROBLEM OF THE BRIDGE

If the objectivity of our knowing is what Lonergan says it is, then there is no "problem of the bridge," the problem that loomed so large in my early philosophical training, the problem of getting from "in here" to "out there."

> If your judgments fall into the pattern we have described, then insofar as those judgments are acts of knowing, you are knowing objects and subjects according to the fulfillment of the conditions. In other words *there is no problem of a bridge.* If you can reach the judgment, you are there . . . [19]

In other words, within the principal notion of objectivity, "the bridge between subject and object is through absolute objectivity positing an absolute realm within which real distinctions occur."[20] Among those real distinctions there is the real distinction between objects, at least one of which is also a subject. The knowing subject might indeed have an experiential "sense" of herself; but to truly "know" herself, there is also needed understanding and good judgment.

> . . . That judgment does not give you a *sense* of yourself; you have to have that sense to be able to make a judgment properly—to go through the argument of chapter eleven. You have to be familiar with your own experience and intelligence and reasonableness. But that familiarity is just the experiential side. When you know yourself through the judgment, you know yourself as objectified. If the subject is not objectified, the subject *qua* subject is not known in that absolute realm.

NOTES

1. "Cognitional. Structure," *CWL 4 Collection*, 211.
2. *CWL 3 Insight*, 380 (356).
3. *CWL 3 Insight*, 373 (348-349).
4. *CWL 3 Insight,* 373 (349).
5. *CWL 3 Insight*, 376 (352).
6. See *CWL 5 Understanding and Being*, 147: "Might there not be something so totally different from our categories of knowing that it could not possibly fall within the range of knowing of this type? At least we raise the question. . . . Is there an a priori limit to the questions we can ask, to the sort of thing we can desire to know? We can ask if there is anything beyond our total range. If we ask that, we have already asked a question about existence with regard to what lies beyond any hypothetical range one might like to set. Our range of interest extends beyond any finite limit that one cares to set. The mere fact that we make a hypothesis about a finite limit, any finite limit, to the range of possible questions reveals the unrestricted character of our knowing."
7. *CWL 5 Understanding and Being*, 148.
8. *CWL 3 Insight*, 379 (354). Cf. Lonergan's words in a review of a work by Emerich Coreth on metaphysics: "Thus Fr. Coreth would accept the principle, *Nihil in intellectu nisi prius fuerit in sensu*. But he would have to distinguish, say, between the way there is nothing in a box and the way there is nothing in a stomach. When there is nothing in a box, the box does not feel empty; when there is nothing in a stomach, the stomach does feel empty. Human intelligence is more like a stomach than like a box. Though it has no answers, and so is empty, still it can ask questions." "Metaphysics as Horizon," *CWL 4 Collection*, 201.

9. *CWL 3 Insight,* 380-381 (356).

10. *A Second Collection*, 269.

11. *CWL 3 Insight*, 400 (376).

12. *CWL 3 Insight*, 401 (376).

13. *CWL 3 Insight,* 401 (377).

14. *A Second Collection*, 76.

15. In *CWL 5 Understanding and Being*, 175-176, Lonergan brings up the case of illusions and hallucinations: "He does not have the freedom of control of the sensitive processes that permit correct judgment. You cannot settle this question of the difference between the given and the abnormally produced by saying that when you are normal you are able to take a look to see what is there, and when you are not normal you look and see what is not there. In either case, all you have is the look, and to know whether you are normal or abnormal you would have to have a super-look in which you would look not merely at your looking but at what it was looking at. The difficulty would recur with regard to the super-look. Some super-looks might be normal and others abnormal. There is no solution on the side of the look. The solution has to be on the side of inquiry, intelligence, working out the characteristics of abnormal and normal states, and making the judgment that when these characteristics arise the man is out of his head, and he will not be held responsible for what he says and does."

16. *CWL 3 Insight,* 404 (380).

17. *CWL 3 Insight,* 402 (378).

18. *CWL 3 Insight,* 402 (378).

19. *CWL 5 Understanding and Being*, 172 (my emphases).

20. *CWL 5 Understanding and Being*, 173.

Chapter Ten

Metaphysics

. . . there are those that resentfully and disdainfully brush aside the old questions of cognitional theory, epistemology, metaphysics. I have no doubt, I never did doubt, that the old answers were defective. But to reject the questions as well is…worse than mere neglect of the subject, and it generates a far more radical truncation. It is that truncation that we experience today not only without but within the Church, when we find that the conditions of the possibility of significant dialogue are not grasped, when the distinction between revealed religion and myth is blurred, when the possibility of objective knowledge of God's existence and of his goodness is denied.[1]

The four chapters on metaphysics were tough going. Part of me was amazed that any intelligent person would still believe in this stuff.

Metaphysics? What's metaphysics? Surely it's some esoteric field without any evident connection to ordinary living? Surely it's remote from the lives of real men and real women? Surely you can't be serious? Surely even within the Catholic Church that old insistence on a scholastic metaphysics has surrendered to engagement with the "real world?"

As it turned out, however, metaphysics for Lonergan just flowed from his cognitional theory and epistemology. If it was in fact true that the structure by which we de facto know anything flows through the processes of experiencing, understanding and judging (= cognitional theory), and that in fact through that activity we arrive at being (= epistemology), then it also follows that the structure of being proportionate to our knowing activity will parallel the structure of our knowing. In fact, Lonergan defines metaphysics as "the integral heuristic structure of proportionate being." He speaks in these chapters about "proportionate being," because he has not yet raised the question of transcendent being. Proportionate being is that towards which the pure desire to know directs our experiencing, understanding and judging. The structure of such proportionate being can be designated heuristically, and as it turns out, the heuristic terms designating the structure of proportionate being could be couched in terms I was familiar with from the scholastic tradition. Just as our knowing consists in experiencing, understanding and judging, so the known proportionate to our knowing will have a potential element, a formal element and an actual element.

judging	—	act
understanding	—	form
experiencing	—	potency

In Lonergan's formulation, however, these traditional scholastic terms will be translated into modern scientifically compatible categories and the "finality of being" will be translated into the upward finality of the scientifically discoverable universe. Such is exemplified primarily in the dynamism of human questioning and secondarily in what the sciences reveal to us of this upward finality. Such a vision, of course, will have a profound effect on one's anthropology, that is, one's vision of the human person. Lonergan ends his reflections on metaphysics with such implications for understanding the growth and development of the person and even the immortality of the person.

The key to all this, however, is one's basic method, one's basic method in metaphysics.

1. METHOD IN METAPHYSICS

As soon as you get into philosophical questions you get into conflicts. Conflicts between materialists, empiricists, idealists, relativists, pragmatists, realists. Consequently, for many the major question becomes simply "Who's to say?" "Who's to say" one philosophy is better than another? "Who's to say" that one metaphysics is true, another not? "Who's to say?" And since we can't determine "who's to say?" it's better to leave these kinds of questions to philosophers and get about our business.

But the fact is that philosophers have been exceptionally intelligent persons and even their mistakes can contribute to clarifying a basic fact. For any given philosophy can possess a significance that extends beyond the particular philosopher's own horizon and can in a real way contribute to the growth of the human family's understanding of itself.[2]

That is Lonergan's point in the chapter on method in metaphysics. A philosophy either gets it right or it doesn't. If it does not, it heads by its own inner logic to a more and more grotesque "counterposition." If it gets it right—especially on the nature of knowing, objectivity and reality—it invites further development.

For example, it might be the case that for the most part Plato, Aristotle and Aquinas got it right and, to the extent that they got it right, their work invites development. And it might also be the case that to a significant degree David Hume got it wrong, and to that extent his "counterpositions" invite reversal.

This, then, is Lonergan's basic method in metaphysics: by means of his basic stance on knowledge, objectivity and reality to distinguish *positions* as developing that basic stance and *counterpositions* as inviting its reversal. It will be a basic *position*,

1) if the real is the concrete universe of being and not a subdivision of the "already out there now";
2) if the subject becomes known when it affirms itself intelligently and reasonably and so is not yet known in any prior "existential" state; and
3) if objectivity is conceived as a consequence of intelligent inquiry and critical reflection, and not as a property of vital anticipation, extroversion, and satisfaction.[3]

On the other hand, it will be a basic *counterposition* if it contradicts any of these basic positions. As such, it will invite reversal. The conflict involved in a counterposition, then, is the conflict between content and performance: a conflict between the unintelligent and irrational content one is defending and the performance of attempting to do that intelligently and reasonably. The only coherent way to maintain a counterposition is that of the animal; for animals not only do not speak but also do not offer excuses for their silence. Counterpositions invite reversal, then, not merely because of an explicit contradiction with anyone else's thought, but in virtue of the implicit contradiction with the processes of one's own thought.

Lonergan gives Descartes' philosophy as an example. The basic position is the *cogito, ergo sum*, the implicit self-knowledge in all human knowing. On the other hand, the basic counterposition is the affirmation of the *res extensa*;

it is real as a subdivision of the "already out there now;" its objectivity is a matter of extroversion; knowing it is not a matter of inquiry and reflection. This counterposition invites reversal, not merely in virtue of its conjunction with the other component in Cartesian thought, but even when posited by itself in anyone's thought.

The history of philosophy, then, is a series of contributions to a single but complex goal: uncovering the structure of the human mind and, with it, the basic structure of the universe. "Reason" then, as humanity's awareness of its own intellectual capabilities, has gradually emerged in the persons of Parmenides and Pythagoras, Plato and Aristotle, Aquinas and Newman, etc.—and might we add, Lonergan?

In a section entitled "The Dialectic of Method in Metaphysics," Lonergan contrasts his method with other methods: methods of deduction, of universal doubt, empiricist methods, "common sense eclecticism" and scientism. For differences in metaphysical positions can be studied by examining differences in method.[4] There are, for example, the *deductive methods*, such as the metaphysics of "all possible worlds" of the medieval theologians, or Kant's transcendental deduction of "what the mind must be like" if it can arrive at Newton's scientific world-view. Lonergan's response to Kant is that he does not seem to have envisioned the problem in its full generality. It is not enough to account for Newton's deduction alone—Einstein's or for any other type of deductive system. What has to be accounted for is a series of concrete deductions, none of which is certain and each of which is only the best available scientific opinion of its time. Lonergan uses the analogy of a universal machine tool to describe the mind.

> The mind is not just a factory with a set of fixed processes; rather it is a universal machine tool that erects all kinds of factories, keeps adjusting and improving them, and eventually scraps them in favor of radically new designs.[5]

In other words, there is not some fixed set of *a priori* syntheses, as Kant would hold, from which all deductions must be made. On the contrary, every act of insight is an *a priori* synthesis and our knowing consists in insight following on insight to complement and correct its predecessor.

Nor is Descartes' "*universal doubt*" an adequate philosophical method, for not even the criterion of indubitability is indubitable.

> It is clear enough that one makes no mistake in accepting the indubitable. It is not at all clear that one makes no mistake in rejecting everything that in fact is true.[6]

And the results of such doubt, such "a leap in the dark" will be illusory. For doubting affects, not the underlying texture and fabric of the mind, but only the explicit judgments that issue from it.

> One can profess in all sincerity to doubt all that can be doubted, but one cannot abolish at a stroke the past development of one's mentality, one's accumulation of insights, one's prepossessions and prejudices, one's habitual orientation in life.[7]

Nor is *empiricism* with its precept, "*Observe the significant facts,*" an adequate method. For it amounts to the assumption that "what is obvious in knowing is what knowing obviously is."[8] Such an empiricist attitude can also affect scholastic philosophers. It can be discerned in Duns Scotus' view of intellectual abstraction as an unconscious co-operation of intellect and imagination in inspecting conceptual contents. Such was the scholastic view of knowing I was taught in my early training.

> Moreover, such intellectual empiricism reaches far beyond the confines of the Scotist school. The objective universals of Platonist thought seem to owe their origin to the notion that, as the eye of the body looks upon colors and shapes, so there is a spiritual eye of the soul that looks at universals, or at least recalls them.[9]

Nor was "*common sense eclecticism*" an adequate philosophical method— although at the time this sounded like something right down my alley. It fit in very well with the 1960s' tendency of "doing your own thing."

> If it rarely is adopted by original thinkers, it remains the inertial center of the philosophic process. From every excess and aberration men swing back to common sense, and perhaps no more than a minority of students and professors, of critics and historians, ever wander very far from a set of assumptions that are neither formulated nor scrutinized.[10]

Such a common sense philosophy lacks the purification and reorientation that only a critical philosophy can provide. Such an eclecticism encourages a wide exercise of judgment, neglecting the fact that understanding is prior to judging. Before one can pass judgment on any issue, one has to understand it. And "unless one endeavors to understand with all one's heart and all one's mind, one will not know what questions are relevant or when their limit is approached."[11] On the contrary, Lonergan summarizes the aim of his own method.

> . . . this procedure yields a metaphysics that brings to contemporary thought the wisdom of the Greeks and of the medieval schoolmen as reached by Aristotle and Aquinas, but purged of every trace of antiquated science, formulated to integrate not only the science of the present but also of the future, and elaborated in accord with *a method that makes it possible to reduce every dispute in the field of metaphysical speculation to a question of concrete psychological fact.*[12]

Finally, Lonergan treats of *scientific method* and the tendency of scientists to make erroneous extra-scientific judgments. Much of that tendency is due to the "traditionalist mentality" among scientists, especially in regard to reductionist interpretations of science. The perennial problem is the polymorphism of human consciousness and the tendency of scientists to misinterpret the meaning of the terms "knowledge," "objectivity" and "reality."[13] On the contrary, the contribution of science and of scientific method to philosophy lies in their unique ability to supply philosophy with instances of the heuristic structures which a metaphysics integrates into a single view of the concrete universe.[14]

In addition, there is a traditional and communitarian dimension to science. A great deal of "belief" goes into the scientific process. Scientific advances are accepted or rejected by the common judgments of the scientific community. The philosopher, on the other hand, has to *personally* decide between different philosophical traditions.

> For while philosophy has had its traditional schools from, it seems, the days of Pythagoras, still the schools have proliferated. Instead of a single tradition with distinct departments as in science, philosophy has been a cumulative multiplication of distinct and opposed traditions. Nor is there anything surprising about this contrast. For in science a single method operates towards a variety of different goals, but in philosophy a single all-inclusive goal is sought by as many different methods as arise from different orientations of the historically developing but polymorphic consciousness of man. Hence, while a scientist is reasonable in entering into the scientific tradition and carrying on its work, a philosopher cannot be reasonable on the same terms; he has to become familiar with different traditions; he has to find grounds for deciding between them; and it is the reasonableness of that decision on which will rest the reasonableness of his collaboration within any single tradition.[15]

That was my challenge as I studied in Rome in the mid-1960s. I was familiar with several philosophical traditions: scholastic traditions, existentialist traditions, and, as I did my doctoral research on Susanne K. Langer, Anglo-American, chiefly empiricist and naturalist, traditions. I was now also being exposed to Bernard Lonergan's philosophy. And I was being asked to decide between them. In words almost descriptive of what I was going through during those days Lonergan wrote:

> It follows that, while the reasonableness of each scientist is a consequence of the reasonableness of all, the philosopher's reasonableness is grounded on a personal commitment and on personal knowledge. For the issues in philosophy cannot be settled by looking up a handbook, by appealing to a set of experiments performed so painstakingly by so-and-so, by referring to the masterful presentation of overwhelming evidence in some famous work. Philosophic evidence is within the philosopher himself.[16]

Nor was this intellectual contest unconnected to what was going on in my life on the level of my own desires.

It is his own grasp of the dialectical unfolding of his own desire to know in its conflict with other desires that provides the key to his own philosophic development . . .

That was where I was at. It was an eminently personal issue.

Philosophy is the flowering of the individual's rational consciousness in its coming to know and take possession of itself. To that event its traditional schools, its treatises, and its history are but contributions; and without that event they are stripped of real significance.

2. INTEGRATING THE SCIENCES

Someone recently mentioned to me that by following the method outlined by Lonergan one enters a large museum filled with all kinds of interesting treasures: the various sciences, the arts, the various dimensions of human culture and consciousness, etc. What Lonergan's philosophy enables you to do is to "find your way" among all these areas. To discover any of these areas in detail you must study that area; but if you would find your way around the whole, you need some guide, some map—some interdisciplinary metaphysics. For Lonergan defines metaphysics in the following way.

Just as the notion of being underlies and penetrates and goes beyond all other notions, so also metaphysics is the department of human knowledge that underlies, penetrates, transforms, and unifies all other departments.[17]

In other words, metaphysics is the discipline that is the "scaffolding" that unites, integrates and transforms all the other disciplines. Metaphysics *underlies* all other departments of knowledge because its basis is the pure desire to know at the root of the all the sciences and all areas of common sense. So also it *penetrates* all other departments of knowledge, for all departments spring from a common source and seek a common compatibility and coherence. Finally, metaphysics *transforms* all other departments, for human consciousness is polymorphic and it always risks formulating its discoveries not as positions but as counterpositions.

In other words, one role of a genuine metaphysics is to transform the results of misconceived science and biased common sense. In so doing metaphysics unifies all other departments, "for other departments meet particular ranges of questions, but metaphysics is the original, total question, and it moves to the total answer by transforming and putting together all other answers."[18] In words reminiscent of John Henry Newman who wrote of philosophy as "the science of sciences," Lonergan says:

Metaphysics, then, is the whole *in* knowledge but not the whole *of* knowledge. A whole is not without its parts, nor independent of them, nor identical with them. So it is that, while the principles of metaphysics are prior to all other knowledge, still the attainment of metaphysics is the keystone that rests upon the other parts and presses them together in the unity of a whole.[19]

In other words, metaphysics builds on the current achievements of the various disciplines. This is why a contemporary metaphysics differs from medieval scholasticism: it deals with different materials, that is, the contemporary developments of scientific and scholarly knowledge.

As we mentioned initially, in these chapters on metaphysics Lonergan prescinds from the question of transcendent being, that is, what lies beyond the limits of human experience. In keeping with his program of addressing one question at a time, he leaves that question to the last chapter of *Insight*. Here his concern is with the structure of "*proportionate being*": that is, "whatever is to be known by human experience, intelligent grasp, and reasonable affirmation." The metaphysical study of such proportionate being moves from a latent stage to a problematic stage, and finally to an explicit stage. Since human knowing heads toward being, so explicit metaphysics aims at clarifying "the integral heuristic structure of proportionate being." The key to such an explicit metaphysics is an adequate self-knowledge by which the latent metaphysics present in human operations becomes explicit. The key is an intelligible and true account of our own intelligence and reasonableness. "The directives of the method must be issued by the self-affirming subject to himself."[20] As Lonergan puts it: *Metaphysics, then, is not something in a book but something in a mind.*[21]

The process from latent through problematic to explicit metaphysics must begin from the person as he or she is in his or her own native disorientation and bewilderment. It cannot begin by appealing to what people know, for what they know is quite often disoriented. Hence, it must begin by appealing to the desire that is prior to knowledge.

Since an appeal to disorientated knowledge would only extend and confirm the disorientation, the appeal must be to the desire that is prior to knowledge, that generates knowledge, that can effect the correction of miscarriages in the cognitional process. Still, it cannot be taken for granted that the subject knows his own desire and its implications; were there such knowledge, the disorientation would be remedied already; and so the initial appeal is to the desire, not as known, but as existing and operative. *The first directive, then, is to begin from interest, to excite it, to use its momentum to carry things along. In other words, the method of metaphysics primarily is pedagogical.*[22]

The method begins from a person's interest and goes on from there. As she proceeds, as she comes to know her own understanding, she will also come to understand the biases that are the sources of her own disorientation and bewilderment and in that process head toward an adequate understanding of herself.

At this point Lonergan made a statement that puzzled me. He states that the transition from latent to explicit metaphysics is based on the *isomorphism* that exists between the structure of the knowing and the structure of the known.

> If the knowing consists of a related set of acts and the known is the related set of contents of these acts, then the pattern of relations between the acts is similar in form to the pattern of the relations between the contents of the acts.[23]

In other word, just by understanding the structure of one's own knowing, one implicitly understands the structure in what can be known. I remember saying to myself:

> I don't know about this. Granted we know by means of experiencing, understanding and judging—why does that determine an *isomorphism*, a similarity of form or structure, between the knowing and the known?

Then I asked the key question:

> Can't I imagine a structure of "the known" different from the structure of my knowing? Why must they be *isomorphic*? Can't I imagine a case where they are not isomorphic, where the structure of the known differs from the structure of my knowing?

This was a question that bedeviled my reading and re-reading of Lonergan's chapters on metaphysics. I did not realize at the time that the question involved an oversight of insight.

3. THE METAPHYSICAL ELEMENTS

What then are the elements of metaphysics? In my undergraduate days I had learned of the Aristotelian "potency," "form" and "act" and those terms found their way into the systematic theology I had studied in Rome. Lonergan developed these terms and wrote of both "conjugate" and "central" potency, form and act: the conjugates that define levels of beings and the central potency, form and act of a particular thing. For example, while the central form of a human person is that which constitutes all the elements of the person into one thing, the conjugate forms of the person pertain to the physical, chemical, biological, psychological and intellectual elements within that one person.

But what exactly do these metaphysical terms refer to? What are they? Lonergan answers succinctly:

Clearly the answer has to be that the elements do not possess any essence, any "What is it?" of their own. On the contrary, they express the structure in which one knows what proportionate being is; *they outline the mold in which an understanding of proportionate being necessarily will flow*; they arise from understanding and they regard proportionate being, not as understood, but only as to be understood.[24]

There follows a very important corollary.

If one wants to know just what forms are, the proper procedure is to give up metaphysics and turn to the sciences; for forms become known inasmuch as the sciences approximate towards their ideal of complete explanation; and there is no method, apart from scientific method by which one can reach such explanation.[25]

This was a shock to my scholastic training. That training had implied that philosophers—and in particular, scholastic philosophers—had some sort of "intuition of forms" or even "intuition of being" that others did not have. To the contrary, Lonergan makes the point that the metaphysician is exposed to the ever-recurrent danger "of discoursing on quiddities without suspecting that 'quiddity' means what is to be known through scientific understanding."[26] Later in the chapter he writes of the "pseudo-metaphysical myth-making" that builds philosophical theories out of the descriptive knowledge of "seeing tables" and "touching chairs," etc.

One takes the descriptive conception of sensible contents, and without any effort to understand them one asks for their metaphysical equivalents. One bypasses the scientific theory of color or sound, for after all it is merely a theory and, at best, probable; one insists on the evidence of red, green, and blue, of sharp and flat; and one leaps to a set of objective forms without realizing that *the meaning of form is what will be known when the informed object is understood.*[27]

Such a blind leaping from descriptive knowledge to philosophical theory is antithetical not only to science, but also to philosophy.

The scientific effort to understand is blocked by a pretense that one understands already, and indeed in the deep, metaphysical fashion. But philosophy suffers far more, for the absence of at least a virtual transposition from the descriptive to the explanatory commonly is accompanied by counterpositions on reality, knowledge, and objectivity.[28]

The upshot is to allow science its freedom to follow out its own questions—a freedom that science has in fact appropriated during these last few centuries. On the other hand, this does not leave the philosopher without a role in relation to science. Rather, the role of the philosopher is to seek the unification and purification of scientific methods and their results and to mold that unity into a vision of the concrete goal of all human knowing.

> If the metaphysician must leave to the physicist the understanding of physics and to the chemist the understanding of chemistry, he has the task of working out for the physicist and chemist, for the biologist and the psychologist, the dynamic structure that initiates and controls their respective inquiries and, no less, the general characteristics of the goal towards which they head.[29]

The value of metaphysical analysis is that it provides the broadest possible set of concepts for dealing with the total goal of all the sciences. "Only the broadest possible set of concepts can provide the initial basis and the field of differences that will be adequate to dealing with a variable set of moving systems that regard the universe of being."[30]

But are these metaphysical elements merely cognitional or are they real? Are they merely the structure in which proportionate being is known? Or are they the structure immanent in the reality of proportionate being?[31] Lonergan's answer is that, because intelligibility is intrinsic to being—since it is the objective of the pure desire to know—the metaphysical elements express the real structure of being. "It follows that potency, form, and act assign not merely the structure in which being is known but also *the structure immanent in the very reality of being*."[32]

Again I was inclined to try to imagine a structure of reality different than the structure of our knowing reality.

4. THE FINALITY OF BEING

As I read through *Insight,* I did not get all the implications of Lonergan's metaphysics, but I did get the general idea. If human knowing consists in a structure of experiencing, understanding and judging, then the known proportionate to our knowing has a similar structure. Conveniently, Aristotelian and Thomistic thought spoke of "potency," "form" and "act." Lonergan retains these metaphysical terms and defines them in relation to the explanatory understanding of ourselves.

> "Potency" denotes the component of proportionate being to be known in fully explanatory knowledge by an intellectually patterned experience of the empirical residue.
>
> "Form" denotes the component of proportionate being to be known, not by understanding the names of things, nor by understanding their relations to us, but by understanding them fully in their relations to one another.

"Act" denotes the component of proportionate being to be known by uttering the virtually unconditioned yes of reasonable judgment.[33]

The existence of different types of heuristic methods indicates that there are different kinds of forms: *conjugate forms* that are the relations between things to be known by classical heuristic structure; and the *central forms* that are the "unity-identity-whole" statistically realized in data which make it possible to move from description to explanation of the same "thing" and to discern change in the same thing.

At this point, Lonergan technically re-casts what he had said earlier in *Insight* about the levels of explanatory knowledge resulting in the knowledge of explanatory genera and species. The issue can be framed by asking for the explanation of the actual existence of distinct sciences. Do the distinct sciences represent merely the dividing up of the same object, "matter?" Or do they reflect the fact that there are indeed higher levels of emerging "things" in the world?

To answer this question there is, on the one hand, the image of the sciences as dealing with the same "body"—"matter"—with every higher level as only a subdivision within the lowest level. On the other hand, there is the challenging fact of insight itself, which cannot be explained by being reduced to the level of experience and imagination. To explain the fact of other patterns of experience, as well as the de facto division of sciences, to explain the simple fact *"that the hypothetical reviser eats and breathes and walks on other things besides men,"* one must posit specifically different genera and species within this emerging world.

As I read this chapter I had in the back of my mind the dramatic vision of the physical universe described by Teilhard De Chardin. For Chardin the universe is a vast upwardly directed dynamism, stretching from the depths of matter to the human person, human community, and ultimately toward the "Omega Point" of divine love. Lonergan's approach was much less "poetic," but it complemented Chardin's wonderfully. Taking the sciences on their own terms as instances of human explanatory understanding, he wove them together into a vision of the whole of human knowing. That emerging vision was powerful.

On the lowest level there was what Lonergan called "prime potency." Each genus is limited by the preceding lower genus and so the lowest genus provides a principle of limitation for the whole domain of proportionate being.[34] Nevertheless, even though potency is conceived as a principle of limitation, it is also connected to the upward finality of all being. In passages reminiscent of Chardin Lonergan writes:

Indeed, since cognitional activity is itself but a part of this universe, so its heading to being is but the particular instance in which universal striving towards being becomes conscious and intelligent and reasonable.[35]

By finality we refer to a theorem of the same generality as the notion of being. This theorem affirms a parallelism between the dynamism of the mind and the dynamism of proportionate being. It affirms that the objective universe is not at rest, not static, not fixed in the present, but in process, in tension, fluid. As it regards present reality in its dynamic aspect, so it affirms this dynamism to be open. As what is to be known becomes determinate only through knowing, so what is to be becomes determinate only through its own becoming. But as present knowing is not just present knowing but also a moment in process towards fuller knowing, so also present reality is not just present reality but also a moment in process to fuller reality.[36]

Indeed, since cognitional activity is itself but a part of this universe, its striving to know being is but the intelligent and reasonable part of a universal striving towards being.[37]

Lonergan works out various characteristics of finality as the dynamism of the real. Among those characteristics two in particular have religious implications. One is that this directed dynamism is realistic.

Men are apt to judge the universe by anthropomorphic standards. They look for the efficiency of their machines, the economy of their use of materials and power, the security of their comprehensive plans, the absence of disease and death, of violence and pain, of abuse and repression that reflects the desires and the aspirations of their hearts. *But human utopias are paper schemes.* They postulate in the universe more perfect materials than those with which it builds. They suppose that the building can be some extrinsic activity apart from the universe itself. They forget that they themselves and all their great achievements and all their still greater hopes and dreams are but byproducts of the universe in its proper expansion in accord with its proper intelligibility.[38]

Furthermore, this finality of the universe is universal.

It is no less the sadness of failure than the joy of success. It is to be discerned no less in false starts and in breakdowns than in stability and progress. It is as much the meaning of aberration and corruption and decline as of sanity and honesty and development. For finality is an immanent intelligibility operating through the effective probability of possibility. Effective probability makes no pretense to provide an aseptic universe of chrome and plastic. Its trials will far outnumber its successes, but the trials are no less part of the program than the successes. Again, in human affairs finality does not undertake to run the world along the lines of a kindergarten; it does undertake to enlighten men by allowing their actions to have their consequences, that by this cumulative heaping of evidence men may learn; and if one tribe or culture, one nation or civilization, does not learn, finality will not stoop to coaxing and pleading; it lets things take their course, that eventually tribes and nations, cultures and civilizations may reach the degree of intelligent and rational consciousness necessary to carry forward the task of finality in transcending limitations.

5. HUMAN GROWTH AND DEVELOPMENT

Previously in *Insight* Lonergan had written of classical and statistical heuristic methods. Now he adds a third method: genetic method. It is this method that has "development" as its basic heuristic notion.

> As classical method anticipates an unspecified correlation to be specified, an indeterminate function to be determined, so genetic method finds its heuristic notion in development. In the plant there is the single development of the organism; in the animal there is the twofold development of the organism and the psyche; in man there is the threefold development of the organism, the psyche, and intelligence.[39]

All organic, psychic and intellectual development is from generic indeterminacy to specific perfection.

> Masses and electric charges, atoms and molecules, are statically systematic; their performance is not a function of their age; there is not a different law of gravitation for each succeeding century. In contrast, organic, psychic, and intellectual development involves a succession of stages; and in that succession the previously impossible becomes possible and the previously awkward and difficult becomes a ready routine. The infant can neither walk nor talk, and once we all were infants. Hence, where the physicist or chemist is out to determine single sets of conjugate forms and consequent schemes of recurrence, the biologist or psychologist or intellectual theorist is out to determine genetic sequences of conjugate forms and consequent sequences of flexible circles of schemes of recurrence.[40]

Hence the outstanding difference between classical and genetic method.

> Classical method is concerned to reduce regular events to laws. Genetic method is concerned with sequences in which correlations and regularities change. Accordingly, the principal object of genetic method is to master the sequence itself, to understand the development, and thereby to proceed from the correlations and regularities of one stage to those of the next.

Lonergan's vision of flexible circles of schemes of recurrence giving rise to successively higher integrations highlights the reason why quantitative methods applicable on lower levels lose their effectiveness when applied to higher levels.

In physics and chemistry, measuring is a basic technique that takes inquiry from the relations of things to our senses to their relations to one another. But when one mounts to the higher integrations of the organism, the psyche, and intelligence, one finds that measuring loses both in significance and efficacy. It loses in significance, for the higher integration is, within limits, independent of the exact quantities of the lower manifold it systematizes. Moreover, the higher the integration, the greater the independence of lower quantities, so that the meaning of one's dreams is not a function of one's weight, and one's ability in mathematics does not vary with one's height.[41]

As one goes up the scale from inorganic to organic, from the organic to the psychic, from the psychic to the intellectual, there exists a greater and greater freedom from the limitations of the underlying levels. Furthermore, the fuller the development on the higher level, the fuller the corresponding development on the lower level. "Thus, organic differentiation reaches its maximum in animals, and psychic differentiation reaches its maximum in man."[42] Or, as he articulates the same principle in other words:

> As it is not in the plant but in the animal that the full potentialities of organic diversity are realized, so it is not in the animal but in man that the full potentialities of a richly diverse and highly integrated sensitive consciousness are attained.

One need only think of a superior athlete — a Tiger Woods, for example — to identify this development of sensitive consciousness influenced and directed by intelligence. Finally, there is the exceptional freedom manifested by the proper development of intellect itself. While the higher system of the organism or of the psyche develops in an underlying material manifold of physical, chemical or biological events that are subject to their own proper laws, intelligence develops not in a material manifold but in the psychic representation of material manifolds. "Hence the higher system of intellectual development is primarily the higher integration, not of the man in whom the development occurs, but of the universe that he inspects."[43]

Within this metaphysical perspective there takes place human development. For a single human action can involve a series of components — physical, chemical, organic, neural, psychic, and intellectual — each occurring in accord with the laws and realized schemes of their appropriate levels. However, while physical and chemical laws tend to be static, higher correlations pertain to what Lonergan calls "systems on the move." Obviously there results the problem of formulating the heuristic structure of the investigation of this triply compounded development.

> What the existentialist discovers and talks about, what the ascetic attempts to achieve in himself, what the psychiatrist endeavors to foster in another, what

the psychologist aims at understanding completely, the metaphysician outlines in heuristic categories.[44]

What the metaphysician outlines in heuristic categories are the various organic, psychic and intellectual systems-on-the-move that constitute the levels of the human person. Furthermore, the initiation of development is one thing; its integrated completion is another. New Year's resolutions are notoriously fragile without the integrated cooperation of one's sensitive perceptiveness and feelings.

> . . . if one sincerely makes an excellent resolution about one's mode or style of behavior, the resolution is apt to remain sterile if the appropriate perceptiveness and feelings are not forthcoming and one does not know how to evoke them. Inversely, a development can begin in one's perceptiveness and feelings, yet it will remain frustrated if one fails to understand oneself, to plan the strategy, and to execute the tactics that secure congenial companionship or employment. Finally, the non-conscious neural basis can send up its signals that express a starved affectivity or other demands for fuller living, but the signals need an interpreter and the interpreter an intelligent and willing pupil.[45]

Hence, in understanding human development there is "the law of integration." The initiative of the development may be organic, psychic, intellectual or external, but the development will remain fragmentary until a certain correspondence between different levels is satisfied.

> The law of integration, then, is a declaration of what is meant by human development. Because man is a unity, his proper development is no more than initiated when a new scheme of recurrence is established in his outward behavior, in his thinking and willing, in his perceptiveness and feeling, in the organic and neural basis of his action. Generally speaking, such an initiation of development invites complementary adjustments and advances, and unless they are effected, either the initiated development recedes and atrophies in favor of the dynamic unity of the subject, or else that unity is sacrificed and deformed to make man a mere dumping ground for unrelated, un-integrated schemes of recurrence and modes of behavior.

One can only think of dieting fads, evoking commitment for a while but eventually surrendering to lower level entrenched habits. Furthermore there is the tension that emerges between the person as he or she is and the dynamic finality of being that calls one to change, to grow, to develop. One feels the tension.

> Now the tension that is inherent in the finality of proportionate being becomes in man a conscious tension. Present perceptiveness is to be enlarged, and the enlargement is not perceptible to present perceptiveness. Present desires and fears have to be transmuted, and the transmutation is not desirable to present desire but fearful to present fear.[46]

Furthermore, because psychic development is so much more extensive and intricate in man than in other animals, it is involved in "a more prolonged tension, and it is open to more acute and diversified crises." As I read this in Rome, I felt that *my* psychic development was indeed involved in acute and diversified crises. Furthermore, it was not just a case of my own personal crises; there were also the demands of a universal order of things.

Intellectual development rests upon the dominance of a detached and disinterested desire to know. It reveals to a man a universe of being in which he is but an item, and a universal order in which his desires and fears, his delight and anguish, are but infinitesimal components in the history of mankind. It invites man to become intelligent and reasonable not only in his knowing but also in his living, to guide his actions by referring them, not as an animal to a habitat, but as an intelligent being to the intelligible context of some universal order that is or is to be.

That is indeed a tall order.

Still, it is difficult for man, even in knowing, to be dominated simply by the pure desire, and it is far more difficult for him to permit that detachment and disin-terestedness to dominate his whole way of life. For the self as perceiving and feeling, as enjoying and suffering, functions as an animal in an environment, as a self-attached and self-interested center within its own narrow world of stimuli and responses. But the same self as inquiring and reflecting, as conceiving in-telligently and judging reasonably, is carried by its own higher spontaneity to quite a different mode of operation with the opposite attributes of detachment and disinterestedness. It is confronted with a universe of being in which it finds itself, not the center of reference, but an object coordinated with other objects and, with them, subordinated to some destiny to be discovered or invented, ap-proved or disdained, accepted or repudiated.

A "destiny" dictated by some universal order of things? Was that order and that destiny basically friendly? That question was put off until later in *Insight*. What is emphasized here is the opposition between the self-centered tendencies of our sensitive being and, on the other hand, the detachment and disinterestedness that characterize our openness to the universe.

Not only is the opposition complete but also it is ineluctable. As a man cannot divest himself of his animality, so he cannot put off the *eros* of his mind.

Nor are the pure desire and the sensitive psyche two things, one of them "I" and the other "It." They are the unfolding on different levels of a single, individual unity, identity, whole. Both are "I," and neither is merely "It." If my intelligence is mine, so is my sexuality. If my reasonableness is mine, so are my dreams.[47]

This was a consolation to read. For *my* sexuality and *my* dreams were certainly me; but so also was my intelligence, an intelligence massively exercised by struggling to read *Insight*. That struggle highlighted what Lonergan called *the law of genuineness*, the admission of the above tension into consciousness.

> Among the topics for questioning are one's own unconscious initiatives, their subsumption under the general order intelligence discovers in the universe of being, their integration in the fabric of one's habitual living.[48]

The whole of *Insight*, then, was an invitation to self-knowledge on every level. At the end of this section Lonergan explains why his treatment of genetic method had to be set within a metaphysical context. For it is only within that context that there can occur the integration of such notions as the finality of being, explanatory genera and species and the emergence and integration of the organic, psychic and intellectual development within the human person.

> . . . because genetic method is concerned with emergent trends, its object can be formulated only by introducing categories in which the notion of emergence and its implications are set forth adequately and with sufficient generality. Finally, it is for this reason that the account of genetic method had to await the discussion of metaphysics; and within this metaphysical context it has been found possible, I believe, to offer a single integrated view that finds its point of departure in classical method yet embraces biology, the psychology of behavior and depth psychology, existentialist reflection upon man, and fundamental elements in the theory of individual and social history, of morals and asceticism, of education and religion.[49]

In his various writings that would follow upon *Insight* Lonergan would pay tribute to and integrate into his metaphysical vision the contributions of such diverse writers as the world historians, Eric Voegelin and Arnold Toynbee; the existentialist and phenomenological philosophers, Karl Jaspers and Max Scheler; the psychologists, Abraham Maslow and Herbert Fingarette; the social ethicist, Gibson Winter; the historians of religions, Friedrich Heiler, Wilfred Cantwell Smith and Mircea Eliade, etc. The point of an adequate metaphysics is to be able to integrate these and other intelligent contributions into a single coherent viewpoint on human development.

6. IMMORTALITY

Within the field of metaphysical explanation there is the question, not only of the unity of the universe, but of the unity of the concrete human person. Previously, Lonergan had spoken not only of schemes of recurrence in the physical world, but also of organic, psychic and intellectual development. In the concrete human person intellectual activity is not only a higher integration of these underlying manifolds, but it is also engaged in understanding the contents of experience.

> By this shift from subjective acts to objective contents, it is headed towards the systematization, not of the particular animal that I am, but of the whole universe of being. And it is within its knowledge of the universe that knowledge of itself is attained, knowledge of its function in the universe is acquired, and the grounds for willing the execution of that function provided.[50]

Such self-knowledge leads to *the distinction between the intelligible and the intelligent.*

> . . . we not only are but also know ourselves. As known to ourselves, we are intelligible, as every other known is. But the intelligibility that is so known is also intelligence and knowing. It has to be distinguished from the intelligibility that can be known but is not intelligent and does not attain to knowledge in the proper human sense of that term.[51]

And herein lies the distinction between the material and the spiritual.

> Let us say that intelligibility that is not intelligent is material, and that intelligibility that is intelligent is spiritual. Then, inasmuch as we are material, we are constituted by otherwise coincidental manifolds of conjugate acts that unconsciously and spontaneously are reduced to system by higher conjugate forms. But inasmuch as we are spiritual, we are orientated towards the universe of being, know ourselves as parts within that universe, and guide our living by that knowledge.

Invoking elements from the first chapter of *Insight*, Lonergan indicates the precise element that differentiates these two types of intelligibility.

> The empirical residue, then, is at once what spiritual intelligibility excludes and what material intelligibility includes . . . the material can be defined as whatever is constituted by the empirical residue or is conditioned intrinsically by that residue.[52]

These explanatory definitions of the material and the spiritual are important, because they get beyond defining the material as what is "already out there now" and the spiritual as what is "already in here now." Furthermore, the spiritual is neither constituted by nor conditioned intrinsically by the empirical residue. Obviously our inquiry and insight demand something into which we inquire and gain insight and commonly that is sensitive experience.

But if sensible experience and so the empirical residue condition inquiry and insight, it is no less plain that that conditioning is extrinsic. Seeing is seeing color, and color is spatial, so that seeing is conditioned intrinsically by the spatial continuum. But insight is an act of understanding, and so far from being conditioned intrinsically by the empirical residue, understanding abstracts from it.[53]

It follows that the central form of the human person is spiritual; it is not intrinsically conditioned by prime potency, the metaphysical ground of the empirical residue. And from the spiritual nature of the human central form, there follows the question of the immortality of the human person. Can the human person exist as a unity without prime potency?

The question is one of possibility. . . . in fact man exists and functions physically, chemically, organically, and sensitively. But the question is whether the breakdown of his organic and sensitive living necessarily is the end of his identical existence. For if his central form is material, then it is conditioned intrinsically by the prime potency that in turn is bound up with his physical, chemical, organic being. But if his central form is spiritual, then it is not conditioned intrinsically by prime potency; and then, absolutely speaking, his central form could be separated from prime potency without ceasing to ground an existing unity and identity.[54]

This was indeed a "modest" conclusion to the question of the immortality of the human person; Lonergan does not dwell on it. The heuristic category of immortality is not "filled in," as the Biblical tradition does. But it is, nevertheless, a momentous conclusion with immense implications. Bound up with it as I struggled with these issues in 1966 was my own religious living and indeed, my own life.

Lonergan's conclusion results from the comprehensive nature of the spiritual. While the material cannot perform the role of the spiritual, the spiritual can perform the role and function of the material.

Were man's central form a material intelligibility, then it could not be intelligent and so could not be the center and ground of man's inquiry and insight, reflection and judgment. Inversely, though man's central form were a spiritual intelligibility, it could be the ground and center of his physical, chemical, organic, and sensitive conjugates; for the spiritual is comprehensive; what can embrace the whole universe through knowledge can provide the center and ground of unity in the material conjugates of a single man.[55]

NOTES

1. "The Subject," *A Second Collection*, 86.
2. *CWL 3 Insight*, 411-412 (386-387).

3. *CWL 3 Insight,* 413 (388).

4. *CWL 3 Insight,* 427 (402).

5. *CWL 3 Insight,* 430-431 (406).

6. *CWL 3 Insight,* 435 (409-410).

7. *CWL 3 Insight,* 436 (410-411).

8. *CWL 3 Insight,* 441 (416).

9. *CWL 3 Insight,* 438 (412-413).

10. *CWL 3 Insight,* 441 (416).

11. *CWL 3 Insight,* 444 (419).

12. *CWL 3 Insight,* 448 (423).

13. *CWL 3 Insight,* 454 (430).

14. *CWL 3 Insight,* 455 (430).

15. *CWL 3 Insight,* 453 (428-429).

16. *CWL 3 Insight,* 453-454 (429).

17. *CWL 3 Insight,* 415 (390).

18. *CWL 3 Insight,* 416 (381).

19. Cf. Lonergan's references to Newman's theorem on the unity of knowledge in *A Second Collection,* 141-142.

20. *CWL 3 Insight,* 423 (398).

21. *CWL 3 Insight,* 421 (396).

22. *CWL 3 Insight,* 422-423. (397-398).

23. *CWL 3 Insight,* 424.

24. *CWL 3 Insight,* 521 (498).

25. *CWL 3 Insight,* 521 (498).

26. *CWL 3 Insight,* 533 (509).

27. *CWL 3 Insight,* 528 (505).

28. *CWL 3 Insight,* 529 (505).

29. *CWL 3 Insight,* 522 (498).

30. *CWL 3 Insight,* 532 (508).

31. *CWL 3 Insight,* 522-523 (499).

32. *CWL 3 Insight,* 525 (501).

33. *CWL 3 Insight,* 457 (432).

34. See *CWL 3 Insight,* 468 (442): "Accordingly, as judgment is limited by insight, and insight by data, so act is limited by form, and form is limited by potency. It will be convenient to introduce the name "prime potency" to denote the potency of the lowest level that provides the principle of limitation for the whole range of proportionate being."

35. *CWL 3 Insight,* 471 (445).

36. *CWL 3 Insight,* 470-471 (445).

37. *CWL 3 Insight,* 470 (445).

38. *CWL 3 Insight,* 473-474 (448).

39. *CWL 3 Insight,* 484 (459).

40. *CWL 3 Insight,* 486 (460-461).

41. *CWL 3 Insight,* 488 (463).

42. *CWL 3 Insight,* 492 (468).

43. *CWL 3 Insight,* 494 (469).
44. *CWL 3 Insight,* 494-495 (470).
45. *CWL 3 Insight,* 496-497 (472).
46. *CWL 3 Insight,* 498 (473).
47. *CWL 3 Insight,* 499 (474).
48. *CWL 3 Insight,* 501 (477).
49. *CWL 3 Insight,* 503-504 (479).
50. *CWL 3 Insight,* 539 (515).
51. *CWL 3 Insight,* 539 (516).
52. *CWL 3 Insight,* 540 (516-517).
53. *CWL 3 Insight,* 541 (517).
54. *CWL 3 Insight*, 542-543 (519).
55. *CWL 3 Insight*, 543 (519).

Chapter Eleven

The Ethical

I will be brief on the ethical implication of Lonergan's metaphysics as he brings these out in chapter eighteen. For the ethical flows from the metaphysical: the "ought" from the "is." Because the universe is a certain way, human activity must fit in with that structure; otherwise disaster looms.

But how understand all this? How understand "conscience?" How spell this out?

Lonergan points to the obvious fact that human understanding takes place within the context of emerging human community. Such community is structured by creative understanding as human beings strive to survive and to progress. Repeating the distinction he had made in the chapter on common sense, Lonergan distinguishes between "the good as the object of desire" and "the good of order." The latter notion arises to the extent that we are capable of insight.

> Besides the good that is simply object of desire, there is the good of order. Such is the polity, the economy, the family as an institution. It is not the object of any single desire, for it stands to single desires as system to systematized, as universal condition to particulars that are conditioned, as scheme of recurrence that supervenes upon the materials of desires and the efforts to meet them and, at the price of limited restrictions, through the fertility of intelligent control, secures an otherwise unattainable abundance of satisfactions.[1]

Oh, so that's "the good of order!"—the good that penetrates the various institutions in my life. It is the good as set in motion through intelligent cooperation through shared insights and patterns of shared activities. People often speak of the necessity of "delayed gratification" in order to achieve something down the road. Well, institutions of their nature demand from individuals "limited restrictions" that result in "an otherwise unattainable abundance of satisfactions."

This good of order is dynamic. It is a "system on the move" that "possesses its own normative line of development. Elements of the idea of order are grasped by insight into concrete situations, are formulated in proposals, are accepted by explicit or tacit agreements, and are put into execution only to change the situation and give rise to still further insights. Such is the wheel of progress.

Still, this normative line of development is only an approximation to the actual course of social development. There are the obvious disturbances brought about by bias. This brings to light a third dimension of the good, that is, value. As Lonergan would put it elsewhere, little children fight over particular goods, grown-ups fight over the good of order. Which good of order is best? Individualism or socialism? Conservatism or liberalism? The politics of the left or the right? We make our choices on the basis of value.

> Individualism and socialism are neither food nor drink, neither clothes nor shelter, neither health nor wealth. They are constructions of human intelligence, possible systems for ordering the satisfaction of human desires. Still, men can embrace one system and reject others. They can do so with all the ardor of their being, though the issue regard neither their own individual advantage nor that of their relatives, friends, acquaintances, countrymen.[2]

In other words, the value, goodness and intelligibility of a particular line of human action can dawn upon the human person in such a way that she becomes willing to initiate a new way of acting and living. "Willingness" and "unwillingness" refer to the antecedent dispositions to make choices and decisions of a particular kind. Unless one has the willingness to give up smoking, one needs to go through the laborious process of being persuaded—and allowing oneself to be persuaded—to give up smoking. Only in this way is the habit of not smoking established. Such is the way that rationality extends itself into the area of human activity.

> The detached, disinterested, unrestricted desire to know grasps intelligently and affirms reasonably not only the facts of the universe of being but also its practical possibilities. Such practical possibilities include intelligent transformations not only of the environment in which man lives but also of man's own spontaneous living.

So it is that the detached and disinterested desire to know would extend its sphere of influence through the field of knowledge into the field of deliberate human acts. So it is that the empirically, intelligently, rationally conscious subject of self-affirmation becomes a morally self-conscious subject. The human person is not only a knower but also a doer. The same intelligent and rational consciousness grounds the doing as well as the knowing; "and from that identity of consciousness there springs inevitably an exigence for self-consistency in knowing and doing."

"An exigence for self-consistency in knowing and doing." How can this exigency be met? It is difficult enough for purely cognitional activities to be dominated by the detached and disinterested desire to know. How can such detachment and disinterestedness be extended into concrete human living? Even though meeting this exigence is obviously difficult—at times excruciatingly difficult—nevertheless the fact of this exigence can be discerned in the many ways people seek to dodge it. And the first and most common escape is to *avoid self-consciousness*: to pour oneself out into "external" activity and to avoid reflection. A second way of dodging this demand for consistency in knowing and doing is rationalization.

> Inconsistency between knowing and doing can be removed by revising one's knowing into harmony with one's doing. Such a revision is, of course, a bold step. Not a little ingenuity is needed to transpose inconsistency between knowing and doing into inconsistency within knowing itself . . . and so the majority of men, instead of attempting rationalization themselves, are content to create an effective demand, a welcoming market, for more or less consistently developed counter-positions presented in myths and philosophies.[3]

The third way of dodging the conscious demand for consistency between knowing and doing is moral renunciation.

> It is content with a speculative acknowledgment of the aspiration to make one's own living intelligent and reasonable. It is ready to confess its wrong doing, but it has given up any hope of amending its ways. If you please, it is very human; yet it is also incompletely human, for the demand for consistency between knowing and doing is dynamic; it asks to be operative; it seeks to extend detachment and disinterestedness into living.

Lonergan, therefore, derives the meaning of the word "ought" from the meaning of the word "is." Because things are the way they are, I can only be fully rational if I live in accord with what is. In the long run, the sanction for the violation of moral consciousness is self-destruction.

The method of ethics, then, parallels the method of metaphysics. Such an ethical method "not only sets forth precepts but also bases them on their real principles, which are not propositions or judgments but existing persons."[4] Such a method, rooted in the dynamics of the person and the structure of being, steers a sane course between relativism and legalism.

. . . finally, because such a method clearly grasps an unchanging dynamic structure immanent in developing subjects that deal with changing situations in correspondingly changing manners, it can steer a sane course between the relativism of mere concreteness and the legalism of remote and static generalities; and it can do so, not by good luck nor by vaguely postulating prudence, but methodically, because it takes its stand on the ever recurrent dynamic generality that is the structure of rational self-consciousness.[5]

This indeed was what I was searching for at the time: some middle course between the "static generalities" often espoused by many religious people, and on the other hand, the total relativism that seemed characteristic of the secular world. Moral values were to be found in the province of developing personhood and conscience.

Because such a human good takes place within the good in general, the objects of our desires are not an isolated manifold but are inextricably bound up with the universe of proportionate being. The intelligible orders that are invented and improved by men are but further exploitations of pre-human intelligible orders and they fall within the universal order of emergent probability.

Such a broad generalization might give rise to the suspicion that one is being tricked into an easy optimism that denies the rather evident fact of evil. Lonergan replies to this objection by starkly re-asserting the transcendence of intelligence over feelings.

Accordingly, it will not be amiss to assert emphatically that the identification of being and the good bypasses human feelings and sentiments to take its stand exclusively upon intelligible order and rational value. Feelings and sentiments are bypassed for, though one begins from objects of desire, one finds the potential good not in them alone but in the total manifold of the universe.

Accordingly, the hedonist will define good and evil merely on the basis of desires and fears, the level of unquestioning experience.[6] Only by allowing questions to emerge can the way be open to the discovery that indifferent objects and even objects of aversion can also be potentially good. Our questioning can raise the possibility that even our pains can be good. This is reminiscent of Ignatius of Loyola's *Spiritual Exercises* where Ignatius counsels "indifference" in regard to "health or sickness, riches or poverty, honor or dishonor, a long life or a short life."

In words that Lonergan would often use through the years, there is "a succession of enlargements of consciousness," a succession of transformations of what consciousness means. Waking replaces dreaming; intelligent inquiry emerges in waking; critical reflection follows upon understanding; and a further enlargement of consciousness consists in the conscious subject (1) demanding conformity of his doing to his knowing, and (2) acceding to that demand by deciding reasonably.[7]

This enlargement and transformation of consciousness sheds light on the notion of *responsibility*. Human freedom possesses not only the negative aspect of excluding necessity but also the positive aspect of responsibility. "Though the act of will is a contingent emergence, it also is an act of the subject; the measure of the freedom with which the act occurs also is the measure of his responsibility for it."[8]

Lonergan begins a section on "the problem of liberation" by pointing to our obvious lack of effective freedom. "Thus, one may be essentially but not effectively free to give up smoking."[9] What is necessary for effective freedom is an ever deepening willingness to seek and implement the good. But what is "willingness?" Willingness is the state in which persuasion is not needed to bring one to a decision.

> Now the function of willingness runs parallel to the function of the habitual accumulation of insights. What one does not understand yet, one can learn; but learning takes time, and until that time is devoted to learning, otherwise possible courses of action are excluded. Similarly, when antecedent willingness is lacking, persuasion can be invoked; but persuasion takes time, and until that time is devoted to persuading oneself or to being persuaded by others, one remains closed to otherwise possible courses of action.[10]

So it is that in the abstract a person may be ready for any good deed or exploit. On second thought, however, "when the pressure is on," when caught unawares, she settles back into narrow and comfortable routines defined by her antecedent willingness. For unless one's antecedent willingness has the height and breadth and depth of the unrestricted desire to know, the emergence of rational self-consciousness involves a restriction upon one's effective freedom.

The point is that effective freedom has to be won. And the key point in reaching such freedom is to reach a willingness to persuade oneself and to submit to the persuasion of others. For only then one can be persuaded to a universal willingness so that one becomes antecedently willing to learn all there is to be learnt about willing and learning and about the enlargement of one's freedom from external constraints and psycho-neural interferences.

> But to reach the universal willingness that matches the unrestricted desire to know is indeed a high achievement, for it consists not in the mere recognition of an ideal norm but in the adoption of an attitude towards the universe of being, not in the adoption of an affective attitude that would desire but not perform but in the adoption of an effective attitude in which performance matches aspiration.[11]

The issue is how to be persuaded to openness when one is not yet open to persuasion? For the human person develops on lower organic and psychic levels before he develops intellectually and rationally. The higher integrations suffer the disadvantage of emerging later; they are the demands of finality upon us before they are realities in us. "They are manifested more commonly in aspiration and in dissatisfaction with oneself than in the rounded achievement of complete genuineness, perfect openness, universal willingness."[12]

For our being is being in process. Human existence is developing and this basic indeterminately directed dynamism of our consciousness gropes toward what does not meet the eye. It is without the settled assurance and efficacy of determined form and so "it tends to be shouldered out of the busy day, to make its force felt in the tranquility of darkness, in the solitude of loneliness, in the shattering upheavals of personal or social disaster."

How many "conversions" take place in response to personal suffering? How often even tragedies are recalled as "blessings in disguise," because in and through them, we grew as persons? There arises then, the issue of moral impotence.

> To assert moral impotence is to assert that man's effective freedom is restricted, not in the superficial fashion that results from external circumstance or psychic abnormality, but in the profound fashion that follows from incomplete intellectual and volitional development. . . . And the less developed one is, the less one appreciates the need of development and the less one is willing to take time out for one's intellectual and moral education.[13]

This consciousness of moral impotence not only heightens the tension between limitation and transcendence but it also can provide ambivalent materials for reflection.

> . . . correctly interpreted, it brings home to man the fact that his living is a developing, that he is not to be discouraged by his failures, that rather he is to profit by them both as lessons on his personal weaknesses and as a stimulus to greater efforts; but the same data can also be regarded as evidence that there is no use trying, that moral codes ask the impossible, that one has to be content with oneself as one is.

This inner tension and its ambivalence are reflected and heightened in the social sphere. As individuals, so societies fail to distinguish sharply and accurately between positions and counterpositions. As individuals, so societies fail to reach the universal willingness that reflects and sustains the detachment and disinterestedness of the unrestricted desire to know.

> But good will is never better than the intelligence and reasonableness that it implements. Indeed, when proposals and programs only putatively are intel-

ligent and reasonable, then the good will that executes them so faithfully and energetically is engaged really in the systematic imposition of ever further evils on the already weary shoulders of mankind.[14]

No doubt, a subtle and protracted analysis can bring to light the components in that polymorphic fact and proceed to a dialectical criticism of any proposal or program. But to whom does it bring the light? To how many? How clearly and how effectively? Lonergan asks Plato's question:

Are philosophers to be kings or kings to learn philosophy? Are they to rule in the name of wisdom subjects judged incapable of wisdom? Are all the members of our democracies to be philosophers? Is there to be a provisional dictatorship while they are learning philosophy?[15]

He summarizes the problem of liberation.

The elements in the problem are basically simple. Man's intelligence, reasonableness, and willingness (1) proceed from a detached, disinterested, unrestricted desire to know, (2) are potentialities in process of development towards a full effective freedom, (3) supply the higher integration for otherwise coincidental manifolds on successively underlying psychic, organic, chemical, and physical levels, (4) stand in opposition and tension with sensitive and intersubjective attachment, interest, and exclusiveness, and (5) suffer from that tension a cumulative bias that increasingly distorts immanent development, its outward products, and the outer conditions under which the immanent development occurs.

Lonergan states the problem succinctly: "Essentially the problem lies in an incapacity for sustained development." The problem is radical, permanent and independent of underlying manifolds. Nor is it primarily a social problem. Even though it results in the social surd and receives from the social surd its aggravating cumulative character, its roots are elsewhere. Hence, a revolution can sweep away old evils and initiate a fresh effort; but the fresh effort will occur through the same common human structure and will lead to essentially the same human results.[16] Nor is the problem to discover a correct philosophy, ethics, or human science.

For such discoveries are quite compatible with the continued existence of the problem. The correct philosophy can be but one of many philosophies, the correct ethics one of many ethical systems, the correct human science an old or new view among many views. But precisely because they are correct, they will not appear correct to minds disorientated by the conflict between positions and counterpositions. Precisely because they are correct, they will not appear workable to wills with restricted ranges of effective freedom. Precisely because they are correct, they will be weak competitors for serious attention in the realm of practical affairs.

The problem is real and its dimensions are the dimensions of human history.

> . . . and the fourth, fifth, and sixth volumes of Arnold Toynbee's *Study of History* illustrate abundantly and rather relevantly the failure of self-determination, the schism in the body social, and the schism in the soul that follow from an incapacity for sustained development.[17]

All along Lonergan has spoken of the need for higher viewpoints. Here again he invokes this category.

> The solution has to be a still higher integration of human living. For the problem is radical and permanent; it is independent of the underlying physical, chemical, organic, and psychic manifolds; it is not met by revolutionary change, nor by human discovery, nor by the enforced implementation of discovery; it is as large as human living and human history. Further, the solution has to take people just as they are. If it is to be a solution and not a mere suppression of the problem, it has to acknowledge and respect and work through man's intelligence and reasonableness and freedom. It may eliminate neither development nor tension yet it must be able to replace incapacity by capacity for sustained development. Only a still higher integration can meet such requirements.

This chapter on ethics explained "the pull of conscience" within me. It put words on the moral impotence and the need for freedom I was experiencing. It opened me up to look for help, for "grace," in becoming not just essentially, but effectively, free. It pointed me toward the mercy and healing grace of God.

NOTES

1. *CWL 3 Insight*, 619-620 (596).
2. *CWL 3 Insight*, 621 (597-598).
3. *CWL 3 Insight*, 622-623 (599-600).
4. *CWL 3 Insight*, 627 (604).
5. *CWL 3 Insight*, 627-628 (604).
6. *CWL 3 Insight*, 630 (606).
7. *CWL 3 Insight*, 637 (613).
8. *CWL 3 Insight*, 642 (619).
9. *CWL 3 Insight*, 643 (620).
10. *CWL 3 Insight*, 646 (623).
11. *CWL 3 Insight*, 647 (624).
12. *CWL 3 Insight*, 648 (625).
13. *CWL 3 Insight*, 650 (627).
14. *CWL 3 Insight*, 652 (629).
15. *CWL 3 Insight*, 653 (630).
16. *CWL 3 Insight*, 654 (631).
17. *CWL 3 Insight*, 655 (632).

Chapter Twelve

God

The question about God is much more important than the proof of God, because at the present time people deny that the question exists.[1]

1. AN UNRESTRICTED ACT OF UNDERSTANDING

Of course, the most significant implication flowing from the self-affirmation of the knower concerned the existence of God. This was the question I had wrestled with as a young man in the 1950s, staying up into the early hours of the morning with my friends in the dormitory at Seton Hall, reflecting on the "proofs" for the existence of God. In Rome in the 1960s a much more existential turn of things had tended to downplay the importance of such proofs. The emphasis was on personal faith, considered deeper than any "proof."

Still, in the midst of the intellectual challenges from atheistic philosophers, Sartre and others, and in the midst of conflicts in the church, the issue of an intellectual vindication of the existence of God remained. I did not articulate it to myself very clearly at the time, but the question remained as an undertow.

Lonergan, however, in chapter nineteen of *Insight* seemed to give the issue another twist. He seemed to say that in order to come to intellectual clarity about the existence of God, you had to come to intellectual clarity about other issues first, primarily the issue of your own self.

As in each of the previous chapters, Lonergan's aim in this chapter is limited. Following Aquinas, his concern is not to know "what God is"—an impossible task—but rather, merely to know "that God is." He begins with the notion of "transcendence" which he says has been implicit in everything

179

so far. For the very being of our humanity is a "going beyond": going beyond experience to understanding and beyond experience and understanding to judging; and beyond any particular realm of common sense, science or philosophy to asking further questions. "Clearly, despite the imposing name, transcendence is the elementary matter of raising further questions."[2]

And these questions we raise are rooted in the detached, disinterested and unrestricted desire to know. Such desire involves the rejection of all obscurantism, all attempts to limit our questioning.

Certainly, this unrestricted desire is accompanied by a limited capacity to attain knowledge and so we have the *fact* that the range of possible questions is greater than the range of possible answers. This fact results in the requirement that we critically survey possible questions so that we can know which questions can and cannot be answered.[3] Among the questions to which answers are possible is the question of transcendent being. For that question is rooted in the "extrapolation" from proportionate being to transcendent being. The question that leads to this extrapolation is "What is being?" and only an unrestricted act of understanding can answer that question.

> For being is completely universal and completely concrete; apart from it, there is nothing; and so knowledge of what being is cannot be had in anything less than an act of understanding everything about everything. . . . Only the content of the unrestricted act of understanding can be the idea of being, for it is only on the supposition of an unrestricted act that everything about everything is understood.[4]

We can answer the question, "What is being?" then, not by having an unrestricted act of understanding, but by determining heuristically a number of features of that unrestricted act of understanding. For one thing, it is absolutely transcendent, for it leaves no question unanswered. Furthermore, it is identical with the intelligible and the good. It is one idea, but it is of the many; immaterial but of the material; non-temporal but of the temporal; non-spatial but of the spatial.

As I read this characterization of the unrestricted act of understanding, I remember thinking how many of these qualifications flowed from the characteristics of insight highlighted in chapter one of *Insight*.

> Again, there is no paradox in affirming that the idea of being is one, immaterial, non-temporal, and non-spatial, yet of the many, the material, the temporal, and the spatial. For what is possible in the content of restricted acts of understanding is not beyond the attainment of unrestricted understanding. But our understanding is one yet of many, for in a single act we understand the whole series of positive integers. Similarly, it is immaterial, for it abstracts from the empirical residue, yet of the material, for it advances in understanding of this universe. Again,

while it is involved in an ordinal time, for it develops, it is not involved in the continuous time of local motion, for its development is not through a sequence of non-countable stages. Finally, while it pertains to a spatially conditioned subject, it is non-spatial, for it deals with the non-countable multiplicity of space through invariants that are independent of particular spatial standpoints.[5]

Lonergan distinguishes between a primary component in the idea of being and a secondary component. The primary component is grasped inasmuch as there is a single act of understanding; the secondary component is understood inasmuch as the primary component is grasped. For the one is not identical with the many, nor the immaterial with the material, nor the non-temporal with the temporal. But in the one idea there are to be grasped many beings; in the immaterial, the material; in the non-temporal, the temporal, etc. "For just as the infinite series of positive integers is understood inasmuch as the generative principle of the series is grasped, so the total range of beings is understood inasmuch as the one idea of being is grasped."

Since the primary component is identical with the unrestricted act of understanding, the primary component consists in the unrestricted act's understanding of itself. The secondary component consists in the unrestricted act's understanding of everything else because it understands itself. The unrestricted act of understanding does not need deduction or prediction to arrive at knowledge of the concrete universe, because it already holds in a single view, in its knowledge of itself, all that can be known about the concrete universe.

> Again, unrestricted understanding could predict only if some events were present relative to it and other events were future relative to it; but unrestricted understanding is non-temporal; it is, so to speak, outside the totality of temporal sequences, for that totality is part of the everything about everything else that it grasps in understanding itself; and as it grasps everything about everything else in a single view, so it grasps the totality of temporal sequences in a single view.[6]

2. CAUSALITY AND THE INTELLIGIBILITY OF BEING

Now "causality" is the connecting link between the idea of an unrestricted act of understanding and the affirmation that there is such an unrestricted act. In general, causality denotes the objective and real counterpart of the questions raised by the detached, disinterested, and unrestricted desire to know. Internal causes are the central and conjugate potency, form and act which Lonergan has analyzed throughout *Insight*. External causes are efficient, final and exemplary. An example of such external causes would be a community building a bridge across a river in order to be in contact with communities on the other side. The final cause would be the use the bridge would have for the community; the efficient cause would be the work of building it; and the exemplary cause would be the design grasped and conceived by the engineer.

But the question can be asked, are such exemplary, efficient and final causes instances of a universally applicable principle, a principle purged of anthropomorphic notions and capable of bearing human knowledge from the realm of proportionate being to that of transcendent being?[7] Lonergan's answer is in the affirmative and the reason is that "being is intelligible." What is apart from being is nothing, and so what is apart from intelligibility is nothing.

> It follows that to talk about mere matters of fact that admit no explanation is to talk about nothing. If existence is mere matter of fact, it is nothing. If occurrence is mere matter of fact, it is nothing.

One cannot, therefore, confine human knowledge within the domain of proportionate being without condemning it to mere matters of fact without explanation and so stripping it of knowledge not only of transcendent but also of proportionate being itself. In other words, every positivism, every assertion of the intelligible without meaning, is involved essentially in the counterpositions.[8]

Such is the core of Lonergan's argument, and it can be given as many applications as there are distinct features of proportionate being.[9] He links his argument to the value of the universe, an actual order whose selection is due to rational choice.[10] Since the universe is "shot through" with contingence, it demands an explanation that is not necessitated and is not arbitrary.[11]

3. CONTINGENT PREDICATION

When the implications of Lonergan's notion of an unrestricted act of understanding are worked out, it becomes obvious that it is one and the same thing to understand what being is and to understand what God is. Lonergan enumerates twenty-six attributes of the notion of God. Among those attributes are the following. The primary intelligible that is God is also the primary truth.

> [B]y identity, it would be a reflective act of understanding grasping itself as unconditioned and therefore correct and true; and so, by identity, the primary intelligible would be also the primary truth.[12]

The primary intelligible and truth is also the primary good to be loved. In a completely perfect spiritual being the primary intelligible is identical not only with an unrestricted act of understanding but also with a completely perfect act of affirming the primary truth and a completely perfect act of loving the primary good. This act of affirming and this act of loving are not distinct from the unrestricted act of understanding, for if they were, then the primary being would be incomplete and imperfect and in need of further acts of affirming and loving to be completed and perfected.

> Hence, one and the same reality is at once unrestricted understanding and the primary intelligible, reflective understanding and the unconditioned, perfect affirming and the primary truth, perfect loving and the primary good.[13]

Lonergan makes the point that, unlike the human person whose development consists in ever further acts, the absolutely perfect primary being does not develop. The unrestricted act understands and affirms and wills contingent beings to be, without any increment or change in its own reality.[14]

How about when we say that "God acts?" or that he does this or that? Does not this mean that God changes? Lonergan's answer is that "contingent predication" concerning God is an "extrinsic denomination." It was an issue he had emphasized in my early theology classes at the Gregorian.

> In other words, God is intrinsically the same whether or not he understands, affirms, wills, causes this or that universe to be. If he does not, then God exists and nothing else exists. If he does, God exists and the universe in question exists; the two existences suffice for the truth of the judgments that God understands, affirms, wills, effects the universe. . . .

Furthermore, though the extrinsic denominator is temporal, the contingent predication concerning God can be eternal.

> For an eternal act is timeless; in it all instants are one and the same instant; and so what is true at any instant is true at every instant. Hence, if at any instant it is true that God understands, affirms, wills the existence of Alexander's horse Bucephalus, then the metaphysical conditions of the truth are the existence of God and the existence of Bucephalus; moreover, though Bucephalus exists only for a short period, still God eternally understands, affirms, and wills Bucephalus to exist for that short period.[15]

Unlike other accounts which ascribe divine control of events to the fact that God by a peculiar activity controls each event, on this account God controls each event because he controls all, and he controls all because *he alone can be the cause of the order of the universe on which every event depends.*[16]

In this light also human knowledge and action take on a new significance. True knowledge not only is true, but it is also an apprehension of the divinely ordained order of the universe. Also, human action consistent with true knowing is also human cooperation with God in the realization of the order of the universe. "Inversely, error becomes a deviation not only from truth but also from God, and wrongdoing takes on the character of sin against God."[17]

Lonergan concludes this section on the notion of God with the characteristic that God is personal.

> An unrestricted act of rational self-consciousness, however objectively and impersonally it has been conceived, clearly satisfies all that is meant by the subject, the person, the other with an intelligence and a reasonableness and a willing that is his own.[18]

4. PROOFS FOR THE EXISTENCE OF GOD

I remember coming to the core of this chapter. It was Lonergan's variation on the "proofs" for the existence of God. In the context of the times and the diffidence about the proofs for the existence of God, I was amazed that he was scaling this peak.

> The existence of God, then, is known as the conclusion to an argument, and while such arguments are many, all of them, I believe, are included in the following general form. *If the real is completely intelligible, God exists. But the real is completely intelligible. Therefore, God exists.* [19]

Lonergan goes on to spell out this argument in detail. Commenting on the premise that the real is completely intelligible, Lonergan notes that the only possibility of complete intelligibility lies in a spiritual intelligibility that cannot inquire because it understands everything about everything. And such unrestricted understanding is the idea of being.[20] And if the idea of being exists, God exists. For if the idea of being exists, at least its primary component exists. But the primary component has been shown to possess all the attributes of God.[21]

Such then, is Lonergan's argument—and it obviously runs counter to "the widely diffused contemporary view that the existence of God cannot be proved." As a set of signs printed in a book, it can do no more than indicate the materials for a reflective grasp of the virtually unconditioned. "To elicit such an act is the work that the reader has to perform for himself."

The whole thing hung together.

> . . . if I am operating in the intellectual pattern of experience, if I am genuine in my acceptance of the domination of the detached, disinterested, unrestricted desire to inquire intelligently and reflect reasonably, then I have no just grounds for surprise if I find myself unable to deny either that there is a reality or that the

real is being or that being is completely intelligible or that complete intelligibility is unrestricted understanding or that unrestricted understanding is God.[22]

The self-affirmation of the knower expands to the affirmation of the existence of God. In a section comparing his treatment with that of Aquinas, Lonergan answers a question that had nagged me all along: whether being or intelligibility was primary.

Among Thomists, however, there is a dispute whether *ipsum intelligere* or *ipsum esse subsistens* is logically first among divine attributes. As has been seen in the section on the notion of God, all other divine attributes follow from the notion of an unrestricted act of understanding. Moreover, since we define being by its relation to intelligence, necessarily our ultimate is not being but intelligence.[23]

He also notes that the five ways in which Aquinas proves the existence of God are so many particular cases of the general statement that the proportionate universe is incompletely intelligible and that complete intelligibility is demanded. In addition, "besides Aquinas's five ways, there are as many other proofs of the existence of God as there are aspects of incomplete intelligibility in the universe of proportionate being."[24]

Historically, the biases and counterpositions entered into the human affirmation of the divine. Eventually, however, these gave way to their own reversal.

So the empires of the Mediterranean basin gathered the gods of their peoples into pantheons; syncretists reduced their numbers; allegorists gave new meanings to their exploits; and philosophers discovered and preached the primacy of the Intelligible and of the One.[25]

But even philosophy itself breaks down: the many gods give way to the many philosophies, and even Scholasticism splinters into many schools. On the other hand, the knowledge of God is both earlier and simpler than any attempt to give it formal expression. Intelligent and reasonable knowledge of God can guide human living.

Again, just as the notion of nature can be misused by the gnostic and the magician yet, if used properly, provides the dynamic base on which the whole of scientific knowledge is erected, so too the notion of God can be corrupted by mythical consciousness and distorted by misplaced practicality yet, if used properly, it supplies the dynamic base on which rise not only the whole of intelligent and rational knowing but also the whole of intelligent and rational living.[26]

Lonergan distinguishes his method from the implicit metaphysics from which it arises. Thus, he states that the critical thinker

...does not allow developments in the notion of God to generate any doubt that it is one and the same being to which all men refer whether they are more or less successful in conceiving him, whether correctly they affirm his existence or mistakenly they deny it.[27]

Lonergan summed up the whole aim of the chapter in this way:

Our subject has been the act of insight or understanding, and God is the unrestricted act of understanding, the eternal rapture glimpsed in every Archimedean cry of Eureka.[28]

5. THE SOLUTION TO THE PROBLEM OF EVIL

In chapter twenty of *Insight* Lonergan outlines the heuristic structure of God's solution to the problem of evil. In other words, given the notion of God outlined in chapter nineteen, what might we expect such a God's response to evil to be?

In defining evil he distinguishes basic sin from physical and moral evil. *Basic sin* is the failure of free will to choose a morally obligatory course of action or its failure to reject a morally reprehensible course of action. It consists in the contraction of consciousness away from willing what one ought. Later on, in the context of the love of God articulated in *Method in Theology*, he will define it as "a radical dimension of lovelessness."[29]

Basic sin is the irrational. Why does it occur? If there were a reason, it would not be sin.

There may be excuses; there may be extenuating circumstances; but there cannot be a reason, for basic sin consists, not in yielding to reasons and reasonableness, but in failing to yield to them; it consists not in inadvertent failure but in advertence to and in acknowledgment of obligation that nonetheless is not followed by reasonable response.[30]

Next, by *moral evils* Lonergan means the consequences of basic sin. From the basic sin of not willing what one ought to will, there follow moral evils of omission and a heightening of the temptation in oneself or in others. From the basic sin of not setting aside illicit proposals, there follow their execution and a positive heightening of tension and temptation in oneself or in one's social milieu.

Finally, by *physical evils* Lonergan means all the shortcomings of a world order that consists, in so far as we can understand it, in a generalized emergent probability. These distinctions are important, for they mean that we cannot lump together basic sin, moral and physical evil.

It is within this context of the fact of evil that in chapter twenty of *Insight* Lonergan deals with what he calls "special transcendent knowledge," that is, knowledge of God's response to the problem of evil. For, since God is the first agent of every event and development, this question inevitably arises about what God is or has been doing about the fact of evil.[31]

There is a theological dimension that must be added to our detached analysis of the compounding of man's progress with man's decline. Bad will is not merely the inconsistency of rational self-consciousness; it also is sin against God. The hopeless tangle of the social surd, of the impotence of common sense, of the endlessly multiplied philosophies, is not merely a *cul-de-sac* for human progress; it also is a reign of sin, a despotism of darkness; and men are its slaves.[32]

In powerful words Lonergan frames the issue:

The reign of sin, then, is the expectation of sin. On a primary level, it is the priority of living to learning how to live, to acquiring the willingness to live rightly, to developing the adaptation that makes right living habitual. On a second level, it is man's awareness of his plight and his self-surrender to it; on each occasion, he could reflect and through reflection avoid sinning; but he cannot bear the burden of perpetual reflection; and long before that burden has mounted to the limit of physical impossibility, he chooses the easy way out.[33]

Such a reign of sin has its social implications. There is the transposition of the inner issue into the outer social milieu. Concrete situations become infected with the social surd and it seems that only in an increasingly limited fashion can intelligence and reasonableness have any real bearing upon the conduct of human affairs.

Finally, dialectical analysis can transpose the issue, but it cannot do so effectively. It goes beyond common sense to a critical human science that supposes a correct and accepted philosophy; but a correct philosophy will be but one of many philosophies, and precisely because it is correct it will be too complicated to be commonly accessible and too alien to sinful man to be widely accepted.

What often struck me as I read these sections of *Insight* is that Lonergan was under no illusions about the influence of his own philosophy. He accepted the fact that for most people his would be just one more voice in a sea of voices.

There is the surd of sin, then, and it is understood inasmuch as one grasps its lack of intelligibility. Since God exists, however, this surd of sin constitutes a problem.

The order of this universe in all its aspects and details has been shown to be the product of unrestricted understanding, of unlimited power, of complete goodness. Because God is omniscient, he knows man's plight. Because he is omnipotent, he can remedy it. Because he is good, he wills to do so. The fact of evil is not the whole story. It also is a problem. Because God exists, there is a further intelligibility to be grasped. . . . No matter how one cares to phrase it, the point seems to remain that evil is, not a mere fact, but a problem, only if one attempts to reconcile it with the goodness of God; and if God is good then there is not only a problem of evil but also a solution.[34]

The affirmation both of a problem and of its solution, implies the existence of a heuristic structure: that is, an object of inquiry that admits antecedent determinations. Even if such a heuristic structure fails to determine a single answer, it can at least offer a set of alternative answers which, through an appeal to the facts, can lead to the determination of the correct answer.

6. CHARACTERISTICS OF THE SOLUTION

Simply put, how would God solve the problem of human evil? What would be the general characteristics of such a solution? Lonergan lines up fifteen features of such a solution; I will highlight and paraphrase some of these. The first ones concern the cosmic and metaphysical aspects of the solution.

1) The solution will be one. For there is one God, one world order, and one problem that is both individual and social.
2) The solution will be universally accessible and permanent. For the problem is not restricted to people of a particular class or of a particular time.
3) The solution will be a harmonious continuation of the actual order of this universe. For there are no divine "afterthoughts."
4) The solution will not consist in the addition of a new genus or a new species. For the problem is a human one. The problem has to be solved for human persons, and introducing a new genus or species would merely be dodging the issue.
5) The solution will consist in the introduction of new "habits" in the human person's intellect, will, and sensitivity. For the problem arises from the nature of development. Because human living is prior to learning and being persuaded, such living is without the guidance of knowledge and without the direction of effective good will. As long as living remains prior to learning, the problem remains. The solution, then, must reverse the priority, and it does so inasmuch as it provides intellect, will, and sensitivity with forms or habits that are operative in living.

6) The relevant habits will be in some sense transcendent or supernatural. For what arises from nature is the problem.
7) These higher habits will be "systems on the move." For they have their place in a harmonious continuation of the actual order of the universe.
8) The solution will come to people through their human understanding and with their consent.

A closer determination reveals the new habits as *habits of faith, of hope and of charity*. To begin with charity, that is, self-sacrificing love of God:

> A man or woman knows that he or she is in love by making the discovery that all spontaneous and deliberate tendencies and actions regard the beloved. . . . It follows that, apart from the surd of sin, the universe is in love with God; and good will is the opposite of the irrationality of sin; accordingly, the man of good will is in love with God . . . to will the order of the universe because of one's love of God is to love all persons in the universe because of one's love of God. . . . [35]

The dialectical method consists in grasping that the social surd neither is intelligible nor is to be treated as intelligible; the corresponding dialectical attitude of will is not to return evil for evil but to overcome evil with good. For it is only inasmuch as people are willing to return good for evil, to love their enemies, to pray for those that persecute them, that the social surd becomes a potential good.

> Again, self-sacrificing love of God and of one's neighbor is repentant. . . . Such repentance is not a merely sensitive feeling of guilt. It is an act of good will following the insights of intelligence and the pronouncements of reasonableness. It is apart from the vagaries of mere feelings, and when they go astray it disapproves them, curbs them, and may seek aid in controlling them. . . . [36]

Since evil is revealed to be not merely a human wrong but also a revolt against God, an abuse of his goodness and love, so repentance becomes *sorrow*. The relationship between the stages in one's living is transformed into a personal relation to the one loved above all and in all. "Finally, good will is *joyful*. For it is love of God above all and in all, and love is joy."

In addition, the heuristic structure of the solution to the problem of evil will involve hope. Besides the charity by which the will itself is made good, there will be *the hope which makes the intellect good*. If the pure desire to know is to be maintained in its purity and not corrupted by the attached and interested desires of human sensitivity and intersubjectivity, if it is not to be overruled by the will's connivance with rationalizations, then it must be aided and reinforced by a deliberate decision and a habitual determination of the will itself.[37]

Finally, the solution to the problem of evil will involve *faith*. Such a form would effectively pull men's minds out of the counterpositions, fix them in the positions, and establish the certitude that God exists and that he has provided a solution which they are to acknowledge and accept.[38]

7. BELIEF

At first sight, this solution seems an impossibility. For the problem arises precisely inasmuch as human knowledge bogs down in the counterpositions. On the other hand, *there is the possibility of arriving at truth not just through immanently generated knowledge, but through belief.* In order to establish the fact that believing is indeed an intelligent and reasonable procedure for arriving at truth, Lonergan provides a long excursus on the nature of belief.

He is convinced that belief and immanently generated knowledge are intimately woven together in our minds. As we saw in the chapter on judgment, there stands in the background of our minds a host of previous judgments and assents that serve to clarify and define, to explain and defend, to qualify and limit, the prospective judgment that one is about to make.

> But if this host is submitted to scrutiny, one finds that one's beliefs are no less operative than one's immanently generated knowledge; and if one pursues the examination, one is forced to the conclusion that, as no belief is independent of some items of immanently generated knowledge, so *there are extraordinarily few items of immanently generated knowledge that are totally independent of beliefs.* One does not simply know that England is an island. Neither does one merely believe it.

The example of believing that England is an island is, of course, from Newman's *Grammar of Assent*. The development of the human mind is by the self-correcting process of learning, and in that process "personal *knowledge and belief practice an unrelenting sybiosis.*" The broadening of individual experience includes hearing the opinions and the convictions of others. The deepening of individual understanding includes the exploration of many new viewpoints.

> The formation of individual judgment is a process of differentiation, clarification, and revision, in which the shock of contradictory judgments is as relevant as one's own observation and memory, one's own intelligent inquiry and critical reflection. So each of us advances from the nescience of infancy to the fixed mentality of old age, and however large and determinate the contributions of belief to the shaping of our minds, still every belief and all its implications have been submitted to the endlessly repeated, if unnoticed, test of fresh experiences,

of further questions and new insights, of clarifying and qualifying revisions of judgment.[39]

The alternative to this collaboration between belief and knowledge is a primitive type of ignorance. To foster such collaboration there exist

. . . the invention and development of languages, the erection of schools and universities, the use of scientific methods and the publication of scientific journals, our domestic, economic, and political institutions, and the whole network of communications of the civilized world with their implicit, and often explicit, reprobation of perjury, deceit, and propaganda.[40]

Of course, there is the need for a critique of one's beliefs. Human life lies under the shadow of evil, an evil that distorts both immanently generated knowledge and beliefs.[41] But a critique of our beliefs is not the same as an exhaustive and explicit analysis of all of our beliefs. For the simple fact is that a man cannot reconstruct his mind by the process of explicit analysis, for such explicit analysis takes more time than the spontaneous procedures of the mind.

. . . it has taken each of us our lifetime to reach by spontaneous procedures the mentalities we now possess; and so if it were necessary for us to submit our mentalities to a total explicit analysis, it would also be necessary for us to have twofold lives, a life to live, and another, longer life in which to analyze the life that is lived.[42]

To critique our beliefs Lonergan recommends the procedure that we find within ourselves just one mistaken belief.

For that discovery enables one to set in reverse the same spontaneous and cumulative process that gave rise to one's mistaken beliefs. So one secures at a stroke the procedure that is both economical and efficacious: it is economical, for it wastes no time examining beliefs that are true; and it is efficacious, for it begins from the conviction that one has made one bad mistake, and it proceeds along the structural lines of one's own mentality and through the spontaneous and cumulative operations of the mind that alone can deal successfully with concrete issues.

This is what happened to me in reading *Insight*. I thought that reality was one way. I came, as I will show in the next chapter, to see that I was seriously mistaken. Here Lonergan relates such a procedure to the universal solution to the problem of evil. If a person has begun to realize that in one area of life he has been seriously mistaken, then his discovery and rejection of one mistaken belief can lead him on to the discovery and the rejection of as many more as the God of truth demands of him.[43]

8. A NEW AND HIGHER COLLABORATION WITH GOD

After touching on the collaboration of people in the attainment of truth through belief, Lonergan resumes outlining the heuristic structure of the solution to the problem of evil. His list of attributes of the solution goes up to "the thirty-first place," but we will touch on only a few of these. Among other things, then, the solution will consist in a new and higher collaboration of people in the pursuit of truth. For in the actual order of the universe human intellectual development takes place within an environment of collaboration that people maintain by their truthfulness, participate in by their beliefs, and contribute to by their immanently generated knowledge.

Furthermore, this new and higher collaboration will be, not simply a collaboration of people with one another, but basically *a human cooperation with God in solving the human problem of evil*. Furthermore, as the problem of evil exists because God respects human freedom, so the existence of the solution *leaves human freedom intact*. In addition, God's solution to the problem of evil, because it will invoke human cooperation, will have its institutional expression.

> Moreover, this survival and preservation, though principally the work of God, will be effected through human channels and in accord with the probabilities, for the new collaboration is part and parcel of the actual order of the universe. But the one human means of keeping a collaboration true to its purpose and united in its efforts is to set up an organization that possesses institutions capable of making necessary judgments and decisions that are binding on all. Accordingly, it follows that God will secure the preservation of faith against heresy through some appropriate institutional organization of the new and higher collaboration.[44]

Furthermore, since the solution will be harmonious with the actual order of the universe, it can be successful only if it touches human sensitivity and intersubjectivity. Consequently, there will be *need for images so charged with affect and feeling that they succeed both in guiding and propelling action*. For human sensitivity needs symbols to unlock its dynamism and bring it into harmony with the vast implications of the pure desire to know, of hope, and of self-sacrificing charity.

> It follows that the solution will be not only a renovation of will that matches intellectual detachment and aspiration, not only a new and higher collaboration of intellects through faith in God, but also a mystery that is at once symbol of the uncomprehended and sign of what is grasped and psychic force that sweeps living human bodies, linked in charity, to the joyful, courageous, wholehearted, yet intelligently controlled performance of the tasks set by a world order in which the problem of evil is not suppressed but transcended.[45]

That mystery must also be an historical fact.

Further, since mystery is a permanent need of man's sensitivity and intersubjectivity, while myth is an aberration not only of mystery but also of intellect and will, the mystery that is the solution as sensible must be not fiction but fact, not a story but history.

Our whole being, then, and every level of our being needs to be touched by a mystery that is at once symbol, sign and psychic force capable of bringing us to a whole new level of living.

It follows, then, that the emergent trend and the full realization of the solution must include the sensible data that are demanded by man's sensitive nature and that will command his attention, nourish his imagination, stimulate his intelligence and will, release his affectivity, control his aggressivity, and, as central features of the world of sense, intimate its finality, its yearning for God.

Furthermore, the solution will have a nature and content and power of its own. To the extent that it goes beyond a minimal solution, God's solution to the problem of evil might involve God's sharing of truths that we could never know if God had not revealed them. In this sense the solution will be absolutely supernatural, for it

not only meets a human need but also goes beyond it to transform it into the point of insertion into human life of truths beyond human comprehension, of values beyond human estimation, of an alliance and a love that, so to speak, brings God too close to man.[46]

Such a supernatural solution will transcend any humanism that revolts against the proffered solution. In the midst of the 1960s with its search for a humanism that did not include God, the following words had a profound effect on me.

For [such a humanism] rests on man's proud content to be just a man, and its tragedy is that, on the present supposition of a supernatural solution, to be just a man is what man cannot be. If he would be truly a man, he would submit to the unrestricted desire and discover the problem of evil and affirm the existence of a solution and accept the solution that exists. But if he would be only a man, he has to be less.[47]

9. IDENTIFYING THE SOLUTION TO THE PROBLEM OF EVIL

Lonergan ends this chapter with a short section on the factual identification of the solution of the problem of evil. He summarizes what the solution will "look like."

There remains the problem of identifying the solution that exists. For if possible solutions are many, the existent solution is one, universally accessible and permanent, continuous with the actual order of the universe, and realized through human acts of acknowledgment and consent that occur in accordance with the probabilities; it is a divinely sponsored collaboration in the transmission and application of the truths of the solution; it is a mystery in the threefold sense of psychic force, of sign, and of symbol; it moves from an initial emergent trend through a basic realization and consequent development to the attainment of an ulterior goal; it is operative through conjugate forms of faith, hope, and charity that enable man to achieve sustained development on the human level inasmuch as they reverse the priority of living over the knowledge needed to guide life and over the good will needed to follow knowledge; it is a new and higher integration of human activity that, in any case, involves some transcendence of human ways and, possibly, complicates the dialectic by adding to the inner conflict between attachment and detachment in man the necessity of man's going quite beyond his humanity to save himself from disfiguring and distorting it.

The task of identifying the solution is not the same for all. Already some have acknowledged the solution and their task is living up to it and bringing forth the fruits of faith, hope and charity. But others will have a notable difficulty in recognizing the solution. The problem of evil and the lack of development can inhibit that recognition.

Nevertheless, the critique of erroneous beliefs is possible. Anyone who has found himself in error on one point can initiate a scrutiny that cumulatively brings to light any other errors in which he happens to be involved. The whole of *Insight* pointed me in this direction. Nor does this critique of beliefs happen without God's grace.

Nor will he labor alone in the purification of his own mind, for the realization of the solution and its development in each of us is principally the work of God, who illuminates our intellects to understand what we had not understood and to grasp as unconditioned what we had reputed error, who breaks the bonds of our habitual unwillingness to be utterly genuine in intelligent inquiry and critical reflection by inspiring the hope that reinforces the detached, disinterested, unrestricted desire to know and by infusing the charity, the love, that bestows on intelligence the fullness of life.[48]

NOTES

1. "Philosophy of God and Theology," *CWL 17 Philosophical and Theological Papers 1965-1980,* 174.

2. *CWL 3 Insight,* 658 (635).

3. *CWL 3 Insight,* 662 (639).

4. *CWL 3 Insight,* 666 (643).
5. *CWL 3 Insight,* 668-669 (645-646).
6. *CWL 3 Insight,* 674 (651).
7. *CWL 3 Insight,* 675 (652).
8. *CWL 3 Insight,* 676 (653).
9. *CWL 3 Insight,* 676 (653).
10. *CWL 3 Insight,* 679 (656).
11. *CWL 3 Insight,* 679-680 (656-657).
12. *CWL 3 Insight,* 681 (658).
13. *CWL 3 Insight,* 681-682 (659).
14. *CWL 3 Insight,* 684 (661).
15. *CWL 3 Insight,* 685 (662).
16. *CWL 3 Insight,* 687 (664). On this whole issue see J. Michael Stebbins, *The Divine Initiative: Grace, World-Order and Human Freedom in the Early Writings of Bernard Lonergan* (Toronto: University of Toronto Press, 1995).
17. *CWL 3 Insight,* 689 (666).
18. *CWL 3 Insight,* 691 (668-669).
19. *CWL 3 Insight,* 695 (672). A shorter commentary on this can be found in Lonergan's paper, "The General Character of the Natural Theology of Insight," *CWL 17 Philosophical and Theological Papers 1965-1980,* 3-9.
20. *CWL 3 Insight,* 696 (673).
21. *CWL 3 Insight,* 697 (674).
22. *CWL 3 Insight,* 698 (675).
23. *CWL 3 Insight,* 700 (677).
24. *CWL 3 Insight,* 701 (678).
25. *CWL 3 Insight,* 704 (681).
26. *CWL 3 Insight,* 706 (683).
27. *CWL 3 Insight,* 708 (686).
28. *CWL 3 Insight,* 706 (683).
29. *Method in Theology,* 243.
30. *CWL 3 Insight,* 690 (667).
31. *CWL 3 Insight,* 709 (687).
32. *CWL 3 Insight,* 714 (692).
33. *CWL 3 Insight,* 715 (693).
34. *CWL 3 Insight,* 716 (694). Lonergan makes the point that he has written *Insight* from a moving viewpoint, that he is only treating of the solution to the problem of evil after he has treated of human progress and human decline: ". . . because this book has been written from a moving viewpoint, we have mentioned first a problem and only later its solution. But it would be an anthropomorphic blunder to transfer this succession to God. There are no divine afterthoughts."
35. *CWL 3 Insight,* 721 (698-699).
36. *CWL 3 Insight,* 722 (700).
37. *CWL 3 Insight,* 723 (701).
38. *CWL 3 Insight,* 724 (702).
39. *CWL 3 Insight,* 728 (706).

40. *CWL 3 Insight,* 729 (707).
41. *CWL 3 Insight,* 736 (714).
42. *CWL 3 Insight,* 738 (716-717).
43. *CWL 3 Insight,* 739 (717-718).
44. *CWL 3 Insight,* 744 (723).
45. *CWL 3 Insight,* 744-745 (723-724).
46. *CWL 3 Insight,* 747 (726).
47. *CWL 3 Insight,* 750 (729).
48. *CWL 3 Insight,* 751 (730).

Part III

INSIGHT INTO INSIGHT

Chapter Thirteen

A Shower of Insights

As I recounted in chapter four, in the spring of 1967 I had been reading and rereading *Insight* for over a year, but this intense study did not take place in a vacuum. The 1960s were a time of great ferment in the Catholic Church and in the whole world—and they were a time of great ferment in me. The Second Vatican Council had inspired and shaken us. Things were no longer neatly packaged. Change was in the air. The conflict between liberals and conservatives reverberated in my own insides. Thrilled to be in Rome during the five years of the Council, I remember very distinctly feeling disillusioned when after the Council we realized that "the same old school" still seemed to be calling the shots. At the same time, a number of us slowly began to realize that the dynamism accompanying the new historical consciousness often did not have roots. As Lonergan once wrote of that new consciousness:

> Far more open than classicist culture, far better informed, far more discerning, it lacks the convictions of its predecessor, its clear-cut norms, its elemental strength.[1]

Such was our situation and it affected the young priests with whom I was studying. Some were leaving the priesthood. Major issues loomed for us all. I was not immune from those issues. My insides began to founder. Fortunately, through the guidance of an older student priest, Father Jim Doyle of Chicago, I began to pray more deeply; and that prayer and that personal sharing began to make all the difference.

This personal conflict in the midst of a changing world provided the context for my continued reading of *Insight*. I was asking the questions: What do you mean by "reality?" What do you mean by "the mind?" by "my mind?" by "me?" What is "insight?"

I was also continuing to write my doctoral dissertation on Susanne K. Langer's philosophy of art. I was aiming at killing two birds with one stone. On the one hand I was interested in learning Lonergan's stuff, and since Lonergan thought highly of Langer, I thought this might be another entree into his thought. On the other hand, I also thought that this dissertation would expose me to the world of American philosophy. It would open me up to how people "out there" thought. In addition, since Langer's area of interest at the time was art and symbolism, and since this was becoming a popular topic among Catholics, particularly in relationship to the Catholic liturgy, I thought that this study would be valuable. Rome itself, of course, was a living museum of art and symbol.

And so I began to research and write the dissertation. The first chapter I dedicated to Langer's early work, influenced by Anglo-American "logical philosophy" and the cultural analyses of the neo-Kantian, Ernst Cassirer. Though Langer was very influenced by the early linguistic analysts—especially Bertrand Russell and Ludwig Wittgenstein—she was also convinced that there was a "formal" or intellectual character to such non-linguistic symbols as art and ritual. That was the point of her *Philosophy in a New Key* (1941) and the lead-in to her major work on art, *Feeling and Form* (1953) This, of course, fit in perfectly with Lonergan's emphasis on insight and with his own writings on aesthetic and artistic consciousness.[2] So chapter two on Langer's theory of art, especially as articulated in *Feeling and Form*, fell quite easily into place.

Chapter three I intended to dedicate to Langer's over-all theory of human mentality, a theory that would shed light on and fill out her theory of art. However, in 1967, as I worked on the dissertation, Langer published *Mind: An Essay on Human Feeling*, a work specifically dedicated to a theory of human mentality. And as I read and re-read this work, I found myself knocked off my pins. Basically what I discovered was a totally naturalistic view of human knowing and human life. In this work Langer reduces all "higher" human intellectual activities, including insight, to imagination, imagination to feelings and feelings to electro-chemical events.[3] And all of these positions cohered with her basic view of human knowing. As I read and re-read Langer's work, I understood that for her knowing is a bi-polar activity in which the "concepts" of scientific or philosophical thinking are the subjective pole, "matter" is the objective pole, and some type of vision or "looking" is the mediating activity. Thus we "see" forms of feeling in works of art; and in metaphorical activity we "see one thing in another," life in the candle flame, death in sleep, etc. This, she asserts, is the basis of all "higher" differentiated activity.[4]

Langer represented the whole modern naturalist tradition in philosophy and as I studied her work, I gradually discovered that there was a gulf separating what she was saying about human knowing and what Lonergan was saying. And what she was saying had consequences. She once spelled out those consequences:

> That man is an animal I certainly believe; and also that he has no supernatural essence, "soul" or "mind-stuff," enclosed in his skin. He is an organism, his substance is chemical, and what he does, suffers, or knows, is just what this sort of chemical structure may do, suffer, or know. When the structure goes to pieces, it never does, suffers, or knows anything again.[5]

This was a thoroughgoing naturalism: it was the assertion that there is nothing beyond what a narrowly conceived empirical method might reveal. In spite of Lonergan's very "generous" reading of Langer—and indeed, most writers—this was a problem for me.

1. CONFLICTING PHILOSOPHIES BECOME A CONFLICT IN ME

The conflicting viewpoints between Langer and Lonergan became a conflict in me. I remember one evening in particular. I was studying in my room sometime in the spring of 1967 as twilight spread over the city of Rome. I remember saying to myself quite clearly:

> Who's right here?—Lonergan or Langer? Both can't be right—between them there's a basic conflict about the human person, the human mind, indeed about reality.

I questioned my own motivation: "If you come down on Lonergan's side, is that because he's a religious, a Jesuit priest, and you yourself are a life-long Catholic and a priest as well?" I could admit all these underlying motivations that might incline me toward a more religiously amenable answer. But the question itself was not directly a religious one. It was a question of *fact*. What were the facts? What was the truth about the human mind? In fact, it was a question about what I was doing then and there. It was a question whose adequate answer I could find only within my own self.

Previously in philosophy courses and in my own reading I had learned many opinions about the mind and about the human person. I had learned what the great philosophers had said. But their sayings and opinions had passed through my own mind and on to test papers without connecting with my own basic self-knowledge. I could regurgitate the various positions, but my opinions were not rooted. They were vulnerable to basic challenges. The challenge I faced that evening in Rome was the challenge of modern naturalism.

In some ways naturalism with its empiricist emphasis was easy to understand—or at least to imagine. Its emphasis on sensation and imagination was rather obvious: the "blooming buzzing confusion" of sense experiences linked together by associative habits. Easy to understand also were the emphases of the other philosophies I found rolling around within me: the traditional scholasticism I had been taught, with its "intuition of being"; Immanuel Kant's emphasis on the knowing subject who cannot intellectually get "out there" to "things in themselves"; and the various existentialist writers who seemed to say, "A pox on all your houses—what counts are your own personal decisions!"

Yet the study of these philosophies was very important for me. For they each represented *people taking a stand.* All represented a challenge to come to a decision about myself and my own "foundations." I was twenty-eight years old and I needed to make some basic decisions on the meaning of "mind" and "reality." Lonergan once wrote about these foundations:

> It is a decision about whom and what you are for and, again, whom and what you are against. It is a decision illuminated by the manifold possibilities exhibited in dialectic. It is a fully conscious decision about one's horizon, one's outlook, one's world-view.[6]

In other words, you had to know something about these possible world-views before you could take a stand in their regard, either positively or negatively. I had been reading around in ancient and modern philosophy during the previous ten years and the major emphases of these various schools were not too difficult to understand.

In contrast, Lonergan's position was difficult to understand. I sensed that he was on to something in his emphasis on understanding. Still, he seemed to imply that there was a residual materialism, or "naive realism," even in someone like myself who had studied many years of Catholic philosophy and theology. I sensed that he was calling for a change *in me* if I were to truly understand what he was talking about.

I knew I had learned something from the study of *Insight.* I had learned something about understanding in mathematics, in science and in common sense. But to a great extent what I had learned had been what *Lonergan* had written. And as Jesus said to Peter when he recounted various views on him, "But who do *you* say that I am?" Similarly I felt the question in me,

> But who do *you* say that *you* are, Dick Liddy? What do *you* say about *your* own knowing? *your* own mind? *your* own self?

This inner dialogue was not about what Lonergan or anyone else had said about knowing; it was rather about what I was coming to know about my own knowing. And the evidence for answering these questions was to be found within me. It was a question of putting the book down and "thinking" about the meaning of the book. As Lonergan wrote,

> Intellectual habit is not possession of the book but freedom from the book. It is the birth and life in us of the light and evidence by which we operate on our own.[7]

And so I kept asking the question "Is this all true?" In particular,

> Is it true, as Lonergan states, that understanding is distinct from imagination? Is my understanding distinct from my imagination? Couldn't understanding be just another form of imagination? Couldn't I imagine that?

And I played many mental games—trying to imagine and re-conceive other explanations for the structure of my own mind. Again and again I said to myself that all the later elements in Lonergan's book, including the existence of God, depended on the correctness of the earlier analyses of insight. And so, as I read the second half of *Insight* I could not help repeating to myself:

> Is the understanding of understanding in the first part of the book correct? The circle, for example, is Lonergan correct on that? Is there a specific act called 'understanding' or is understanding just some kind of "imagining?"

And my imagination threw up on the screen of my mind all kinds of conflicting images and questions: "Perhaps what I call 'understanding' is just a kind of imagination—for example, an imagining of perfectly equal radii?" But that did not seem to make sense. For imagination just "re-presented" the sensitive experiences of seeing the spokes on a wheel or some symbolic radii. The fact that mathematics deals with intelligibilities that can be symbolized but not represented seemed strong evidence for a distinct intellectual level of consciousness. In the example of the circle points and lines cannot, strictly speaking, be imagined; they can only be intellectually symbolized by marks on a page.

But what was this intellectual level? Where was it? "What did it look like?"

Beneath the surface of my mind there percolated an unease that I formulated in the question, "Where is this act?" I was not sure I had a real "handle" on it. I was not sure what insight was *like*. I was not sure I could situate it clearly within my own consciousness. I was not sure I "had" it. In some real way, I was looking for something with a label on it:

"THIS IS THE ACT OF INSIGHT! THIS IS UNDERSTANDING!"
or
"BEHOLD—INSIGHT!"

But the reality turned out to be more subtle.

2. A SHOWER OF INSIGHTS

And that is when I remember having an "Archimedean experience." It was late one afternoon in Rome in the spring of 1967 and I had been working on this stuff for most of the day. So I decided to take a shower.[8] Like Archimedes, I was relaxing in the water as various questions and images went through my head. Then, at one point I remember asking myself: "Where is this act of insight?" And then it hit me:

> You're asking the wrong question!

> Look at the question you're asking! You're asking a question that cannot be answered! You're asking "where?" and that's your attempt to visualize what can't be visualized! You're attempting to imagine what of its nature goes beyond imagination. Indeed, you can be aware of insight; you can understand it in its relationships with other cognitional acts; you can come to judge that understanding correct; but *you can't see it!* The very question you're asking is formulated in imaginative and visual terms and, as such, can't be answered!

That is my formulation now of what I said to myself that afternoon some forty ago. Perhaps my words then were somewhat different; but that was the substance of it. I realized that the question I was asking, that I spontaneously felt could be answered, could not be answered. I was in the shower, in a room, in a place that could be designated spatially. But an explanatory understanding of my own understanding could not be so designated.

And *that* I was understanding! And that's why that moment that afternoon forty years ago stands out in my mind today. It is part of my "psychological present."

An important dimension of my insight, then, was the discovery that *I had not understood.* For a long time while reading *Insight* I had been bothered by an underlying question, a question I hardly realized was in me—a question that was literally part of me, part of "my guts." In the shower it found expression in "*Where is this act of insight?*" But the question had been rolling around within me before that as an uneasy feeling, an unsure-ness that I really had a handle on what I was thinking about. And the question that flowed from that uneasy feeling was a question that as such could not be answered. Perhaps a neurobiologist could indicate certain areas of the brain stimulated by such reflective thinking, but the insight itself cannot be explained by such underlying conditions.[9]

In the critique of beliefs in chapter 20 of *Insight* Lonergan emphasizes the importance of coming to understand even one instance of one's failure to understand.[10] For such an awareness can be an important moment in one's coming to know oneself. It is a single thread linked to other threads affecting the whole fabric of one's mind. That moment in the shower precipitated a whole inventory of instances of misunderstanding and oversight that were principally due to my desire for a "picture" of what I was trying to understand. And that deep-seated habit of wanting to "picture" things had extended itself to wanting a picture of my own understanding.

3. A "STARTLING STRANGENESS" AND THE FEAR OF IDEALISM

As mentioned previously, the introduction to *Insight* speaks of the "startling strangeness" one will experience as one get the point of the book.[11] It is a breakthrough as distinctive as the difference between winter twilight and the summer noon.[12] One has not yet experienced it if one has not yet made the discovery

> . . . that there are two quite different realisms, that there is an incoherent realism half animal half human that poses as a halfway house between materialism and idealism, and on the other hand there is a coherent realism between which and materialism the halfway house is idealism.[13]

Let us diagram that sentence in terms of my own history, for it concerns what happened to me in the shower that day and how I came to interpret it. Previously in my training I had been taught to look at the major schools of philosophy in this way:

Materialism → Realism ← Idealism

"Realism" or a realist philosophy was thought to occupy the sound middle ground between materialism and idealism; it took something of materialism's emphasis on matter and some of idealism's emphasis on mind. It was "half animal, half human." Now Lonergan was saying that such realism is itself incoherent. Because it is "half animal," it is not human enough. The only truly coherent realism is to follow out idealism's emphasis on the priority of mind while purging idealism of its assumption that only by "looking" can one know reality. If reality is attained not merely by sensitive experience but also by understanding and true judgment, then a genuinely progressive diagram of the relationships between the major positions in philosophy would be:

Materialism → Idealism → Critical Realism

Now this was an issue that faced me in the aftermath of my experience in the shower. For I kept asking myself, Is this real? Am I on to anything here?

Or am I just getting wrapped up in my own mind? Am I becoming an idealist? Does this insistence on the intellectual pattern of consciousness lose contact with reality? Or is it the way we really know reality? Lonergan himself noted that in his early years of philosophical study he himself had experienced this fear that he was becoming an idealist.[14] I found that same fear in myself. I feared that somehow I was getting too wrapped up in my own "self" and never reaching reality "out there."

But then I realized that this fear itself involved the same imaginative "inner-outer" schema on the self and on reality that had bedeviled my efforts to figure out "where" insight was. Idealism still holds on to the idea of reality as "out there," and since we do not have any intellectual intuition, any intellectual "look," we consequently cannot get "out there" to "the really real." We are, as it were, trapped in our minds.

If, on the other hand, reality is mediated by reasonable judgment about what we have understood, rooted in a grasp of the sufficiency of the evidence, then we attain reality through the truth of reasonable judgments. And such a reality-ordered process becomes a critical realism through the process of self-appropriation. The breakthrough to understanding the un-imaginability of insight was intimately connected to the breakthrough to a critically realist philosophy.

Lonergan once touched upon this fear of idealism while writing about the early Christian writer, Tertullian, for whom the criterion of the reality of the divinity of the Son of God was that he was made "of the same stuff" as the Father. In that context Lonergan goes on to say:

> Unfortunately, some people have the impression that while Tertullian and others of his time may have made such a mistake, no one repeats it today. Nothing could be further from the truth. For until a person has made the personal discovery that he is making Tertullian's mistake all along the line, until he has gone through the crisis involved in overcoming one's spontaneous estimate of the real, and the fear of idealism involved in it, he is still thinking just as Tertullian did.

He goes on to link this with Saint Augustine's experience.

> It is not a sign that one is dumb or backward. St. Augustine was one of the most intelligent men in the whole Western tradition and one of the best proofs of his intelligence is in the fact that he himself discovered that for years he was unable to distinguish between what is a body and what is real.[15]

4. THE TESTIMONY OF OTHERS

I have not made a study of others who have had experiences similar to mine; that would be a worthwhile project. But I can recall some anecdotal evidence of the "startling strangeness" that overcomes a person when first he experiences an "insight into insight."

There was, for example, the professor of philosophy who told me of an afternoon, many years ago, when he was reading *Insight* on the grounds of the North American College in Rome. "I was absolutely carried away by it," he said. "When I walked up to my room that afternoon, everything was different—everything!"

Another philosophy professor witnessed to the same experience of "everything looking different" after having had a breakthrough in reading Lonergan. It was a breakthrough to "the intelligibility of being" as in the title of the novel, *The Incredible Lightness of Being*. Walking down stairs he marveled that the stairs held him; and as he drove his car he marveled at "the lightness of being."

These experiences have a strange similarity to some accounts of religious experience, such as that recounted by Jonathan Edwards:

> After this my sense of divine things gradually increased and became more lively, and had more of that inward sweetness. The appearance of everything was altered; there seemed to be, as it were, a calm, sweet cast, or appearance of divine glory in almost everything.[16]

Still, the experience we are focusing on was primarily intellectual; but it had its sensible overtones. One can hardly have an experience of "startling strangeness" without it affecting all of one's being. Another student of *Insight* remembers attending the horse-races at a track in Dublin. "In the middle of the races," he said,

> I began to think of the meaning of "reality." Then it hit me—like a ton of bricks. I realized I understood what Lonergan was talking about!—and it was quite different than our ordinary meaning of "reality." I can remember that moment quite vividly.

Another person told me he remembers very distinctly the turning point in his own journey. "I was in a class at Boston University," he said.

> The professor was a very open man, encouraging us in our own opinions, while at the same time going on about his own. And his opinions on philosophy and human knowing were quite distinct from what *Insight* held. I remember saying to myself: "I *know* he's wrong. I know I hold a whole set of positions on consciousness, insight, etc., that are in opposition to what he's teaching." Perhaps it was his teaching itself that so set up the contrast for me. I can remember that moment years back quite clearly. It was a key moment in my own self-knowledge.

And Philip McShane writes about his experience, not while reading *Insight*, but while reading Lonergan's articles, *Verbum: Word and Idea in Saint Thomas*.

I recall vividly the strangeness of the beginning of my own escape, and the concomitant shift in sensibility, when I was 26, with four years of mathematical science and two years of philosophy behind me. The pivotal text, oddly enough, was not *Insight,* but the fifth element in the general notion of inner word in the first of the *Verbum* articles. Since then I have found it easy to keep track of the few students I have helped towards and into that strangeness, and I have no doubt that Maslow's statistic, "less than 1 % of adults grow," holds sway for the population of philosophers with regard to this bridge. The statistic can change only if we seriously and incarnately make this bridge a topic, and the difficulty of its crossing a topic.[17]

There is also the testimony of the Jesuit, William Ryan, whose breakthrough, like my own, took place in relation to Lonergan's favorite example, the circle.

Then in 1963 I went to Europe for Tertianship and for doctoral studies in philosophy at Louvain. In Louvain, for the first time, I read Father Lonergan's *Insight* from cover to cover. Shortly afterwards, I ran into a quaint phrase of his: "An insight into a circle has no bumps or dents." I was astonished. I grasped cleanly that an insight is not just more sensing, like staring at the bumps and dents on a wheel. And finally I grasped that by having insights and recognizing them, one enters into the world of Lonergan's method, the world where sensing and insights perform such radically disparate functions.[18]

Another of Lonergan's students, Giovanni Sala recounts how important Lonergan's insistence on judgment was for his own breakthrough. For years he had studied Kant's philosophy and was convinced, along with most neo-scholastic philosophers, that the only guarantor of the transcendence and objectivity of our knowledge was some kind of intellectual intuition. His encounter with Lonergan as his teacher in Rome, however, threatened his naïve realism.

It was therefore a cause of amazement and confusion to me when later, as a student at the Gregorian University, I heard Lonergan speaking repeatedly of the *"vim judicii existentialis quo per verum judiciium cognoscitur existens" [the power of an existential judgment by which through a true judgment an existent is known]* or of *"verum absolute positum quo innotescit ens" [an absolutely posited truth by which being is known].* My first reading of *Insight* could not restore firm ground under my feet after Lonergan had called my realism into question, a realism that rested on nothing other than the principle of intuition! For years I remained stranded in midstream, so to speak, until gradually the indirect approach through the study of theology, a few seminars with Lonergan . . . the study of the articles "The Concept of *Verbum* in the Writings of St. Thomas Aquinas" (which gave me an easier access to Lonergan's thought because of my neo-scholastic background), and another round of wrestling with *Insight*, revealed to me the truth, indeed the extreme simplicity, of the thesis that knowledge of reality occurs through the performance of our intentionality.[19]

Sala sums up his discovery:

The surprising thing about this insight, which came to me at the end of a long search and in which the scales of intuitionism fell from my eyes, was that, in spite of all the complex particular forms and instances of human knowledge in all its various branches, the core of this doctrine proved to have a disarming simplicity: we know reality because and to the extent that we attentively observe the relevant data of experience, bring the data to an intelligible unity, and take the trouble of weighing the evidence for and against our interpretation of the data with intellectual honesty. Every human being who wants to know how it stands with reality spontaneously does precisely this! This same insight made it possible for me to see the chasm that intuitionism of every sort sets up between the cognitive acts which we de facto perform and the postulated intuition of the fact itself, whether it be Kant's merely sensible intuition or the neo-scholastic intellectual intuition.

Other students of *Insight* find it difficult to recall particular moments in their philosophical journey. Sometimes they explain this in terms of never having had to "unlearn" an inadequate philosophy—such as the particular brand of neo-scholasticism I was taught. The very effort expended on learning a particular philosophy as well as the break from that philosophy perhaps makes the breakthrough particularly vivid.

Still, the basic breakthrough to an understanding of understanding is not just from one or another explicit philosophy to Lonergan's philosophy. Rather, it is a breakthrough from the spontaneous, implicit, "philosophy" we carry with us from childhood to truly understanding ourselves and the world mediated by meaning.[20] In several places Lonergan outlines Jean Piaget's analysis of the intellectual development of children and their progressive "de-centering" as gradually they are able to imagine themselves as fitting within larger worlds of reality. One such development is learning to fit into the "already out there now" world of common sense and such development is necessary for mental health. But to consider that the only world and the only criterion of reality is to shut oneself off from the universe revealed by understanding and true judgment.

From that preliminary learning in infancy and childhood there can be formed a notion of what is real. The real is what satisfies several sensorimotor or perceptual schemes of operations. And there can be a great philosophic block against going beyond that notion of reality. . . . To throw any doubt upon the convictions about reality formed in infancy is to be an idealist, a Platonist, a Kantian, a relativist, or God knows what. . . . [21]

This break from the whole world of common sense feeling would seem to be the basic cause for the "startling strangeness" that Lonergan describes in the introduction to *Insight*. Elsewhere he speaks of this event as "being dazed and disoriented" for a while as one becomes accustomed to a whole new view of things. He is speaking of how we can neglect our very selves as we get caught up in a verbalism or a conceptualism of any kind—that is, in an inadequate or truncated view of who we truly are. The movement out of such a counter-position is not an easy one:

The transition from the neglected and truncated subject to self-appropriation is not a simple matter. It is not just a matter of finding out and assenting to a number of true propositions. More basically, it is a matter of conversion, of a personal philosophic experience, of moving out of a world of sense and of arriving, dazed and disorientated for a while, into a universe of being.[22]

That was how I felt—dazed and disoriented. Everything was different. I now understood what Lonergan was talking about. Other parts of *Insight* began to fall into place like one piece after another in a very big puzzle. In particular, difficulties about the "isomorphism between the structure of knowing and the structure of being" fell into place. I had been trying to "imagine" a structure of being diverse from the structure of knowing being. Here again, the difficulty had been one of imagination. Every effort to imagine that "being" was not intelligible, I discovered to be just that—an image. That which I sought, the intelligibility of everything, the object of my inquiring intelligence, cut through every such imagination.

My question in the shower, "Where is this insight?" was a question that came out of my connection to the earth—out of my whole early human development of orienting myself in the "already out there now world." It was a major achievement to overcome that life-long orientation in just this one area. There were many other areas where the weight and force of "the already out there now real" still exercised its powerful sway. It still does. And yet a Rubicon had been crossed. An interior point of gravity had shifted within me. And though in my thinking and acting I have through the years fallen below that point, still, from that moment onwards I *knew* that reality is more than what I imagined—and that *I* am more.

5. INTELLECTUAL CONVERSION AND AUTOBIOGRAPHY

Towards an autobiography, a first step is a diary. Day by day one records, not every event that occurred—one has other things to do—but what seems important, significant, exceptional, new. So one selects, abbreviates, sketches, alludes. One omits most of what is too familiar to be noticed, too obvious to be mentioned, too recurrent to be thought worth recording. Now as the years pass and the diary swells, retrospect lengthens. What once were merely remote possibilities, now have been realized. Earlier events, thought insignificant, prove to have been quite important, while others, thought important, turn out to have been quite minor.[23]

So what am I doing in this book? What have I been doing in these previous pages? I have been trying to "tell my story." I've been describing my process of self-appropriation. It's part of my "memoirs," a contribution to my autobiography—my attempt to objectify what was going on within me at a certain period in my life.

But one's story can change. I don't think I kept a diary during those years, but I have checked my letters from that time to my family and I cannot find any mention in them of this key event in my life. Of course, it is not something you would naturally have written home about! But I was busy telling them of other events in Rome at the time—the Council, papal ceremonies, etc. I had many concerns in those days, and my "insight into insight" was just one of those concerns. And when afterwards I came home to the States to teach, I also became involved in many other things: spiritual director and rector of the seminary, Acting Chancellor of the university, university professor, etc. Consequently, although the breakthrough I have recounted above became very important in my life, it need not have become so. Someone could have had an experience similar to mine, but other "dominant concerns" could have swamped it. They did threaten to do so from time to time in my own life.

So the life of the mind is connected to the life of the heart and the heart's decisions. The reason that insight in the shower is still so important to me is that through the years I have followed up on it. Right from the beginning, decisions flowed from that "insight into insight." Those decisions involved continuing to read Lonergan, to teach what I learned, to stay in "Lonergan studies," to go to the Lonergan Workshop, to join the Woodstock Theological Center, to write books and articles about Lonergan, etc., etc. It is because of those subsequent decisions that that event in the shower in Rome has become ever more significant.

And there is a further aspect to the matter and that is the social and communal dimensions. For in highlighting what happened to me I have not perhaps highlighted sufficiently the fact that there were others studying *Insight* in Rome in the 1960s and I would sometimes speak with them about what we were learning—our difficulties, our insights. And just as Lonergan himself benefited in his self-understanding from so many others, so our thinking—even about ourselves—takes place within a communal and historical context. Peter Berger once brought out this need for community if we are to take our moments of self-knowledge seriously. Speaking of religious conversion, he noted:

> It is only within the religious community, the *ecclesia*, that the conversion can be effectively maintained as plausible. This is not to deny that conversion may antedate affiliation with the community . . . But this is not the point. To have a conversion experience is nothing much. The real thing is to keep on taking it seriously; to retain a sense of its plausibility. *This* is where the religious community comes in. It provides the indispensable plausibility structure for the new reality. In other words, Saul may have become Paul in the aloneness of religious ecstasy, but he would remain Paul only in the context of the Christian community that recognized him as such and confirmed the "new being" in which he now located this identity.[24]

So to a significant degree it is "the Lonergan community" that has helped me to continue to take seriously that moment so long ago and, even more importantly, to make decisions that followed up on that moment. Through the years that community has helped me to see the innumerable implications in this breakthrough from picture thinking. This element of community is also very helpful in introducing others to the meaning of an "insight into insight." Thus, Lonergan once wrote about the effectiveness of a "seminar" approach to these questions:

> Everyone will have his own difficulties. There is an advantage, then, to having a seminar on the subject. It gives people a chance to talk these things out . . . to talk them out with others. There is a set of concrete opportunities provided by the seminar that cannot be provided by any mere book. The more you talk with another and throw things out, the more you probe, and the more you express yourself spontaneously, simply, and frankly, not holding back in fear of making mistakes, then the more quickly you arrive at the point where you get things cleared up.[25]

In addition, these moments of "startling strangeness" that have happened to others in "the Lonergan movement" take place in an historical context, a context of progress, decline and redemption.

> There is social and cultural process. It is not just a sum of individual words and deeds. There exists a developing and/or deteriorating unity constituted by co-operations, by institutions, by personal relations, by a functioning and/or malfunctioning good of order, by a communal realization of originating and terminal values and disvalues. Within such processes we live out our lives.[26]

So seemingly purely personal questions—such as the meaning of "insight"—have not only personal intellectual implications, but they lead to questions that are social, cultural and political. Lonergan himself drew out some of these cultural implications in *Insight, Method in Theology*, and his other writings, including his writings on economics. As he says in *Method in Theology*:

> Still intellectual conversion alone is not enough. It has to be made explicit in a philosophic and theological method, and such an explicit method has to include a critique both of the method of science and the method of scholarship.[27]

So also, in the last pages of his *Method in Theology* Lonergan makes a pitch for a critical approach to the human sciences based on intellectual conversion. Just as the natural sciences, history and philosophy need a dialectical critique based on such conversion, so also do the human sciences.[28] Such a purification can lead to significant healing of the human family's understanding of herself and creative policies for human development. In such a way intellectual conversion can find application-insertion-relevance in the contemporary world situation.

So in a sense what happened to me in Rome was "nothing much." Whether or not it was an "intellectual conversion" that lived up to Lonergan's high standards still remains a question for me. And indeed, just as there are stages of moral and religious conversion, so one can speak analogously of stages in intellectual conversion, at least insofar as one allows that experience to gradually influence all of one's intellectual life.

> In any individual at any given time there may exist the abstract possibility, or the beginnings, or greater or lesser progress, or high development of intellectual or moral or religious conversion.[29]

Still, on an apologetic level, this breakthrough to my own mind in the mid-1960s was also a breakthrough to convictions about the issues treated at the end of *Insight*, especially the possibility of ethics, moral impotence, the existence of God and the need for God's solution to the unintelligibility of sin. Somewhere Lonergan remarks that through the breakthrough to one's own mind "You're almost all the way home," that is, home to the question of God and to identifying God's solution to the problem of human living. Speaking about the search for "the unknown god" among the ancients, particularly in Plato and Aristotle, he remarked:

> Insofar as they reached the unknown god, they were already within the horizon of being, of being that is immaterial beyond all knowledge. And you have the long-winded approach in *Insight* because people today do not know about the unknown

god. You have to open up their minds, let them find out what their own minds are before they can begin to be open to thinking of anything beyond this world.[30]

That was my experience. My insight into my own insight, culminating that afternoon in the shower, opened the door to finding my way, with God's help, through the turbulent 1960s—and ever since.

Lonergan himself was rather blasé and off-handed about his own intellectual conversion. He mentioned it once in a discussion on the history of philosophy.

> So there was considerable room for development after Aristotle and you get it in St. Thomas when he distinguishes existence from essence and makes them really distinct; and to make them distinct really you have to have something equivalent to an intellectual conversion even if you don't know what is meant by an intellectual conversion. I had the intellectual conversion myself when in doing theology I saw that you can't have one person in two natures in Christ unless there is a real distinction between the natures and something else that is one. But that is the long way around.[31]

Besides showing Lonergan's reticence at autobiography, the tenor of this passage illustrates that he had other very important things to attend to than the details of his own life. His concern was what he could concretely contribute to the world. Still, that moment in Rome in 1935 was foundational both for his writing of *Insight* as well as for all his later writings. That experience reproduced in him something similar to what had happened to Saint Augustine in the summer of 389 when he came to realize that the word "real" went beyond the meaning of the word "body."

> My mind was in search of such images as the forms of my eye was accustomed to see; and I did not realize that the mental act by which I formed these images, was not itself a bodily image. (*Confessions* 7, 1)

So the dates of 389, 1935, 1967 and 2006 are connected. They remind me of Eric Voegelin's words about a "Gospel":

> A Gospel is neither a poet's work of dramatic art, nor an historian's biography of Jesus, but the symbolization of a divine movement that went through the person of Jesus into society and history.[32]

NOTES

1. *A Second Collection*, 92.
2. See in particular *CWL 3 Insight*, 207-209 (184-185). Also, *CWL 10 Topics in Education*, 208-232.

3. Susanne K. Langer, *Mind: An Essay on Human Feeling* (Baltimore: Johns Hopkins, 1967). See Richard M. Liddy, *Art and Feeling: An Analysis and Critique of the Philosophy of Art of Susanne K. Langer* (Ann Arbor: University Microfilms, 1970).

4. See my review of Susanne K. Langer, *Mind: An Essay on Human Feeling, Volume I* in *International Philosophical Quarterly*, vol. 10, n.3 (1970), 481-484. Also Richard Liddy, "Susanne K. Langer's Philosophy of Mind," *Transactions of the Charles S. Peirce Society*, Vol. XXXIII, No. 1 (Winter, 1997), 149-160.

5. Susanne K. Langer, *Philosophy in a New Key* (New York: New American Library, 1948), 44.

6. *Method in Theology*, 268.

7. *CWL 2 Verbum*, 193.

8. Someone once told me of one of Rollo May's books on human creativity where he specifically speaks of "the shower experience." I have not been able of locate the reference. Someone else referred to "the three 'b's'—the bed, the bath and the bus—all places in which you're relaxed and insights can emerge.

9. As Lonergan replied when asked about the biological basis of thought: "The biological basis of thought, I should say, is like the rubber-tire basis of the motor car. It conditions and sets limits to functioning, but under the conditions and within the limits the driver directs operations." *A Second Collection*, 35.

10. *CWL 3 Insight*, 737-739 (713-718).

11. *CWL 3 Insight*, 32 (xxviii).

12. *CWL 3 Insight*, 18 (xix).

13. *CWL 3 Insight*, 32 (xxviii).

14. See *Caring About Meaning, Patterns in the Life of Bernard Lonergan*, ed. Pierrot Lambert, Charlotte Tansey, Cathleen Going (Montreal: Thomas More Institute, 1982), 110-11. There is also a reference to this fear of idealism in Lonergan's seminar on method in theology from 1962, now available as CDs from the Lonergan Research Institute in Toronto.

15. "Consciousness and the Trinity," *CWL 6 Philosophical and Theological Papers 1958-1964*, 130.

16. Quoted in William James, *The Varieties of Religious Experience* (New York: New American Library, 1958), 199.

17. Philip McShane, *Creativity and Method: Essays in Honor of Bernard Lonergan*, ed. Matthew Lamb (Milwaukee: Marquette University Press, 1981), 548. See also Philip McShane, *Economics for Everyone* (Halifax: Axial Press, 1998), 36: "What, then, do I mean by a concept, a serious explanatory concept, such as we struggle towards in these chapters? I can perhaps appeal to the description that I regularly, in the past twenty years, invited my students of philosophy to ponder over. There are two characteristics of a serious explanatory concept. You will remember the weeks, months, even years, that you spent—with feats of curiosity, not feats of memory—in struggling towards it. You will be able, even years later, to speak of it illuminatingly, through illustrations, for perhaps ten hours. Maybe you are led by this to suspect that serious explanatory concepts are rare achievements? And certainly they are not passed on from generation to generation in compact learned nuggets."

18. William F. Ryan, "Personal Tribute," *Compass: A Jesuit Journal*, special issue honoring Bernard Lonergan, Spring 1985, 7.

19. Giovanni B. Sala, *Lonergan and Kant: Five Essays on Human Knowledge*, trans. Joseph Spoerl, ed. Robert Doran (Toronto: University of Toronto Press, 1994) xvi-xvii.

20. See Lonergan's reference in *Verbum: Word and Idea in Aquinas*, 20-21: "For the materialist, the real is what he knows before he understands or thinks: it is the sensitively integrated object that is reality for a dog; it is the sure and firm-set earth on which I tread, which is so reassuring to the sense of reality; and on that showing intellect does not penetrate to the inwardness of things but is a merely subjective, if highly useful, principle of activity."

21. *CWL 10 Topics in Education*, 169-170.

22. *A Second Collection*, 79.

23. *Method in Theology*, 182-183.

24. Peter Berger, *The Social Construction of Reality* (New York: Doubleday, 1966) 158.

25. *CWL 5 Understanding and Being,* 18.

26. *Method in Theology*, 184.

27. *Method in Theology*, 318. So also, *Insight* 22: "For the appropriation of one's own rational self-consciousness, which has been so stressed in this introduction, is not an end in itself but rather a beginning. It is a necessary beginning. . . ."

28. *Method in Theology*, 365-367.

29. *Method in Theology*, 326.

30. Transcript by Nicholas Graham of discussion at Lonergan Workshop, Boston College, June 13, 1978.

31. Transcript by Nicholas Graham of discussions at Lonergan Workshop, June 13, 1978.

32. Eric Voegelin, "The Gospel and Culture" in *Jesus and Man's Hope*, ed. Donald G. Miller and Dikran Y. Hadidian, Vol. II (Pittsburgh: Pittsburgh Theological Seminary, 1971), 92.

Chapter Fourteen

Encountering Bernard Lonergan

S ince that "shower experience in Rome," one of my greatest joys has been to read Bernard Lonergan's writings. I find them healing and consoling. Many times, overwhelmed and distracted, I find in his writings clarity of thought and consolation.[1]

Not that reading Lonergan has been easy. My experience is often similar to my first experience of reading *Insight*: an initial period of floundering about, followed by the subtle joy of dawning insight. Often through the years, in picking up and reading something by him I would feel, "This is boring. Why's he going down this obscure alley? What relevance do these questions have?" Then slowly I would begin to catch on, to get the point, to see the relevance. I would compare later sections of articles or chapters with earlier ones and connections would begin to be made. Eventually I would find myself "putting on the mind of Lonergan" as I catch on to the way he is asking questions and the precise angle he is trying to illuminate.

> . . . the process of learning is marked by an initial period of darkness in which one gropes about insecurely, in which one cannot see where one is going, in which one cannot grasp what all the fuss is about; and only gradually, as one begins to catch on, does the initial darkness yield to a subsequent period of increasing light, confidence, interest, absorption.[2]

This was my experience in reading Lonergan's *Method in Theology*, which he published in 1972. But before treating that work, let me add some history. Lonergan returned from Rome to Canada in 1965 to face a very serious operation in which one of his lungs was removed. William Mathews has recounted the story of this very painful period in Lonergan's life, a period in which he suffered deeply, but also a period in which he experienced the ministrations of a very loving religious sister.[3] In September of 1966 he wrote to Fred Lawrence:

217

I assure you that I have had plenty of experience of the obscurity and power of faith. I was sixteen years in the order before there was question of my getting more than a B.A.; I was almost forty when my first article was published and over fifty when my book came out. What carried me on over the years was my trust that what God wants will be done; it also carried me through my pneumectomy and thoracoplasty last year; my *Method in Theology* is advancing very slowly but I feel confident that it will be done.[4]

It was at that time in the late 1960s, as he began to recover physically, that he resumed the project he had envisioned years previously, the project of writing a book on method in theology. Even *Insight* was just a step toward such a project. He commented on this long range goal in an interview published in 1979.

In 1926, I was sent to England to study philosophy at Heythrop College and at the same time to prepare for an external degree at London University. A year later, aged twenty-two, I wrote the Canadian Jesuit Provincial asking that my field of study be shifted to general methodology. I didn't know anything about methodology at the time, but forty-five years later I published a book on method in theology. All along I was interested in method and learning more about it.

Asked what the response of the provincial was, Lonergan replied:

The provincial said "no!" In the same year at Heythrop I had to preach to two hundred and fifty students during supper. I took as my text "You may hear and hear but not understand. You may look and look but you will never see." (*Acts* 28, 26) Our superior advised that, while my doctrine was true enough, it would be better not to preach it, and I never have but the idea remained fruitful. It became, in *Insight*, "inverse insight," understanding that there is nothing to be understood . . . In *Method in Theology* that idea became "dialectic," again the negation of intelligibility somewhere along the line. In *Grace and Freedom* sin is a surd, an irrational. In other words, the idea I had in the sermon is something which fructified later on in life even though it was an idea that received a dose of cold water at the time. I knew there was something there, but what it was took me years to figure out. I haven't exhausted the issue yet.[5]

How is this possible that some understand and others do not? Or that some are tone-deaf when it comes to religion and others are not? And that some who originally are tone-deaf change and begin to understand and perhaps become quite religious? And how do these basic changes affect one's "method" of reading texts and stating the meaning of texts? It could be said that all of Lonergan's analyses of conversion, of conflicting horizons, of the breakthrough to the startling and strange experience of taking "mind" seriously—all of these themes in Lonergan's writings are the outcome of his early efforts to understand the meaning of *Acts* 28, 26.

Two years after I returned from Rome in 1967 and began to teach at Immaculate Conception Seminary in New Jersey, Lonergan gave a workshop on method in theology in Toronto. A classmate from Brooklyn, John Strynkowski, and I flew to Toronto for the workshop which took place at the Jesuit Regis College then located in Willowdale, a beautiful suburb outside of Toronto. These were beautiful surroundings for summer days and in between the sessions in which Lonergan lectured, we were able to use the pool. Lonergan himself would come down in the afternoons and lay by the pool in the warm sun—still recovering from his serious operation. While in Toronto I asked Father Lonergan if he would visit our seminary in New Jersey and give a lecture, which he immediately agreed to do. In early November, 1969, he wrote to me:

> In connection with my talk at the Seminary on the evening of the 18th (Topic: "Faith and Beliefs): I am due at LaGuardia on American Airlines flight 410 at 3:59 p.m. on the afternoon of November 18. My plans to visit relatives in Philadelphia on the 19th have not worked out. Could you let me stay until the 20th when I go on to Washington?
>
> > In Domino,
> > Bernie Lonergan

And so I was delighted to have Father Lonergan's company for several days in November of 1969. I picked him at LaGuardia Airport and drove him to the seminary—then called "Darlington" after the beautiful section in the Ramapo Mountains of northeast New Jersey where it was located. As we drove through the little town of Ramsey near the seminary, he said to me, "Could you pull over? I want to get something at that liquor store." By the time I had parked the car he was across the street buying a bottle of Johnnie Walker Black Label. "It helps me sleep," he said. I found out later that since his operation he had not been able to sleep and his doctor had recommended that he take a shot of whiskey every night.

The lecture Lonergan gave that night to a crowded audience was entitled "Faith and Beliefs" and was one he had prepared for the first plenary session of the American Academy of Religion the month before in Boston. In that talk Lonergan spoke of the experience of "falling in love with God" and "being in love with God." It was rather remarkable to hear this exigent philosopher-theologian who had so often invoked differential equations and "long chains of reasoning" here speaking of falling in love! He spoke of our human capacity for self-transcendence, for getting beyond ourselves.

> Now capacity becomes achievement when one falls in love. Then one's being becomes being-in-love. Such being-in-love has its antecedents, its causes, its conditions, its occasions. But once it has occurred and as long as it lasts, it takes

over. It becomes the first principle. From it flow one's desires and fears, one's joys and sorrows, one's discernment of values, one's decisions and deeds.[6]

He distinguished three levels of such being in love: the love of intimacy, of one's fellow human being and the love of God—as in St. Paul's statement: "The love of God has been poured into our hearts through the Holy Spirit who has been given to us." (*Romans* 5, 5). "Faith" is the knowledge born of such love, as in Pascal's statement, "the heart has reasons which reason knows not of."

Being in love with God, as experienced, is being in love in an unrestricted fashion. All love is self-surrender, but being in love with God is being in love without limits or qualifications or conditions or reservations. . . . Because that love is the proper fulfilment of our capacity, that fulfilment brings a deep-set joy that can remain despite humiliation, failure, privation, pain, betrayal, desertion. Again, that fulfilment brings a radical peace, the peace that the world cannot give. That fulfilment bears fruit in a love of one's neighbor that strives mightily to bring about the kingdom of God on this earth. On the other hand, the absence of that fulfilment opens the way to the trivialization of human life in the pursuit of fun, to the harshness of human life arising from the ruthless exercise of power, to despair about human welfare springing from the conviction that the universe is absurd.[7]

After the talk, one of the seminarians said to me, "You know, I never thought I would be able to understand Lonergan; but when he spoke tonight about falling in love with and being in love with God, I knew what he was talking about!"

Of course, in the question and answer session Lonergan's sometimes "testy" self came out. For example, when someone asked him to "explain the problem of evil," he quickly replied, "Read chapter nineteen of my book, *Insight*. Next question?" The audience gasped.

After the talk, I introduced him to my mother and father who were in the audience and he was very kind to them. Then he joined a number of .the priests in the recreation room and chatted with us for a while. William Keeler from Harrisburg, PA, presently the Cardinal Archbishop of Baltimore, was visiting at the time and was present at that little soiree. Lonergan entertained us with stories about the Jesuits in Rome.

The next day I asked him what he would like to do and he suggested we see a movie and so, along with a friend, Father Charlie Gusmer, we saw Woody Allen's film, "*Take the Money and Run.*" It was the first Woody Allen film I had ever seen and I remember saying to myself "This is the stupidest movie I've ever seen—and here I am sitting next to this genius!" Afterwards, he remarked on how much he liked it!

His conversations those days touched on topics that in one way or another would appear in his later writings. For example, I remember him commenting on the new types of faucets in the sink of the room where he was staying, and years later I would remember this conversation as I plowed through his writings on economics. Economic cycles accelerate on the basis of new practical insights—railroads in the 19th century, electronics at the end of the 20th, etc.

At another meal he spoke with our faculty about Gibson Winter's 1966 book, *Elements for a Social Ethic: The Role of Social Science in Public Policy,* in which Winter outlined four styles of social science: the physical, the functional, the voluntarist, and the intentional. Each style is appropriate for dealing with different types of social reality. For example, the physical or behaviorist style is helpful for dealing with traffic problems in a congested city, but it is certainly not very helpful in dealing with more human issues of meaning, the focus of the intentional style. Lonergan's point was to reflect on how Christian theology might interact with the social sciences and with social policy. His own philosophy aimed at providing the bridge. As he was to write sometime later:

> Just as a social philosophy and a social ethic can be inserted between social science and social policy, so too a philosophy of religion and its extension into a theology can be inserted between empirical religious studies and the policies of religious groups.[8]

1. *METHOD IN THEOLOGY*

In 1972 Lonergan published *Method in Theology* in which he extended what he had done in *Insight* to modern historical scholarship and to theology. My journey from *Insight* passed through *Method in Theology*. In that work Lonergan undertook to analyze the massive cultural shifts that had overtaken not only Catholic writers but also all others writing in a Western cultural idiom since the 19th century. Chief among those cultural shifts was the prevalence and even hegemony of historical scholarship. Such scholarship had created immense problems for Catholic theologians. What if stories from the Hebrew Scriptures were just mythological accounts rooted in the ancient near East? What about the story of the Magi in the New Testament? The miracles of Jesus? The resurrection? What is a "myth?" and how does it relate to "reality?" Indeed, what is "history?"

These were important questions—for some of the answers that were being given seemed to take the heart out of the Christian message. Many who faced these questions experienced personal crises. As Timothy Fallon, a Jesuit, described his experience of studying philosophy in the late 1950s:

> It was with indescribable anguish that it slowly dawned on me that if Thomas
> Aquinas had the truth, it was not evident to a very wide circle of excellently
> trained and eminent philosophers and perhaps should not be so evident to me. . .
> . This raised serious questions not only about the philosophy of being and doing
> but also about what I was doing being a Roman Catholic.[9]

And the basic issue often came down to conflicts over the meaning of
words like "reality," "knowledge" and "objectivity." These terms recur again
and again in historical writing. Here again understanding understanding was
the key. It was the key to understanding what "historical knowledge" meant.
It was the key to understanding what is meant by "objective history." It was
the key to understanding the relationship of historical scholarship to reality,
to religion and to theology.

> Since the beginning of the century theologians have been incorporating more
> and more historical study into their theology. . . . But mere history is not the-
> ology, and the task of doing genuine history and on that basis proceeding to
> theology confronts Catholic theologians with the most basic and far-reaching of
> problems, the problem of method in theology.[10]

In a lapidary statement Lonergan once remarked, "All my work has been
introducing history into Catholic theology."[11] The Second Vatican Council
signaled the acceptance by the Catholic Church of modern historical consciousness.[12] If the Church were to speak to the people of this age, it had to
take such consciousness seriously.

How to do that? Lonergan does it in *Method in Theology* by developing the
basic notions taken from *Insight*, that is, the levels of human consciousness,
and by applying those notions to the study of history and the relationship of
such study to religion, and religious doctrine. But this is not an easy process.
In fact, as I read and re-read *Method in Theology* in 1972, I went through a
process similar to the one I had gone through in reading *Insight*. The first time
I read it through, in fact, I remember saying to myself,

> What a dry book! Who's going to be interested in this? Why in the world does
> he have to set it up this way? Why does he say this in this place?—and that in
> that?

Gradually, however, I came to understand the interlocking structure of the
book, its fundamental terms and relations based ultimately upon the basic
structure of human consciousness. Those terms and relations are applied
to understanding the various "functional specialties" in historical theology,

an insight Lonergan himself had in February, 1965.[13] It was, in fact, his discovery of the structure of historical understanding. These functional specialties—research, interpretation, history, dialectic, foundations, doctrines, systematics and communications—are all linked together by the dynamic structure of human consciousness. They are interlocking ways in which the we seek to understand the Word of God coming to us out of the past and, having heard the Word, how we would speak that Word to the future. They can be schematized in this way:

Hearing the Word from the Past	Speaking the Word in the Present
Dialectic (conflicts)	Foundations (objectifying conversion)
History	Doctrines
Interpretation	Systematics
Research	Communications

Central to *Method in Theology* are the categories of religious, moral and intellectual conversion. Religious conversion consists in falling in love with God, the move from a basic lovelessness to radical love. Moral conversion consists in beginning to make choices on the basis of values instead of on the basis of desires and fears. Finally, "intellectual conversion" is shorthand for the experience *Insight* sought to mediate.

And so, as with *Insight*, I spent a lot of time studying *Method in Theology*, reading it from every angle, and especially from the angle of conversion: intellectual, moral and religious. Gradually, as I began to penetrate the book, its pieces began to fall into place. One day, in the early 1980s when I was back in Rome as Spiritual Director of the North American College, I remember taking an afternoon walk out to the Catacombs of Saint Sebastian on the Via Appia Antica. I had with me a copy of *Method in Theology* and, after visiting the catacombs, I spent some time sitting outside in the garden reading. At one point I remember saying to myself,

This whole book is about intellectual conversion!—but it's about intellectual conversion as applied to understanding religious and moral conversion in history! It's an application of the point of *Insight* to understanding progress, decline and redemption! Without intellectual conversion you don't have the personal tools necessary to talk clearly about religion and morality in history!

It was an insight reflecting Lonergan's insight of February 1965—just as my insight in the shower in 1967 reflected what he had experienced in the mid-1930s—and what Aquinas had experienced in the 13th century and Augustine in the fourth.[14] Insights have a way of transcending time.

Another way to formulate this insight into *Method in Theology* would be to say that that work is the application of an absolutely basic set of categories and relationships (experiencing, understanding, judging, deciding) to understanding the developing understanding of human community and the Word of God in history. On the basis of the intellectual conversion facilitated by *Insight*, it aims at helping us discern genuine conversion in history. This movement from the theme of *Insight* to the central theme of *Method in Theology* is evident in the words of another Jesuit, Bernard Tyrrell:

> While studying at Fordham University in 1961 two Jesuits, Joe Flanagan and Al Fritch, introduced me to *Insight* and to Lonergan's articles on the "word" in Aquinas. I recall distinctly the moment when, after a conversation with Joe Flanagan about the meaning of a passage in the Aquinas articles, I suddenly experienced that flash of insight which made all the difference and as the beginning of my intellectual conversion. Lonergan writes of the "startling strangeness" of this moment of insight into insight and the accuracy of his observation is validated by the vividness of my memory of that epiphanic moment at Fordham.
>
> Again, I recall hearing Father Lonergan lecture on religious and moral conversion in 1968 at Boston College. I remember being deeply shaken by the insight that the religious and moral conversion of the theologian is as important for doing good theology as the intellectual conversion of the philosopher is for doing good philosophy. This moment of transformative understanding has served ever since as a religious and moral imperative for me in my writing and teaching.[15]

Conversion—religious, moral and intellectual—determines the horizon within which we do our research, how we will interpret other writers and persons, and what stand we will take as we read conflicting histories. Our level of conversion is our "foundations." By our conversion—or lack thereof—we constitute ourselves on a quite basic level. Only deepening conversion can help us to understand the "saints" and converted persons of the past. Only deepening conversion can help us positively influence others in the present and the future.

Another key aspect of *Method in Theology* is Lonergan's attention to the whole area of human feelings and to our growing discernment of values through feelings. Besides "non-intentional" feelings, such as hunger and fatigue, there are also "intentional feelings" that arise from the apprehension of objects. We are thrilled by the stories of heroes, we despise villains. We fall in love with some people; we avoid others. "Such feeling gives intentional consciousness its mass, momentum, drive, power. Without these feelings our knowing and deciding would be paper thin."[16]

Such feelings can reflect a scale of values, an *ordo amoris*, as Augustine put it, a right order of loving that subordinates satisfaction and fears to a hierarchy of vital, social, cultural, personal and religious values. The recognition of such a scale of values—and its obverse in disvalues—can help us in the whole area of moral and religious living. It can help us relate cultural values—the meanings and values we attribute to our concrete living—to the rest of our living, especially our moral and religious living. Intellectual conversion can have a profound effect on the discernment of such cultural values—and on our whole lives. Such conversion is "counter-cultural" to many of the values by which our world lives. It is a dimension of Jesus' "Repent! The Kingdom of God is at hand!"

In pages central to *Method in Theology* Lonergan defines intellectual conversion as moving us beyond the myth of knowing as "taking a good look."

> Intellectual conversion is a radical clarification and, consequently, the elimination of an exceedingly stubborn and misleading myth concerning reality, objectivity, and human knowledge. The myth is that knowing is like looking, that objectivity is seeing what is there to be seen and not seeing what is not there, and that the real is what is out there now to be looked at.[17]

Lonergan goes on to say that this myth of knowing as looking overlooks the distinction between the world of immediacy and the world mediated by meaning. The world of immediacy is the infant's world of what is seen, heard, touched, tasted, smelt, felt. But this world is but a tiny fragment of the world mediated by meaning.

> For the world mediated by meaning is a world known not by the sense experience of an individual but by the external and internal experience of a cultural community, and by the continuously checked and rechecked judgments of the community. Knowing, accordingly, is not just seeing; it is experiencing, understanding, judging, and believing. The criteria of objectivity are not just the criteria of ocular vision; they are the compounded criteria of experiencing, of understanding, of judging, and of believing. The reality known is not just looked at; it is given in experience, organized and extrapolated by understanding, posited by judgment and belief.

Lonergan notes that this position, issuing in a philosophy of critical realism, is not just a philosophical nicety.

> Now we are not discussing a merely technical point in philosophy. Empiricism, idealism, and realism name three totally different horizons with no common identical objects. An idealist never means what an empiricist means, and a realist never means what either of them means.[18]

Just as there are radically divergent interpretations of modern science according to scientists' horizons—materialist, relativist, etc.—so such foundational positions enter into the interpretation of history. They determine, for example, what we mean by historical facts.

What are historical facts? For the empiricist they are what was out there and was capable of being looked at. For the idealist they are mental constructions carefully based on data recorded in documents. For the critical realist they are events in the world mediated by true acts of meaning.

Similarly, what is myth?

What is a myth? There are psychological, anthropological, historical, and philosophic answers to the question. But there also are reductionist answers: myth is a narrative about entities not to be found within an empiricist, an idealist, a historicist, an existentialist horizon.

In other words, an intellectual conversion is needed to understand the meaning of history, the meaning of historical facts, the meaning of myth—in fact, the meaning of most of what our minds are involved in as we question, understand, judge and believe. It is a lack of clarity about such subjects—including what we are involved in with so much of our lives—that has afflicted not only enemies of religion, but even outstanding Christian scholars.

In both Barth and Bultmann, though in different manners, there is revealed the need for intellectual as well as moral and religious conversion. Only intellectual conversion can remedy Barth's fideism. Only intellectual conversion can remove the secularist notion of scientific exegesis represented by Bultmann.[19]

It is to apply intellectual conversion to the processes of doing history and modern theology that Lonergan wrote *Method in Theology*. Such an application to historical scholarship can free theology from materialistic undertows and aid it in its service to human and religious love. At every step of the way the presence or absence of intellectual conversion can help or hinder us as we try to hear the Word of God coming to us out of the past and as we strive to speak and live that Word in today's world.

The aim of *Method in Theology*, then, is, with the help of the intellectual conversion, to aid us in understanding our religious and moral conversions in history. Or, to put it another way, it helps us to truly encounter other historical figures and in such encounters to allow those others to enlighten us and our own self-understanding as we ourselves influence the world.

Through *Method in Theology*, as previously through *Insight*, I was encountering Bernard Lonergan and his mind. And he was helping me to encounter others from the past—Augustine, Aquinas, Newman, etc.—as well as religious and cultural figures in the present. Such encounters change a person. They change the way we look at things, the way we look at ourselves, the way we look at God.

Such changes are explicated in the functional specialization "foundations."

Foundations as a functional specialty aims at objectifying conversion and broadly speaking, could be exemplified by what Augustine was aiming at in his *Confessions* and Newman in his *Apologia pro vita sua*. Newman subtitled the latter "*A History of His Religious Opinions*" and in that work he catalogues the conflicting religious positions of his day. Out of those conflicts his conversion to Catholicism was forged. Lonergan also aimed at objectifying conversion in *Insight* and *Method in Theology*, but he did so in line with the explanatory ideals of modern scientific consciousness. Where both Augustine and Newman aimed at articulating their conversions, they did so in a way that employed common sense terms about human mentality. They did not reach the ideal of an explanatory understanding exemplified by Lonergan's writings.

What Lonergan aimed at in *Insight* and *Method in Theology* was an articulation of conversion in an explanatory way influenced by the ideals of modern science: that is, the ideal of an interlocking set of terms and relations in which the terms fix the relations and the relations fix the terms and insight fixes both. Such were the terms and relations involved in an explanatory understanding of a circle. Such were the terms and relations involved in an understanding of human consciousness.

It was the emergence of modern scientific consciousness that allowed Lonergan to transpose the achievements of Augustine and Newman into what he called "the third stage of meaning." The first stage of meaning, that of common sense, was transcended by the second stage of theory—finding expression in Aristotle, Thomas Aquinas and modern scientific consciousness. The third stage takes advantage of that theoretical achievement to seek an explanatory account of human interiority—the whole realm that Lonergan sought to explore.[20]

The Greeks needed an artistic, a rhetorical, an argumentative development of language before a Greek could set up a metaphysical account of mind. The Greek achievement was needed to expand the capacities of commonsense knowledge and language before Augustine, Descartes, Pascal, Newman could make their commonsense contributions to our self-knowledge. The history of mathematics, natural science, and philosophy and, as well, one's own personal reflective engagement in all three are needed if both common sense and theory are to construct the scaffolding for an entry into the world of interiority.[21]

2. FURTHER ENCOUNTERS

In August of 1972 I wrote a review-article on *Method in Theology* for *America* magazine. Sometime later in the Georgetown library, I came across the following letter that Lonergan wrote to a friend, in which he said:

> My thanks for the clippings from *America*. Richard Liddy is a former pupil of
> mine and is teaching in the seminary at Darlington, N.J. He has had me there to
> talk, and I discovered that I was very well known there by the seminarians, as
> many of their professors are former pupils of mine.[22]

In June of 1973 I was asked to participate in a session on Lonergan's
Method in Theology at the Catholic Theological Society of America meeting
in New York. I was expected to give a positive review of Lonergan's work
while Msgr. Austin Vaughan of New York was to give a critical assessment.
Lonergan himself was in the audience. Vaughan's reflections included a criticism of Lonergan for not being sufficiently "Catholic" in his methodology,
at least for not bringing in more explicitly theological principles. My own
remarks consisted in absolving Lonergan of that charge in the light of what
he was specifically aiming at; for his was a method aimed at bringing to light
the personal principles of whoever is broaching these issues. During the question and answer session I suggested that Father Lonergan himself respond and
afterwards I wrote this account.

> Father Lonergan noted that there is a notion of method that is at least minimally
> theological and yet allows theology to encompass many areas not otherwise
> comprehended. Thus, *Method in Theology* can be viewed as theological to the
> extent that it is grounded in Romans 5, 5: "The love of God has flooded out
> hearts through the Holy Spirit that has been given to us." At the same time that
> minimal notion enables you to conceive method as spreading out to encompass
> other religions and other areas of human experience to the extent that the Holy
> Spirit is operative in those areas as well.

In his remarks Lonergan gave a very powerful presentation of his own classicist training and upbringing and of his life-long quest to introduce "history"
into Catholic theology. Afterwards he sent me the following note:

July 31, 1973

Dear Dick,
Many thanks for your note of July 1st.
    Permit me to congratulate you again and most warmly on the very effective
paper you read at the CTSA meeting. Like your book review in *America* it will
contribute notably to the fortunes of *Method in Theology*.
    I am glad some people found my jerky remarks at the end of the session ac-
ceptable. I would like to feel that they might serve to extricate me from the cocoon of abstractions in which, in the minds of some, I am supposed to dwell.
    Wishing you all good things and keeping you in my prayers,

Bernie Lonergan

"The cocoon of abstractions!" For this man abstractions could be eminently enriching when they flowed from insight! In October of 1973 Lonergan was presented with the *John Courtney Murray Award* of the Catholic Theological Society of America at America House in New York. He sent me the following invitation:

Dear Dick,
J C Murray Award, brief presentation at 4:00 pm followed by cocktails until 6:00 pm in La Farge Lounge, second floor, America House, 106 W 56th, on Wednesday, October 24.
I shall be honored if you can follow up your review and your paper at CTSA with your presence. In any case all the best,

Bernie Lonergan

Of course, I attended the presentation and have several pictures taken with him—himself in jacket and tie, myself in clericals, and both of us holding drinks!

Several years later Lonergan moved from Toronto to Boston College as Visiting Distinguished Professor. It was during this time that Fred Lawrence of the theology department at Boston College initiated the Lonergan Workshops in which for a number of years Lonergan gave lectures and responded to questions. These question sessions were fascinating and wonderful experiences, filled with off-handed remarks on his own work as well as on many issues in the church and the world. Charles Hefling once described these sessions and Lonergan's "mellowing' in his handling of questions.

Recently, as I was reading through the transcripts of his dialogue sessions, one thing I could not help noticing was Lonergan's persistence and patience. The workshop has always welcomed participants at every level of interest and expertise, and so it was not surprising to find that their questions have run the gamut of sophistication. There are elementary questions, recondite questions, questions precisely framed and questions floundering in their wordiness, questions posed by dubious critics and questions from admiring fans. From another point of view, I was struck by how often questions on the same topics—feelings, Newman, liberation theology—came up year after year. From Lonergan's point of view, though, to judge from his answers, the main thing was that each of them *was* a question, someone's own unique quest for understanding, to be honored and taken seriously as such. Often enough, he might simply have answered by referring to one of his published works. But he never did. Even if he had already discussed the matter in print, he always tried to give it some new twist, some allusion or example, or turn of phrase that might help someone get the point. I remember his saying, with reference to a section of *Method in Theology* that goes over ground covered in an earlier chapter, "It won't hurt to have another go at it, eh?" It didn't. For me, at any rate, Lonergan's variations on his own themes often made it possible to hear the theme for the first time.[23]

I remember one night in June of 1979 when I brought two friends to one of his lectures at Boston College entitled "*Horizons and Transpositions.*" As I listened to him speak that night I said to myself,

> I don't understand what he's getting at! He's over my head! And I've been studying this stuff for years! How could others like Colin and Rose understand what he's saying?

Since then, I've read and re-read that talk, each time discovering in it new insights.

One afternoon in February of 1978 while he was living at St. Mary's Hall at Boston College I took him out to dinner at Valle's Steakhouse on nearby Beacon Street. He was dressed in a gray suit and tie. He seemed somewhat feeble. During our conversation he spoke about his own childhood and being bored one slow summer day and someone saying to him, "Well, what do you do when you're bored? Well, you read a book!" So he read his first book, Robert Louis Stevenson's *Treasure Island*—then going on to reading Dickens and others.[24] Apparently he loved his aunt Minnie, his mother's sister who lived with them. "I had two mothers," he said.

He also talked about his life at St. Mary's Hall. "The average age is 60!" The Jesuits there had a regular "Holy Hour"—besides being interested in "Lawrence Welk and the Patriots!" He noted that there were only 17 Jesuits at home at Christmas. "They all have families," he said. But then he added, "We have a good minister"—implying that they were well taken care of. That seemed to sum up everything.

At the time he was running a seminar on Christology which he described as on "Nicea, Thomas Aquinas and Theology as 'Praxis.'" The seminar apparently began with 22 present and only 10 remained for the duration. "No females," he said. One of the students was an Anglican priest about whom he said, "He has Newman's problem—figuring out where the Councils end? With Nicea?" "But I don't want to rush him," he added.

One thing he spoke about was the work he was presently doing in economics, an area of study which he had begun as a young man at the time of the depression. He remarked on how impressively printed were the current textbooks in macro-economics such as Robert J. Gordon's beautifully designed *Macroeconomics.* I asked him what the point of his study was and he replied:

> Well when you're driving a car you can't step on the gas and the brakes at the same time—otherwise you're in trouble! The same way with the economy: you can't manipulate interest rates at the wrong time and in such a way that you're stepping on the gas and the brakes at the same time. Otherwise, you're in for booms and slumps. There's a way an exchange economy should run—a pure cycle—and if you don't respect it, you're in for trouble.

He also gave me a primer on inflation with the scenario of unions asking for larger salaries, company managers imprudently negotiating and government pouring more money into the economy. He also gave me a run-down on economics gurus, such as the Polish economist, Michael Kalecki, who worked at Cambridge and with whose ideas he felt a great affinity; and, above all, the Austrian economist, Joseph A. Schumpeter, who, like Lonergan, emphasized the importance of "new ideas" in economic development. Depressions, he said, were the result of "spent ideas."

Sometime later, at a reception at the Catholic Theological Society of America meeting in Toronto I naively said to him, "There seems to be so much going wrong with the economy these days; isn't there some way we could get your ideas 'out there?'" To which he responded with a smile, "Well, these kinds of things take a long time to catch on, you know."

It is amazing to trace the trajectory of Lonergan's thought: from an early interest in scientific and philosophical method to the self-appropriation of the knower, to method in history and theology, to method in the social sciences and finally, method in economics. And what was the purpose of it all? Ultimately, all of his work was for the conversion and transformation of the person and of the world. As he wrote in *Method in Theology*:

> The church is an out-going process. It exists not just for itself but for the human family. Its aim is the realization of the kingdom of God not only within its own organization but in the whole of human society and not only in the after life but also in this life.[25]

Such an outgoing thrust towards the world should involve a knowledge of economic realities. Commenting in 1974 on Cardinal Danielou's plea for the church to speak to the poor, he said:

> Cardinal Danielou speaks of the poor. It is a worthy topic, but I feel that the basic step in aiding them in a notable manner is a matter of spending one's nights and days in a deep and prolonged study of economic analysis.[26]

Intellectual conversion, then, can be at the service of faith and of the world. It can help extend one's divinely inspired loving to ever wider circles. As Patrick Byrne said of "PULSE," a service program at Boston College that was influenced by Lonergan's work:

> Not only was the program's distinguishing feature inspired and informed from the beginning by Father Lonergan's work, but its uniqueness and successes can be traced to the fact that he, unlike any other contemporary thinker, was able to make it clear that while the pursuit of truth is a proximate goal of philosophy, theology and the sciences, their most fundamental intentionality is the transfor-

mation of the human social situation.[27]

After noting that the PULSE program involves reading classic works as well as contemporary writers, Byrne notes:

> Yet the PULSE approach to these texts is different from what is commonly found in academic classrooms. In PULSE the texts are treated as *transformational* rather than *informational*. That is, the reading material is presented as raising questions every human being faces *en route* to what Lonergan has described as the project of "producing the first and only edition of oneself," and as setting forth fundamental options for just, happy and holy living. . . . The extent to which the PULSE faculty succeeds is in large part due to the way Lonergan has shown how the unrestricted desire for human self-transcendence, its distortions in bias, and its redemption in the loving transformation of God's grace underlie every human being's thoughts and actions.

3. FINAL ENCOUNTERS

In 1980 I returned as spiritual director to the North American College in Rome. That summer, back home in the States, I visited Lonergan at Saint Mary's Hall at Boston College. His health was beginning to fail at the time and I remember waiting for him as a nurse took care of him. Afterwards we had a cup of tea together as we talked in the little room beside the refectory at St. Mary's. The previous year I had made one of Ira Progoff's *Intensive Journal* workshops and Lonergan was very interested in Progoff and his work. He questioned me about the workshop and wanted to know all about my experience. It was the only time I ever felt I was teaching him anything!

Afterwards as we left I asked him to say hello to a friend who had given me a ride to Saint Mary's, Rosemary Nadeau. Rosemary greeted him and said how much I had spoken of him through the years. But Lonergan quickly replied, "Oh, but Father Liddy is in charge of the spiritual formation of the future priests of America!" It was a moment of humility—and of love.

Bernard Tyrrell, S.J. recounted a similar moment:

> My most recent encounter with Bernie Lonergan was in his room at Boston College in June 1982 when he told me he was going to have a serious operation and asked for my prayers. I gave him an awkward hug and left his room sad and yet hopeful because Bernie showed such serenity and trust in God. I have always experienced a certain awe in his presence and I am grateful to him for those various times when he spontaneously broke the barrier of master-disciple relationship and let me experience his quiet affection and simplicity of heart.[28]

Sometime around 1982, on a snowy night in winter, a priest friend of mine, Father Jim Rafferty, also a faculty member at the North American College, was walking with another priest near Saint Mary's. They caught up with a couple of people walking ahead of them and one was Father Lonergan. When Jim told him that he was a colleague of Dick Liddy's in Rome, Lonergan exclaimed, "Dick Liddy? Dick Liddy? I know Dick Liddy!" It was a moment Rafferty loved to recount.

Soon afterwards, because of his failing health, Lonergan returned to Canada to the Jesuit infirmary in Pickering, Ontario.[29] When I heard of his death on November 26, 1984, I said to myself that I just had to be there. So I flew to Toronto and attended the funeral at the Jesuit Church of Our Lady of Lourdes on the evening of November 29, 1984. His faithful friend through the years, Father Fred Crowe, gave the homily and, as I sat listening in the church that night, two Cardinals of the Church sat in my line of vision to the altar: Cardinal Emmet Carter, Archbishop of Toronto, and Cardinal George Flahiff, retired Archbishop of Winnepeg. I remember thinking to myself:

> What a tribute to this great man! I really hope that in the years to come the Church will recognize his humility, his holiness and his greatness.

At the same time I thought that probably few of us at the funeral grasped the full significance of the event and of the man. "Doctor of the Church" is a title often given centuries later to great teachers in the church. There were some of us at that funeral that sensed that in centuries to come Bernard Lonergan, through his writings, would still be teaching in the church. In some small college, in some great university, in the study of some home, women and men would pour over his writings to grasp how the world of divine faith links up with human transformation and God's beautiful world.

The next day I drove from Toronto to the Jesuit cemetery at Guelph where he was to be buried. As the body was to be brought to the burial plot, Father Crowe asked me and some of Father Lonergan's other students to carry the coffin to the grave. Later on, I wrote the following words:

> Last Friday morning, November 30, 1984, I had the privilege, along with some of his other students, to carry the body of Bernard Lonergan, S.J. to his final resting place in the simple unpretentious Jesuit cemetery in Guelph, Ontario. As we lowered his body into the grave, my whole life passed in front of me and I had the deep and distinct impression of the great privilege of encountering this great man. Not only had he been my teacher and later my friend with whom I shared meals, but on a deeper level I had witnessed from within his penetrating thought linking the Christian past to the present and the future.

Not too many people were at the simple Jesuit cemetery in Guelph that day—perhaps forty or fifty. The weather was cold and gray, and the burial could have been that of any number of ordinary people who were buried that day. It was—as was the life of Father Lonergan—unpretentious. The simple gravestone, similar to that given every other member of the Society of Jesus, recounted the basic parameters of his life:

Rev. B. J. Lonergan, S.J.
Born Dec. 17, 1904
Entered July 29, 1922
Died, Nov. 26, 1984

At the end of the ceremony drops of earth were scattered over the casket, prayers were said, and all of us left to continue our own lives—and to carry on his heritage.

NOTES

1. Robert Doran in an unpublished paper given at the 2006 Lonergan Workshop, "Ignatian Themes in the Thought of Bernard Lonergan," reported conversations with two Jesuits who spoke of the experience of "consolation" they felt after reading chapters of *Insight*.

2. *CWL 3 Insight*, 31 (6).

3. See William Mathews, "A Biographical Perspective on Conversion and the Functional Specialties in Theology," *Method: Journal of Lonergan Studies*, Vol. 16 (Fall, 1998), 133ff.

4. Quoted in Fred Lawrence, "Lonergan: A Tribute," in the *Boston College Bi-weekly*, January 17m 1985, 8.

5. "Initiating Fruitful Questions for Myself?" *The Question as Commitment: A Symposium*, ed. Elaine Cahn and Cathleen Going (Montreal: Thomas More Institute/77, 1979), 10.

6. "Faith and Beliefs," *CWL 17 Philosophical and Theological Papers 1965-1980*, 38.

7. *CWL 17 Philosophical and Theological Papers 1965-1980*, 38-39.

8. "The Example of Gibson Winter," *A Second Collection*, 189.

9. *Compass*, March 1985, 8.

10. "Belief: Today's Issues," *A Second Collection*. 96. Other citations along this same line can be found in Frederick E. Crowe, *Lonergan* (Collegeville, MN, 1992), 98.

11. "Bernard Lonergan in Conversation," in J.M. O'Hara (ed.), *Curiosity at the Center of One's Life: Statements and Questions of R. Eric O'Connor* (Montreal: 1984) 427. In the same interview he also says "The meaning of Vatican II was the acknowledgment of history."

12. See Lonergan's statement that the new age in Catholic theology "dates not

from 1965 when the second Vatican council closed, but rather from 1845 when Newman completed his *Essay on the Development of Christian Doctrine.*" Bernard Lonergan, "A New Pastoral Theology," *CWL,* Vol. 17, *Philosophical and Theological Papers 1965-1980,* 238.

13. See William Mathews, "A Biographical Perspective on Conversion and the Functional Specialties in Theology," 133ff.

14. See Richard Liddy, *Transforming Light: Intellectual Conversion in the Early Lonergan.*

15. *Compass,* Spring 1985, 7.

16. *Method in Theology,* 29-30.

17. *Method in Theology,* 238.

18. *Method in Theology,* 239.

19. *Method in Theology,* 318.

20. *Method in Theology,* 261.

21. *Method in Theology,* 261-262. For the three stages of meaning, common sense, theory and interiority, see *Method in Theology,* 85-99.

22. Letter of Bernard Lonergan to Maria Shrady, February 29, 1972. From the Maria Shrady Letters, Georgetown University archives.

23. *Compass,* 12.

24. See Valentine Rice, "The Lonergan Family," *Compass,* Spring 1985, 4-5.

25. *Method in Theology,* 363-364.

26. "Sacralization and Secularization," *CWL 17 Philosophical and Theological Papers 1965-1980,* 280.

27. *Compass,* 12.

28. *Compass,* 8.

29. Robert Doran has some beautiful reflections on Lonergan's last days in his talk, "On the 100th Anniversary of the Birth of Bernard Lonergan," at the meeting of the Catholic Theological Society of America in 2004. See CTSA Proceedings 59/2004, 166-170.

Epilogue

Lonergan Workshop 2006

Glimpses of heights . . .
    "Being"
            opened up by words
                  Beauty
                         unplumbed
"Strange"
        beyond the ordinary
            "startling"
                  vision
                       complicated
                            (because we are complex persons)
                              yet amazingly simple—
Touching everything that is mine
        my experience
            history
                autobiography
Opening to others
        to beauty
            and the lure of love
Calling
        in the midst of world history
            Iraq
                and scandals . . .
Calling us into the universe—
        Luring us into You. . . .

Bibliography

1. BASIC WORKS BY BERNARD LONERGAN

Collected Works of Bernard Lonergan (hereafter *CWL*) Vol. 1, *Grace and Freedom: Operative Grace in the Thought of Saint Thomas Aquinas.* Edited by Frederick Crowe and Robert Doran. Toronto: University of Toronto Press, 2000.

CWL, Vol. 2, *Verbum: Word and Idea in Aquinas, Collected Works of Bernard Lonergan,* Vol. 2, Edited by Frederick Crowe and Robert Doran. Toronto: University of Toronto Press, 1997.

CWL, Vol. 3, *Insight.* Edited by Frederick Crowe and Robert Doran. Toronto: University of Toronto Press, 1992.

CWL, Vol. 4, *Collection, Collected Works of Bernard Lonergan.* Edited by Frederick Crowe and Robert Doran. Toronto: University of Toronto Press, 1988.

CWL, Vol. 5. *Understanding and Being.*, Edited by Elizabeth Morelli and Mark Morelli, revised and augmented by Frederick Crowe. Toronto: University of Toronto Press, 1990.

CWL, Vol. 6, *Philosophical and Theological Papers 1958-1964.* Edited by Frederick Crowe and Robert Doran. Toronto: University of Toronto Press, 1996.

CWL, Vol. 7, *The Ontological and Psychological Constitution of Christ.* Edited by Michael Shields, Frederick Crowe and Robert Doran. Toronto: University of Toronto Press, 2002.

CWL, Vol. 10, *Topics in Education, Collected Works of Bernard Lonergan.* Edited by Frederick Crowe and Robert Doran. Toronto: University of Toronto Press, 1993.

CWL, Vol. 15, *Macroeconomic Dynamics.* Edited by Frederick Lawrence, Patrick H. Byrne, and Charles C. Hefling. Toronto: University of Toronto Press, 1993.

CWL, Vol. 17, *Philosophical and Theological Papers 1965-1980.* Edited by Robert Doran and Robert Croken. Toronto: University of Toronto Press, 2004.

CWL, Vol. 18, *Phenomenology and Logic: The Boston College Lectures on Mathematical Logic.* Edited by Philip McShane. Toronto: University of Toronto Press, 2001.

CWL, Vol. 21, *For a New Political Economy.* Edited by Philip McShane. Toronto: University of Toronto Press, 1998.

The Lonergan Reader. Edited by Elizabeth Morelli and Mark Morelli. Toronto: University of Toronto Press, 1997.

Method in Theology. London: Darton, Longman & Todd, 1972 (reprinted by University of Toronto Press, 1990).

A Second Collection. London: Darton, Longman & Todd, 1974 (reprinted by University of Toronto Press, 1996).

A Third Collection. Papers by Bernard Lonergan, S.J., edited by Frederick E. Crowe, S.J. New York: Paulist, 1985.

The Way to Nicea: The dialectical Development of Trinitarian Theology. Trans. Conn O'Donovan. London: Darton, Longman & Todd, 1976.

B. Lonergan, *De Deo Trino, Pars Systematica* (Rome: Typis Pontificiae Universitatis Gregorianae, 1964)

De Deo Trino, Pars analytica. Rome: Typis Pontificiae Universitatis Gregorianae, 1961.

De Verbo Incarnato. Rome: Typis Pontificiae Universitatis Gregorianae, 1961 with later revisions.

"The Original Preface to *Insight,*" published in *Method: Journal of Lonergan Studies,* Vol. 3/1 (March 1985), 5.

2. RELATED LONERGAN WORKS: INTERVIEWS

Caring About Meaning: Patterns in the Life of Bernard Lonergan. Eds. Pierrot Lambert, Charlotte Tansey, Cathleen Going. Montreal: Thomas More Institute, 1982. (Series of interviews with Bernard Lonergan).

Eric O'Connor, ed. *Curiosity at the Center of One's Life.* Montreal: Thomas More Institute, 1987, 371-384. (Interviews with Bernard Lonergan).

"Questions with Regard to Method: History and Economics," March 31, 1980. In *Dialogues in Celebration,* ed. Cathleen M. Going. Montreal: Thomas More Institute, 1980, 286-314.

Participation in *The Question as Commitment: A Symposium.* Ed. Elaine Cahn and Cathleen Going. Montreal: Thomas More Institute Papers/77, 1979. Reproducing discussions of 1977 with Eric Voegelin, Frederick Lawrence, etc.

3. WORKS CITED AND OF RELATED INTEREST

Patrick Allitt. *Catholic Converts: British and American Intellectuals Turn to Rome.* Ithaca, NY: Cornell University Press, 1997.

Berger, Peter. *The Social Construction of Reality.* New York: Doubleday, 1966.

Bloom, Harold. *The Western Canon: The Books and Schools of the Ages.* New York: Harcourt Brace and Co., 1994.

Brinton, Crane. *The Shaping of the Modern Mind.* New York: New American Library, 1953.

Brown, Peter. *Augustine of Hippo.* Berkeley: University of California Press: 1969.

Butterfield, Herbert. *The Origins of Modern Science, 1300-1800.* New York: The Free Press, 1957. 2nd.ed., 1965.

Byrne, Patrick. "The Fabric of Lonergan's Thought." *Lonergan Workshop 6.* Atlanta: 1986.

Castro-Klarén, Sara. "The Paradox of the Self in *The Idea of the University.*" Pp. 318-338 in *The Idea of the University,* edited by Frank Turner. New Haven: Yale University Press, 1996.

Compass: A Jesuit Journal, published by the Upper Canada Province of the Society of Jesus, special issue on Bernard Lonergan, S.J., Spring 1985.

Connor, James L., and Fellows of the Woodstock Theological Center. *The Dynamics of Desire: Bernard J. F. Lonergan on the Spiritual Exercises of St. Ignatius of Loyola.* St. Louis: The Institute of Jesuit Sources, 2006.

Cronin, Brian. *Foundations of Philosophy.* Nairobi, Kenya (PO Box 49789): Consolata Institute of Philosophy, 1999. This excellent introduction to Lonergan can also be accessed on line at the Washington D.C. Lonergan Institute: http://www.lonergan.org/.

Crowe, Frederick E. *Appropriating the Lonergan Idea.* Ed. Michael Vertin. Washington, D.C.: Catholic University of America Press, 1989.

———. "For a Phenomenology of Rational Consciousness," *Method: Journal of Lonergan Studies,* 18 (Spring 2000), 67-90.

———. *Christ and History: The Christology of Bernard Lonergan.* Ottawa: Novalis, Saint Paul University, 2005.

———. *Lonergan* (*Outstanding Christian Thinkers Series*), Collegeville, MN, The Liturgical Press, 1992.

Dennett, Daniel. *Consciousness Explained.* Boston: Little, Brown, 1991.

———. *Breaking the Spell: Religion as a Natural Phenomenon.* Penguin, 2006.

Denziger, H. and A. Schönnmetzer, *Enchiridion Symbolorum.* 32nd ed. Freiburg, 1963.

Doorley, Mark. *The Place of the Heart in Lonergan's Ethics.* Lanham, MD: University Press of America, 1996.

Doran, Robert. *Proceedings of the Catholic Theological Society of America,* 59/2004, 166-170.

———. *Theology and the Dialectics of History.* Toronto: University of Toronto Press, 1990.

———. *What Is Systematic Theology?* Toronto: University of Toronto Press, 2005.

Dulles, Avery. *A Testimony to Grace.* New York: Sheed & Ward, 1946.

Dunne, *Lonergan and Spirituality: Towards a Spiritual Integration.* Chicago: Loyola University Press, 1985.

Dyson, Freeman."Innovation in Physics." Pp. 259-260 in *Physics,* edited by Rapport and Wright. New York: Washington Square Press, 1965.

Einstein, Albert. *Essays in Science.* NY: Philosophical Library, 1934.

Farrell, Thomas J., and Paul A. Soukup, eds. *Communication and Lonergan: Common*

Ground for Forging the New Age. Kansas City, MO: Sheed & Ward, 1993.

Fitzpatrick, Joseph. *Lonergan and the Analytical Tradition.* Toronto: University of Toronto Press, 2005.

Flanagan, Joseph, *Quest for Self-Knowledge.* Toronto: University of Toronto Press, 1997, 18-23.

Gilson, Etienne. *Realisme thomiste et critique de connaissance.* Paris: Vrin, 1939; English trans. By M.A. Wauck, *Thomist Realism and the Critique of Knowledge.* San Francisco: Ignatius Press, 1986.

———. *Being and Some Philosophers.* Toronto: Pontifical Institute of Medieval Studies, 1949.

Hammarskjold, Dag. *Markings.* New York: Knopf, 1966.

Gleason, Philip. *Contending With Modernity.* New York: Oxford University Press, 1995.

Gregson, Vernon, ed. *The Desires of the Human Heart.* New York: Paulist Press, 1988.

Hedin, Raymond. *Married to the Church.* Indiana University Press, 1995.

Hefling, Charles C. *Why Doctrines?* Boston: Cowley Publication, 1984.

———. "On Apprehension, Notional and Real." Unpublished paper presented at the Lonergan Workshop, Boston College, March 18-19, 1988.

James, William. *The Varieties of Religious Experience.* New York: New American Library, 1958.

Jaspers, Karl. "Philosophical Autobiography." Pp. 3-94 in *The Philosophy of Karl Jaspers. Library of Great Philosophers, Vol. IX.* Ed. Paul Arthur Schilpp. Chicago: Open Court Publishing Co., 1957, augmented 1981.

———. "On My Philosophy." Pp. 131-158 in *Existentialism from Dostoyevsky to Sartre.* Ed. Walter Kaufmann. New York: Meridian Books, 1956.

Johnston, William. *Silent Music: The Science of Meditation.* NY: Harper & Row, 1974.

Kenaris, Jim, and Mark Doorley, *In Deference to the Other: Lonergan and Contemporary Continental Thought.* Albany, NY: State University of New York Press, 2004.

Kenny, Anthony. *A Path From Rome.* Oxford: Oxford University Press, 1986.

Komonchak, Joseph, *Foundations in Ecclesiology*, (Supplementary issue of the, Vol. 11, F. Lawrence, ed., Boston College, 1995).

Lamb, Matthew, ed. *Creativity and Method.* Milwaukee: Marquette University Press, 1981.

Langer, Susanne K. *Philosophy in a New Key.* New York: New American Library, 1948.

———. *Feeling and Form.* New York: Charles Scribner's, 1953.

———. *Mind: An Essay on Human Feeling. Volume I.* Baltimore: Johns Hopkins Press, 1967. Volume II and Volume III published in 1972 and 1982 respectively. Abridged edition of three volumes 1988.

Lawrence, Fred. "Lonergan: A Tribute," *Boston College Biweekly*, January 17, 1985, 8.

———. "Bernard Lonergan." *New Catholic Encyclopedia.* Second Edition, Vol. 8, Washington, DC: Catholic University of America, 2003. 772-775.

Liddy, Richard, *Transforming Light: Intellectual Conversion in the Early Lonergan*

(Collegeville, MN: The Liturgical Press, 1993).

————. Review of Susanne K. Langer, *Mind: An Essay on Human Feeling, Vol I,* in *International Philosophical Quarterly,* Vol. 10,n.3 (1970) 481-484.

————. "Susanne K. Langer's Philosophy of Mind." *Transactions of the Charles S. Peirce Society,* Vol. XXXIII, No. 1 (Winter, 1997), 149-160.

Lyonnet, Stanislaus. *St. Paul: Liberty and Law* (Rome: Pontificio Istituto Biblico, 1962) 244.

Mathews, William A., *Lonergan's Quest: A Study of Desire in the Authoring of Insight.* Toronto: University of Toronto Press, 2005.

————. "A Biographical Perspective on Conversion and the Functional Specialties in Lonergan," *Method: Journal of Lonergan Studies,* Vol 16, no. 2 (Fall 1998), 133-160.

McCarthy, Michael H. *The Crisis of Philosophy.* Albany: SUNY Press, 1990.

McCool, Gerald A. "Neo-Thomism and the Tradition of St. Thomas," *Thought,* Vol. 62, No. 245 (June 1987), 131-146.

————. *Catholic Theology in the Nineteenth Century: The Quest for a Unitary Method.* New York: Seabury, 1977.

————. *From Unity to Pluralism: The Internal Evolution of Thomism.* New York: Fordham University Press, 1989.

McShane, Philip, *Creativity and Method: Essays in Honor of Bernard Lonergan,* ed. Matthew Lamb (Milwaukee: Marquette University Press, 1981), 548.

————. *Economics for Everyone.* Halifax: Axial Press, 1998.

Merton, Thomas, *The Seven Storey Mountain.* New York: New American Library, 1952.,

Meyer, Ben F., *The Aims of Jesus* (London: SCM Press, 1979). Lonergan and the interpretation of the Scriptures.

————. *Reality and Illusion in New Testament Scholarship* (Collegeville, MN: The Liturgical Press, 1994.

Meynell, Hugo A. *An Introduction to the Philosophy of Bernard Lonergan.* Toronto, University of Toronto Press, 1991.

Miller, Jerome. *In the Throe of Wonder.* Albany, NY: State University of New York Press, 1992.

Morris, Charles R., *American Catholic.* (New York: Random House, 1997.

Murphy, Francis X., "Out of the Catacombs," *America,* September 11, 1999, 15-17.

Newman, John Henry. *Apologia pro vita sua.* London: Longmans, Green, and Co., 1913.

————. "'Biglietto' Speech." Rome: Libreria Spithöver, 1879.

————. *A Grammar of Assent.* London: Longmans, Green, & Co., 1913.

————. *An Essay on the Development of Christian Doctrine.* London: Longmans, 1894, 40.

O'Brien, John A., *The Road to Damascus.* Garden City, NY: Doubleday, 1949.

————. *Where I Found Christ.* Garden City, NY: Doubleday, 1950.

Rynne, Xavier, *Vatican Council II.* New York: Farrar, Straus and Giroux, 1968.

Sala, Giovanni B. *Lonergan and Kant: Five Essays on Human Knowledge,* trans. Joseph Spoerl, ed. Robert Doran. Toronto: University of Toronto Press, 1994

Shea, William, "Horizons on Bernard Lonergan," *Horizons* (Journal of College Theology Society) 15/1 (1988), 77-107.

Shook, L.K. "Gilson, Etienne Henry." *New Catholic Encyclopedia,* Second Edition, Vol. 6, Washington, DC: Catholic University of America, 2003, 227-228.

Spaccapelo, Natalino. *Fondamento e Orizzonte: Scritti di Anthropologia e Filosofia.* Rome: Armando Editore, 2000.

Stebbins, Michael. *The Divine Initiative: Grace, World-Order, and Human Freedom in the Early Writings of Bernard Lonergan.* Toronto: University of Toronto Press, 1995.

Terry J. Tekippe, *What is Lonergan Up to in Insight? A Primer.* Collegeville, MN: The Litrugical Press, 1996.

———. *Bernard Lonergan's Insight: A Comprehensive Commentary.* Lanham, MD, University Press of America, 2003.

Tracy, David. "Reasons to Hope for Reform," *America,* October 14, 1995, 12-18.

Voegelin, Eric. *Autobiographical Reflections.* Ed. Ellis Sandoz. Baton Rouge, LA: Louisiana State University Press, 1989.

———. "The Gospel and Culture" in *Jesus and Man's Hope,* ed. Donald G. Miller and Dikran Y. Hadidian, Vol. II (Pittsburgh: Pittsburgh Theological Seminary, 1971), 92.

Walsh, James J. *The Thirteenth: Greatest of Centuries.* New York: Fordham University, 1952.

Whitehead, Alfred North. *Introduction to Mathematics* (NY: Oxford University Press, 1958), 24-25).

Index

About the Author

Richard M. Liddy is the University Professor of Catholic Thought and Culture and Director of the Center for Catholic Studies at Seton Hall University. He is also a member of the Religious Studies Department. He is a graduate of Seton Hall University and Immaculate Conception Seminary in New Jersey and the Gregorian University in Rome, where he studied under Bernard Lonergan. He was ordained to the Catholic priesthood in December 1963. His doctoral dissertation in philosophy was on the American philosopher of art, Susanne K. Langer. In 1993 he published *Transforming Light: Intellectual Conversion in the Early Lonergan*. He has also written on the thought of John Henry Newman and he is interested in the topics of art, education, formation and church leadership.